Human Trafficking

Other books in the Contemporary Debates series:

Human Trafficking

Examining the Facts

Laura J. Lederer

BLOOMSBURY ACADEMIC
NEW YORK • LONDON • OXFORD • NEW DELHI • SYDNEY

BLOOMSBURY ACADEMIC
Bloomsbury Publishing Inc, 1359 Broadway, New York, NY 10018, USA
Bloomsbury Publishing Plc, 50 Bedford Square, London, WC1B 3DP, UK
Bloomsbury Publishing Ireland, 29 Earlsfort Terrace, Dublin 2, D02 AY28, Ireland

BLOOMSBURY, BLOOMSBURY ACADEMIC and the Diana logo are trademarks of
Bloomsbury Publishing Plc

First published in the United States of America 2024
Paperback edition published 2026

Library of Congress Control Number: 2023950486

ISBN: HB: 978-1-4408-8120-6
PB: 979-8-7651-1530-5
ePDF: 979-8-2161-8295-5
eBook: 978-1-4408-8121-3

Series: Contemporary Debates

Typeset by Newgen KnowledgeWorks Pvt. Ltd., Chennai, India

For product safety related questions contact productsafety@bloomsbury.com.

To find out more about our authors and books visit www.bloomsbury.com
and sign up for our newsletters.

Modern life begins with slavery …

—Toni Morrison

Let the people know the facts and the country will be safe.

—Abraham Lincoln

Contents

Illustrations

How to Use This Book

Human Trafficking: Examining the Facts is part of Bloomsbury Academic's Contemporary Debates reference series. Each title in this series, which is intended for use by high school and undergraduate students as well as members of the general public, examines the veracity of controversial claims or beliefs surrounding a major political/cultural issue in the United States. The purpose of this series is to give readers a clear and unbiased understanding of current issues by informing them about falsehoods, half-truths, and misconceptions—and confirming the factual validity of other assertions—that have gained traction in America's political and cultural discourse. Ultimately, this series has been crafted to give readers the tools for a fuller understanding of controversial issues, policies, and laws that occupy center stage in American life and politics.

Each volume in this series identifies twenty to forty questions swirling about the larger topic under discussion. These questions are examined in individualized entries, which are in turn arranged in broad subject chapters that cover certain aspects of the issue being examined, for example, history of concern about the issue, potential economic or social impact, or findings of latest scholarly research.

Each chapter features a collection of individual entries. Each entry begins by stating an important and/or well-known "Question" about the issue being studied, that is, "How widespread is sex and labor trafficking in the United States?" "What barriers do trafficking survivors face to escape and obtain care?" and "How are the experiences of trafficking survivors being incorporated into anti-trafficking work?"

The entry then provides a concise and objective one- or two-paragraph "Answer" to the featured question, followed by a more comprehensive, detailed explanation of "The Facts." This latter coverage provides quantifiable, evidence-based information from respected sources to fully address each question and provide readers with the information they need to be informed citizens. Importantly, entries will also acknowledge instances in which conflicting or incomplete data exists or legal judgments are contradictory. Finally, each entry concludes with a "Further Reading" section, providing users with information on other important and/or influential resources.

The ultimate purpose of every book in the Contemporary Debates series is to reject "false equivalence," in which demonstrably false beliefs or statements are given the same exposure and credence as the facts; to puncture myths that diminish our understanding of important policies and positions; to provide needed context for misleading statements and claims; and to confirm the factual accuracy of other assertions. In other words, volumes in this series are being crafted to clear the air surrounding some of the most contentious and misunderstood issues or our time—not just add another layer of obfuscation and uncertainty to the debate.

Acknowledgments

I had help completing this book and need to acknowledge the time and efforts of so many. First a thank you to my interns, McKamie Chandler and Malaz Namir. McKamie assisted in the early drafts of two of the articles in this book. Malaz did much of the hard work on formatting the citations, references, and the index. Thank you also to John Foster-Bey, Chris Wetzel, and McKamie Chandler for the original charts in the article on Barriers to Escape. Thank you to Stanley Stinson, a Street Medicine nurse in Detroit, for the raw data on trafficking and commercial sex in Detroit, from which we hope to continue to gain insight and write articles. Thank you to my family, John Foster-Bey, Lianna Foster-Bey, and Jenna Imani Foster-Bey, and especially to my grandson, Kye Foster-Bey, who keeps my spirits buoyed and propels me optimistically in a future that I hope will be slavery-free. Finally, a huge thank you to my editor at Bloomsbury, Kevin Hillstrom, who did much more than a simple editing—he contributed thoughts as to the overarching themes and content of the book, suggestions for substantive content, and in many places a thoughtful sentence or turn of phrase. This in addition to the many sentences he edited for grammatical correctness and readability. No book sees the light of day without a good editor, and I had one here.

Numbers Never Lie? Estimating the Nature and Scope of Human Trafficking

It is a difficult task to identify how many people are trafficked in the United States, in other individual countries, and around the globe. Trafficking is an underground criminal activity, making traffickers hard to identify and victims hard to count. In addition, every country has its own definition of human trafficking, and definitions vary widely: finding and settling on one definition is almost impossible.

Another problem is that experts cannot agree upon one method of collecting information; only recently are some undertaking a comparative analysis of the different methods being utilized. Furthermore, the numbers are always changing from year to year, so maintenance of a continuous database—of cases, case law, law enforcement actions, victims, victim services, and other information—is a challenging undertaking. This is true even for relatively small populations (e.g., cities, states, or regions); the challenge is even greater at national and international levels. Yet even with all these challenges, social scientists and anti-trafficking advocates are making strides in quantifying the scale and extent of both labor and sex trafficking.

This chapter examines some of the controversies and continuing debates about the nature and scope of the problem of human trafficking. We ask and answer questions that have been raised since the passage of the Trafficking Victims Protection Act (TVPA) in the United States, and the ratification of the UN Protocol to Prevent, Suppress, and Punish Trafficking in Persons in the United Nations: Do we know how many people are trafficked around the world? Do we have an idea of the scope of the problem in the United States? Everyone talks about sex trafficking, but what about labor trafficking—how big a problem is it in our country and around the world?

We also look briefly at the common methods for measuring human trafficking and ask if they are working and discuss the importance of anecdotal information gathered from stories of survivors in combatting human trafficking.

We can't say in the case of human trafficking that numbers never lie, because we don't have the full story on the numbers yet. This is a concern because as Walk Free (WF)—a nongovernmental organization (NGO) anti-trafficking organization—has stated, "You can't solve a problem if you can't measure it. Knowing how and where modern slavery occurs is key to eradicating it." Compiling data on the nature and scope of human trafficking not only provides a baseline of information, it also gives researchers and law enforcement benchmarks and other means to measure the effectiveness of various anti-trafficking measures and policies.

Q1. How Many People Are Trafficked in the United States and Around the World?

Answer: Unknown. Since the passage of the TVPA in 2000, researchers have discovered much more about the prevalence of human trafficking. However, no one really knows how many people are trafficked in any one country, including the United States, nor do we have a global number. There are a number of reasons for this, chief among them that human trafficking is an underground criminal activity and therefore difficult to detect and count. Other reasons include differences in the ways countries define human trafficking, differences in methodologies used to gather information on human trafficking, inadequate funding to set up and conduct complex random sample, and the fact that the forms of trafficking and modus operandi of the traffickers change every year.

The Facts: On October 28, 2000, after more than three years of discussion and debate, Congress passed the Trafficking Victims Protection Act of 2000 (TVPA). The new law was a "whole-of-government" approach and equipped the US government with new tools and resources to create a comprehensive and coordinated campaign to combat human trafficking. In 1997 US authorities estimated that 700,000 to 2 million women and children were being trafficked in this way each year (Laczko 2002).

In the years leading up to the passage of the new law, both the House and the Senate held hearings about the problem. During those hearings, legislators often asked experts about the nature and scope of the problem of human trafficking. In one hearing alone in 1999, the numbers quoted varied wildly from as few as 17,000 trafficking victims in the United States, to 50,000 globally, to 20,000 trafficked in one country alone (Thailand), to 1 million trafficked globally (US Congress 1999). That same year, well-known anti-trafficking advocate Kevin Bales published *Disposable People*, which claimed that 27 million people were trapped in modern-day slavery around the world (Bale 2012). The methodologies for obtaining those claims and findings, however, were not readily apparent.

Since then, researchers, investigators, and advocates know much more about the scale of the problem of human trafficking. One privately funded NGO called Walk Free produces the most widely accepted estimates of the nature and scope of human trafficking. The 2022 Walk Free Report estimates there are 49.6 million people around the globe living in situations of modern slavery on any given day (Walk Free 2022). The US Department of State, the United Nations, and most other NGOs cite these statistics to describe the problem. The estimates are based on a jointly developed methodology practiced by WF and the ILO (International Labor Organization). According to the Walk Free Report, "the calculations are derived from multiple data sources, as no single source was sufficiently reliable" (Walk Free 2022). The principal sources are data from 143 nationally representative household surveys conducted by ILO and WF, as well as the Counter Trafficking Data Collaborative (CTDC) anonymized case dataset on victims of trafficking collected by the International Organization for Migration (IOM) and its partners in the process of providing protection and assistance services to trafficked persons (ILO 2022).

History

Following the passage of the TVPA, the US government made a single attempt to obtain international and global statistics on human trafficking. Based on CIA estimates, it claimed that somewhere between 700,000 and 2 million women and children were trafficked each year (Lee 2011, 17). Those figures were used for a few years and then revised downward, revisiting figures produced by the Clinton Administration in 1997 which estimated that 45,000–50,000 women and girls were trafficked *into* the United States annually. According to Heather Clawson, an early researcher, The 2002 Annual Trafficking in Persons Report stated that 50,000 females were trafficked into the United States for sexual exploitation; the first year the estimate clearly indicated it did not include labor trafficking or adult males. In earlier reports, no distinction was made between those trafficked for sex or labor or whether these persons were men or women (Clawson 2007). The Clinton administration also estimated 700,000 were trafficked annually globally (Clawson 2007: US Department of State 2002).

Although the United Nations Protocol to Prevent, Suppress, and Punish Trafficking in Persons, Especially Women and Children was adopted by the United National General Assembly on December 12, 2000, it did not enter into force until December 25, 2003. Numerous UN agencies estimated the global size of the problem including the United Nations International Children's Emergency Fund (UNICEF), the United Nations International Development Fund for Women (known as UNIFEM), and the United Nations and the United Nations International Drug Control Program (UNDCP, now known as the United Nations Office on Drugs and Crime—UNODC). Other UN agencies and intergovernmental agencies also published their own estimates including the ILO and IOM. In 2004 United Nations Educational, Scientific and Cultural Organization (UNESCO) published a Trafficking Statistics Project that documented over a dozen different governmental, intergovernmental, and NGO estimates (Lee 2011, 18).

In 2004, an investigative journalist named Peter Landesman published an investigative report in *New York Times Magazine* titled, "The Girls Next Door" (Landesman 2004). He used the CIA estimate of 18,000–20,000 people trafficked into the United States per year, and quoted Kevin Bales, who said the number was "at least 10,000 a year" to describe the seriousness of the problem in the United States (Landesman 2004). The furor that followed was unexpectedly negative. Over the next eighteen months (from January 26, 2004, the day after the article was published, to June 6, 2005, the *New York Times* was heavily criticized for publishing Landesman's statistics, which they decried as inflated or unprovable. The outcry was so great that the *New York Times* published a note about it, acknowledging that there was disagreement among experts about the nature and scope of human trafficking in the United States (Slate 2004).

Ironically, although there is still no national estimate of human trafficking in the United States, over two dozen states have conducted their own studies, usually at the request of the attorney general, and the numbers from those reports far outweigh the numbers that Landesman reported in his article. For example, in Texas, the Governor's Office funded a 2017 report on human trafficking in the state. It found an estimated 313,000 victims of human trafficking in the state of Texas alone—79,000 minors and youth victims of sex trafficking and 234,000 adult victims of labor trafficking (University of Texas 2016). Other states

How Trafficking in Persons Occurs

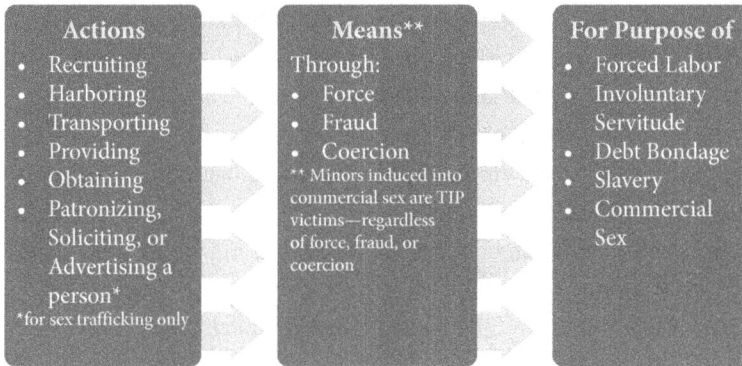

Figure 1 The AMP Model: How trafficking occurs

have published similar numbers, which, when taken in the aggregate, confirm Landesman's findings (US Department of State 2022).

Difficulties Estimating Nature and Scope of the Problem of Human Trafficking

There are many reasons why it is difficult to obtain good information about the prevalence of human trafficking in the United States and globally. They include varying definitions of trafficking, the difficulty of measuring underground criminal activity, and different methodologies for collecting and estimating data.

Definitions

Today, the US Department of State says that "trafficking in persons," "human trafficking," and "modern day slavery" are umbrella terms—often used interchangeably—to refer to a crime whereby traffickers exploit and profit at the expense of adults and children by compelling them to perform labor or engage in commercial sex (US Department of State 2022). The legal definitions of sex trafficking, forced labor, commercial sex, involuntary servitude, and debt bondage can be found in the Definitions section of the TVPA, and in the US Criminal Code.[1]

The US definition of human trafficking is best represented by the "AMP Model" (Figure 1). It describes human trafficking as having three elements—Action,

[1] TVPA of 2000, 22 U.S. Code § 7102.

Means, and Purpose, all of which need to be present for trafficking to occur. Actions include recruiting, harboring, transporting, or soliciting trafficked persons. Means refers to the ways in which traffickers prey on victims, that is, through force, fraud, or coercion. Purpose refers to the type of trafficking involved, including forced labor, debt bondage, and forced prostitution and other forms of commercial sex.

Other countries have their own definitions of human trafficking, as does the United Nations. The UN definition of trafficking is similar to the US definition, but it includes a number of types of trafficking not recognized in the US definition, including organ removal and forced marriage. The UN also has an "AMP Model," which varies slightly from the US model.

It is easy to see how, with even these two different definitions, it might be difficult to gather basic data on the nature and scope of the problem.

Underground Criminal Activity

In August 2022, the Congressional Research Service (CRS) produced a report entitled *Criminal Justice Data: Human Trafficking*. In it, they noted that "Perpetrators of trafficking intentionally conceal their illicit activities—including from entities such as law enforcement agencies that the federal government relies on to measure the prevalence of trafficking. The concealed nature of trafficking contributes to the inability to precisely measure its prevalence" (CRS 2022, 2).

In the United States, the three ways we measure criminal activity are by official police reports, surveys that uncover victims, and self-reporting by victims and offenders. The DOJ administers two statistical programs to measure the magnitude, nature, and impact of crime in the nation: the FBI's Uniform Crime Reporting (UCR) Program and the Bureau of Justice Statistics' National Crime Victimization Survey (NCVS). In the best of worlds, these two data-gathering methods allow a scientific and fairly accurate method of extrapolating underreported criminal activity. For example, it is said that only one out of ten women report being raped. The FBI can make that statement because it compares reported rapes from the UCR Program with the number of rapes that are self-reported in the National Crime Victimization Survey. They can extrapolate from the reported rapes the total number of rapes in the United States.

According to the Human Trafficking Institute (HTI), which tracks and analyzes federal case law on human trafficking across the United States, the DOJ has prosecuted 3,127 cases of human trafficking since the law was passed in 2000 (HTI 2022). But this represents only the successful prosecutions, not all the traffickers at work in the United States. In addition, there are still difficulties in estimating the true number of human trafficking cases and, further, the number of victims in each case.

For example, in 1998, a case called *U.S. v. Cadena* was a "wake-up call" for the United States about whether trafficking was occurring here; sixteen defendants were charged with criminal conspiracy to lure young women and girls from Mexico, some as young as fourteen years old, into the United States. The victims were promised good jobs in the United States and then forced into prostitution in Florida. The Cadenas were a family-run criminal organization. Though only a handful of victims testified, it is thought that that one ring trafficked hundreds of victims over a period of years (US Department of Justice 2015). Similarly large labor trafficking networks have been uncovered in Guam (a territory of the United States) and Hawaii. However, prosecutions reflect only those incidents that come to the attention of law enforcement and where law enforcement officials successfully investigate, charge, prosecute, and convict traffickers.

The FBI began collecting "certain human trafficking data" as part of the UCR Program in 2013 (CRS 2022, 3). These include "case clearances" and arrests for two categories of human trafficking: commercial sex acts and involuntary servitude (CRS 2022, 3).[2] But state reporting to the UCR is voluntary, and information about human trafficking trickled in slowly from thirteen states in 2013 to forty-seven states and Puerto Rico in 2020. Still, using this data, in 2020, states reported 2,023 incidents of human trafficking—1,693 sex trafficking and 329 involuntary servitude and 1 unspecified. There were 393 offenders arrested in conjunction with these incidents. Twenty-six of the offenders were juveniles. There was no report on the number of victims from these cases (CRS 2022, 4).

In the same way, because of its covert nature, the international magnitude of the problem is difficult to ascertain. The 2020 edition of the United Nations Office of Drugs and Crime (UNODC) *Global Report on Trafficking in Persons* is based on information from official statistics on the detected cases of trafficking in persons collected from 148 countries. The countries covered encompass more than 95 percent of the world's population. The reported number of victims is 49,032. However, it must be stated again that these are only the detected cases as reported by official government points of contact (UNODC 2020). The UNODC, which is the lead agency in tracking implementation of the Protocol to Prevent, Suppress, and Punish Trafficking in Persons, has also collected 489

---

[2] According to the FBI, case clearances are defined as cases where an offense is cleared by an arrest, charge and turn-over to prosecutors for prosecution, or otherwise solved for crime reporting purposes.

cases of human trafficking from 71 countries. Those cases have a total of 2,963 victims and 1,576 offenders. This is a start, but it is a very small number of cases compared to the regional and country-by-country estimates of the problem.

New Methodologies

Walk Free

In 2010 a new NGO was formed in Australia with the goal of providing a picture of the scale and depth of modern slavery. Since its inception it has produced four global estimates of modern-day slavery, with additional breakdowns by region, age group, and gender. In their latest report, issued in 2022, they found that on any given day in 2021, 49.6 million people were in modern slavery (ILO 2022).

WF uses cutting-edge prevalence estimation techniques to measure slavery around the world, including nationally representative surveys in partnership with Gallup, risk-model extrapolation, and multiple systems estimation (ILO 2022). The group's 2022 report's global estimates were produced using data from surveys in 143 sample countries. Findings were drawn from interviews with over 185,000 respondents, administrative data from the IOM, and data from ILO sources. The resulting estimates have a global and regional focus.

They also produce a Global Slavery Index that examines the scale of modern slavery at a country level. The index presents a thoroughly researched, detailed picture of modern slavery as it exists across industries and countries today (Walk Free 2023). It also indicates the actions governments are taking to combat modern slavery and the risks that populations face around the world. Because they have partnered with the ILO and IOM, two large world-renowned and venerated intergovernmental organizations, their findings have generally been accepted and utilized by governmental, intergovernmental, and NGOs alike.

Prevalence Estimations

In 2021 a new initiative, the Prevalence Reduction Innovation Forum (PRIF), was formed at the University of Georgia to build a global community of researchers in the science of human trafficking prevalence estimation, with a focus on documenting the robustness of various methodological approaches in human trafficking prevalence research. It is distinguished by its precise focus on specific countries considered to be "global trafficking hotspots," including Brazil, Costa Rica, Morocco, Pakistan, Tanzania, and Tunisia (Gallant 2022). These "mezzo"-focused estimation projects hold hope for a better and more detailed understanding of the nature and scope of human trafficking in each country and even localities within countries (Gallant 2022).[3] The first results from these projects are forthcoming.

Further Reading

Bales, Kevin. 2012. *Disposable People: New Slavery in the Global Economy.* Berkeley: University of California Press.

Clawson, Heather. 2007. *Estimating Human Trafficking Into The United States: Development of a Methodology Final Phase Two Report,* U.S. Department of Justice, Document No. 221035. https://www.ojp.gov/pdffiles1/nij/grants/221035.pdf. Accessed July 1, 2023.

CRS (Congressional Research Service). 2022. *Criminal Justice Data: Human Trafficking.* (R47211): 1–17. https://sgp.fas.org/crs/misc/R47211.pdf. Accessed September 19, 2023.

Gallant, André. 2022. "David Okech Talks Combatting Human Trafficking, Globally and Locally." University of Georgia Research, February 15. https://research.uga.edu/news/david-okech-talks-combatting-human-trafficking-globally-and-locally/. Accessed July 1, 2023.

HTI (Human Trafficking Institute). 2022. *Federal Human Trafficking Report.* https://traffickinginstitute.org/federal-human-trafficking-report/. Accessed July 1, 2023.

ILO (International Labor Organization). 2022. *Walk Free, International Organization for Migration. Review of Global Estimates of Modern Slavery: Forced Labour and Forced Marriage.* Geneva: International Labor Organization, Walk Free, International Organization for Migration.

Laczko, Frank, Amanda Klekowski von Koppenfels, and Jana Barthel. 2002. "Trafficking in Women from Central and Eastern Europe: A Review of Statistical Data," in *New Challenges for Migration Policy in Central and Eastern Europe,* ed. F. Laczko, I. Stacher and A. Klekowski von Koppenfels, The Hague: Asser Press.

Landesman, Peter. 2004. "The Girls Next Door." *New York Times,* January 25.

Lee, Maggy. 2011. *Trafficking and Global Crime Control.* London: Sage, 17–18. https://doi.org/10.4135/9781446269152.

Slate. 2004. "Press Box: Assessing Landesman." https://slate.com/news-and-politics/2004/01/assessing-landesman.html. Accessed September 19, 2023.

Trafficking Victims Protection Act of 2000, 22 U.S. Code § 7102—Definitions. https://www.law.cornell.edu/uscode/text/22/7102#:~:text=threats%20of%20serious%20harm%20to,abuse%20of%20the%20legal%20process. Accessed June 25, 2023.

---

[3] Mezzo-level practice is interventions with organizations and communities or neighborhoods. Mezzo-level prevalence estimations hold promise for better information about trafficking at a community level, and therefore better designed programs informed by the information gathered at the mezzo level. For example, in Sierra Leone, PRIF conducted the largest-scale mezzo research by sampling 4,000 households in four districts.

University of Texas at Austin. 2016. *Human Trafficking by the Numbers: The Initial Estimate of Prevalence and Economic Impact for Texas, Final Report.* University of Texas at Austin.

UNODC (United Nations Office on Drugs and Crime). 2020. *Global Report on Trafficking in Persons.* United Nations publication, Sales No. E.20.IV.3 https://www.unodc.org/documents/data-and-analysis/tip/2021/GLOTiP_2020_15jan_web.pdf. Accessed June 25, 2023.

US Congress. House. 1999. Committee on International Relations and Human Rights. *Trafficking of Women and Children in the International Sex Trade: Hearing before the Subcommittee on International Operations and Human Rights.* 106th Cong., 1st sess., September 14.

US Department of Justice. 2015. "Mexican National Sentenced to Five Years for Participating in a Brutal Family-Run Sex Trafficking Organization." Federal Bureau of Investigations, May 18. https://www.fbi.gov/contact-us/field-offices/miami/news/press-releases/mexican-national-sentenced-to-five-years-for-participating-in-a-brutal-family-run-sex-trafficking-organization. Accessed June 25, 2023.

US Department of State Archive. n.d. "Clinton Administration Anti-Trafficking Initiatives."

US Department of State. 2022. "Fact Sheet: Understanding Human Trafficking."

Walk Free. 2023. Global Slavery Index. https://www.walkfree.org/global-slavery-index/#the-scale. Accessed June 25, 2023.

Q2. How Widespread Is Sex and Labor Trafficking in the United States?

Answer: The US Department of Health and Human Services (HHS) Office of Trafficking in Persons (OTIP) states that although there is still no rigorous prevalence estimate of human trafficking within the United States, cases of human trafficking have been reported in all fifty states and the District of Columbia, on tribal land, and within US territories. The little information we have comes from a few national efforts at data collection, and some state-specific efforts, including examining the cases that have been prosecuted and studies that individual states have done to ascertain the nature and scope of human trafficking in their own state. To date, the federal government has not conducted a nationwide study on human trafficking in the United States, relying instead on inaccurate and conflicting numbers from international and intergovernmental organizations.

The Facts: There are a number of national, state, and local efforts to collect data that will help map the prevalence of human trafficking in the United States.

US Government Efforts

Annual Attorney General's Report

Each year since 2017, the US Attorney General (AG) has published a report to Congress outlining US government efforts to address human trafficking. The AG's office spends over six months doing "in-reach" to the twenty-one US government agencies that play a vital role in combating human trafficking. The report reflects information from various components of the DOJ, as well as information reported to the DOJ by other US government agencies and departments involved in anti-trafficking efforts. The report uses the 3P framework, which proposes Prevention, Prosecution, and Protection and Assistance, as a tri-partite approach to countering human trafficking, to summarize the accomplishments and deliverables of the US government (Trafficking Victims Protection Act 2000).

In 2020, the AG reported the following under "Prosecutions":

- The FBI initiated 663 human trafficking cases (619 for sex trafficking, 41 for labor trafficking, and 3 for both sex and labor trafficking) and arrested 121 subjects for human trafficking violations (compared to 607 initiated cases and 350 arrests in FY 2019).
- DHS ICE Homeland Security Investigations (HSI) initiated 947 cases related to human trafficking and reported 1,746 criminal arrests, 873 criminal counts charged in indictments, and 400 criminal counts in federal, state, and local convictions (a decrease from 1,024 initiated cases, 2,197 criminal arrests, 1,113 criminal counts charged in indictments, and 691 criminal counts in federal, state, and local convictions in FY 2019).
- US Attorneys' Offices, DOJ's Human Trafficking Prosecution Unit (in the Civil Rights Division), and DOJ's Child Exploitation and Obscenity Section and Money Laundering and Asset Recovery Section (in the Criminal Division) together brought 210 human trafficking cases, charged 337 defendants, and obtained 309 convictions (a decrease from 220 filed cases, 343 defendants charged, and 475 convictions in FY 2019).
- The US Department of Defense (DoD) investigated 160 human trafficking or trafficking related incidents (an increase from 65 total human trafficking

or trafficking-related cases reported in FY 2019), including 48 sex trafficking or related incidents and 112 labor trafficking or related incidents (US Attorney General Report 2020).

It also reported the following actions related to protection and assistance services and programs for victims of trafficking:

- The Federal Bureau of Investigation (FBI) Victim Services Division's 171 victim specialists provided services to human trafficking victims in 564 cases. Services included crisis response, victim support and assistance, needs assessment, victim notification, and service referrals.
- For the one-year period from July 1, 2019, to June 30, 2020, DOJ Office for Victims of Crime (OVC) grantees reported 5,968 new clients who began receiving OVC-funded services for trafficking victims and 3,886 existing clients from previous reporting periods who required ongoing services (an increase from 5,090 new clients and 3,285 existing clients in the 12 months prior). The 9,854 clients represented an all-time high number of clients receiving OVC-funded services during a one-year period.
- The HHS, which operates two grant assistance programs for human trafficking victims, issued 508 Certification Letters to foreign national adults and 673 Eligibility Letters to foreign national children who have experienced human trafficking and met specific eligibility rules to allow them access to federally funded benefits and services (an increase from the 311 Certification Letters issued to foreign national adults and a decrease from the 892 Eligibility Letters issued to foreign national children in FY 2019).
- An HHS-funded victim assistance grant provided case management services to 1,457 foreign national victims of trafficking and 884 US citizens and Lawful Permanent Residents who have experienced human trafficking (an increase from 968 foreign national victims and 825 US citizens and Lawful Permanent Residents served in FY 2019).
- The US Department of Homeland Security (DHS) Immigration and Customs Enforcement's (ICE) Victim Assistance Program assisted 423 identified human trafficking victims (a slight decrease from the 428 victims assisted in FY 2019).
- DHS ICE granted 117 Continued Presence requests and issued 56 extensions to victims of human trafficking (compared to 125 granted requests and 48 extensions in FY 2019).
- DHS US Citizenship and Immigration Services (USCIS) provided immigration relief to human trafficking victims by granting USCIS

provided immigration relief to human trafficking victims by granting T nonimmigrant status to 1,040 victims and 1,018 victims' family members (an increase from 500 victims and 491 victims' family members granted T nonimmigrant status in FY 2019). USCIS met the statutory cap of 10,000 grants of U nonimmigrant status for victims of certain qualifying criminal activity (which may include human trafficking) and approved 7,212 petitions for their eligible family members, for a total of 17,225 approved petitions (a decrease from 17,856 approved petitions in FY 2019). Projects funded by the US Department of State's (DOS) Office to Monitor and Combat Trafficking in Persons (TIP Office) provided more than 5,200 trafficking victims with short-term to long-term services, including shelter, medical and psychosocial care, repatriation, legal aid, and reintegration assistance (an increase from 3,500 victims served in FY 2019). The T and U visas provide legal status to certain victims of human trafficking (T Visas) who assist law enforcement authorities in the investigation or prosecution of trafficking crimes, and to victims of an enumerated list of "qualifying criminal activities" who have suffered substantial physical or mental abuse, and possess information concerning that crime, and who have been, are being, or are likely to be helpful to law enforcement or government officials (U visas) (Trafficking Victims Protection Act 2000).

- The US Department of State Diplomatic Security Service's (DSS) Victims' Resource Advocacy Program supported approximately 95 human trafficking victims.
- The Legal Services Corporation, an independent nonprofit corporation established by Congress to provide financial support for civil legal aid to low-income Americans, recorded 287 human trafficking case closures in calendar year 2020 (an increase from 243 human trafficking cases closed in calendar year 2019).
- In August 2020, EEOC settled a Title VII lawsuit with national origin and race discrimination claims against employers that hired Thai farm workers through a farm labor services company. A federal court had previously entered a default judgment against the labor services company and ordered damages to the workers who were subjected to "an unrelenting sense of imprisonment." The settlement with the farms provides $325,000 for 105 workers and requires the farms to institute accountability measures for farm labor contractors, training, review of policies and procedures, and reporting of violations (US Attorney General Report 2020).

Unfortunately, the *Attorney General Annual Report on Trafficking in Persons* reports data only for a one-year period.

National Efforts to Combat Trafficking

Human Trafficking Institute

The HTI is a nonprofit organization that focuses on empowering justice systems to combat human trafficking effectively. The institute works to ensure that governments and law enforcement agencies have the tools, training, and resources necessary to investigate and prosecute human trafficking cases. Every year HTI publishes a federal human trafficking report (Lane et al. 2023). This report includes a summary of all federal human trafficking cases prosecuted in a given year. From 2001 to 2021, the report stated that the federal government prosecuted over 2,500 cases of human trafficking, including cases in all fifty states, the District of Columbia, on tribal land, and within US territories. Just in the year 2022, HTI reported 178 sex trafficking cases and five labor trafficking cases. Within the cases filed in 2022, there were 363 identified victims, of which at least 34 percent were minors.

While the report is a helpful resource for prosecutors and investigators, it only shows cases that have arisen in the federal system and does not include cases that have been adjudicated in state systems or unreported or uninvestigated cases. As such, the report can't be used to precisely quantify the prevalence of human trafficking in the United States.

National Human Trafficking Hotline

The National Human Trafficking Hotline ("the Hotline") is a helpline in the United States that provides support, information, and resources related to human trafficking. It serves as a confidential and toll-free hotline for victims, survivors, and individuals seeking help or reporting potential cases of human trafficking. Each year the Hotline publishes an annual report providing an analysis of the data received through "substantive signals" that year (National Human Trafficking Hotline 2023). Substantive signals are the communications the Hotline receives through phone calls, emails, texts, webchats, and online tips, which excludes non-substantive communications such as hang-ups or wrong numbers. The report typically includes information such as the number of trafficking cases reported, the types of trafficking (such as sex trafficking or labor trafficking), state-by-state statistics, victim demographics, recruitment methods, and the industries involved.

For example, in 2021, the Hotline reported receiving 51,073 substantive signals. From those signals, the Hotline identified 10,360 potential trafficking cases in the United States. Nearly 75,000 cases implicated sex trafficking scenarios, 1,066 implicated labor trafficking, and 400 implicated both labor and sex trafficking. However, it is important to remember that the Hotline is only able to report data based on the calls it receives. If a victim is unaware of the Hotline or does not call, this data will not be reported. In 2023, 36 state attorneys general sent a letter to Congressional leaders informing them of an issue with the National Human Trafficking Hotline and requesting their assistance to preserve the critical joint federal-state effort to end trafficking (National Human Trafficking Hotline 2023).

Since 2007, Polaris (formerly Polaris Project) has operated the National Human Trafficking Hotline with funding authorized by Congress. Many states rely on the National Hotline to forward tips of suspected human trafficking to local law enforcement to arrest traffickers, safely recover victims, and uncover evidence of trafficking rings and operations.

Legislators discovered that Polaris only forwards tips to state law enforcement about adult victims in limited circumstances. Critics assert this practice is contrary to what Polaris advertises, to what states and organizations have come to expect from this partnership, and to the intent of Congress, which provides funding. In some cases, states have discovered a delay of up to several months before the Hotline shared tips with. Many states, federal agencies, and organizations have actively engaged the public in utilizing the Hotline for tips on trafficking to gather additional intelligence on trafficking operations, disrupt these criminal activities, and recover victims. State attorneys general noted that these newly discovered Polaris practices dramatically diminish the value of the Hotline to any of these efforts. After meetings with legislators, though, Polaris indicated that it would not revise its policies (National Association of Attorneys General 2023).

In their letter to Congress, the attorneys general wrote,

> It appears to us that the Hotline is not performing the services it is already funded to perform. Without changes to Polaris's operating procedures, our state anti-trafficking initiatives gain little from participation in the National Hotline. As such, individual states may be forced to establish their own state hotlines, as some already have begun to do. A nationally run hotline not only achieves cost-efficiencies, but also ensures a uniform approach and allows for the collection of cross-state information with regard to human trafficking tips.

The debate about the mission and purpose of the Hotline continued in reporting by journalists who interviewed survivors. They argued that the Hotline is suffering an identity crisis: is it a law enforcement reporting Tip Hotline, or is it a Support Hotline that offers crisis intervention, empathetic listening, and warm handoffs to designated local service providers. Many survivors noted that they would be less likely to call the National Human Trafficking Hotline if they knew that it might make a report to law enforcement without their request or consent (Shammas 2023).

State-Specific Anti-Trafficking Efforts

Many states have specialized human trafficking task forces coordinated by the state's governor or attorney general. These task forces typically consist of professionals from various agencies and organizations, including law enforcement, prosecutors, social services, victim advocates, and other relevant stakeholders. The primary purpose of these task forces is to coordinate statewide efforts, implement effective strategies to prevent human trafficking, investigate cases, prosecute offenders, and provide support to survivors. In an effort to understand the extent of human trafficking, some states have organized research surveys and studies. These studies can be conducted independently or in partnership with an academic institution or an NGO. Here are some examples:

Texas

In 2016 the Texas Office of the Governor funded a benchmark study of the prevalence of human trafficking in Texas conducted by the University of Texas at Austin (Busch-Armendariz et al. 2016). The Texas report used a mixed-methods approach, analyzing Texas-specific data from the National Human Trafficking Hotline, administering a survey to a wide range of professionals working in human trafficking-related fields, such as law enforcement, policy development, immigration assistance, fields of human trafficking, and so on, conducting focus groups and interviews with both professionals in human trafficking-related fields and persons in populations with a high risk of trafficking, such as migrant workers or at-risk youth. The report then used statistical algorithms to convert this information into approximate rates of human trafficking in Texas. The report estimated that there are approximately 234,000 victims of labor trafficking and 79,000 minor victims of sex trafficking in Texas, with a total of 313,000 victims. However, the report did not include approximations of adult victims of sex trafficking, leaving what is likely a large population unreported.

New York

The New York State Interagency Task Force on Human Trafficking publishes an annual report on human trafficking in New York (The New York State Interagency Task Force on Human Trafficking n.d.) In its report, the New York Task Force compiled information gathered from 2007 to 2020. In that time period, the task force has identified 1,841 confirmed victims, of which 68 percent are sex trafficking victims, 26 percent are labor trafficking victims, and 6 percent are both. The task force also identified the geographic locations of the victims, reporting that 38 percent of all victims were trafficked in New York City.

Minnesota

The Minnesota legislature passed a statute mandating the creation of an anti-human trafficking task force and the publication of annual reports assessing trafficking in Minnesota. In its 2019 report, the Department of Health and Safety published its findings from a 2017 survey administered to those most likely to come in contact with victims of trafficking, primarily service providers and law enforcement (Minnesota Office of Justice Programs and Minnesota Statistical Analysis Center 2019). In this survey, law enforcement identified 21 labor trafficking victims and 401 sex trafficking victims. In the same survey, service providers identified 394 labor trafficking victims and 2,124 sex trafficking victims. The survey also collected data regarding the age of victims, the race and ethnicity of victims, and the trafficking venue.

Florida

Florida's attorney general serves as chair of Florida's Statewide Council on Human Trafficking. Rather than focusing on victim rates, the council's 2022 annual report highlighted prosecutorial and investigative efforts in a nine-month period (Statewide Council on Human Trafficking Florida 2022). Between January and September 2022, Florida investigated, charged, or sentenced 150 targets for human trafficking-related charges.

Arizona

Arizona's Human Trafficking Council works with and helps to fund the Office of Sex Trafficking Intervention Research (STIR) at Arizona State University (Arizona Human Trafficking Council 2021). STIR publishes reports on trafficking in Arizona as it relates to specific issues or contexts. For example, in its 2021 Youth Experience Survey, STIR surveyed eighty-nine homeless young adults and found that nearly a quarter of the participants experienced sex trafficking and nearly a quarter experienced labor exploitation (Roe-Sepowitz 2021). In another study, STIR published a county-specific report on child sex trafficking. In a four-year period, the Maricopa County Child Sex Trafficking Collaborative identified 291 child victims of sex trafficking (Roe-Sepowitz 2020). The ages of the victims ranged from five to seventeen years. These studies are helpful for understanding the contexts in which trafficking occurs and guiding policymakers and law enforcement agencies. However, they merely confirm that trafficking exists rather than indicating the extent or prevalence of trafficking.

Conclusion

Understanding the prevalence of human trafficking in the United States is challenging for several reasons. Trafficking typically happens through underground and clandestine criminal networks that target the most vulnerable members of society for trafficking. Even if they could report their situation to law enforcement authorities, health providers, social workers, or others they may come in contact with, they often refrain out of fear of retaliation from traffickers; fear of deportation or other legal problems; anxiety about being returned to an abusive home, jail, or foster care placement; and fear that traffickers might cause harm to family or loved ones.

In addition to reporting issues, many states have decided to focus on only one or two types of trafficking, usually those types they deem most egregious. A number of states are pursuing robust investigations and prosecutions of child sex trafficking and forced labor but not adult sex trafficking (the recruiting, transporting, harboring, provision, obtaining, patronizing or soliciting of a commercial sex act through force, fraud, or coercion in the federal definition). Further, each state has its own definition of trafficking, which makes aggregation of data almost impossible.

Only a few states are publishing full records of the cases of human trafficking investigated and prosecuted at the state level, and currently, no organization is gathering data from all fifty states on state-generated cases.

Finally, most reports, at both the federal and state level, are annual, going from fiscal year to fiscal year. Since the investigation, charging, prosecution, and conviction in cases runs across fiscal years, and victim services are also going beyond a fiscal year, gathering can be difficult.

Further Reading

Arizona Human Trafficking Council. 2021. *Annual Report.* https://www.goo
gle.com/url?q=https://goyff.az.gov/file/1862/download?token%3DUlV7w
ZC_&sa=D&source=docs&ust=1689199906849082&usg=AOvVaw3_P34DtQFfP
UGChLRh0We1. Accessed September 19, 2023.

Busch-Armendariz, Noël, Nicole Levy Nale, Matt Kammer-Kerwick, Bruce Kellison,
Melissa Irene Maldonado Torres, Laurie Cook Heffron, and John Nehme. 2016.
*Human Trafficking by the Numbers: The Initial Benchmark of Prevalence and
Economic Impact for Texas.* Austin, TX: Institute on Domestic Violence and Sexual
Assault. https://traffickinginstitute.org/wp-content/uploads/2023/06/2022-Fede
ral-Human-Trafficking-Report-WEB-Spreads_compressed.pdf. Accessed July
1, 2023.

Lane, Lindsey, Angela Gray, Alicen Rodolph, and Brittany Ferrigno. 2023. *2022 Federal
Human Trafficking Report.* Fairfax, VA: Human Trafficking Institute. https://trafficki
nginstitute.org/wp-content/uploads/2023/06/2022-Federal-Human-Trafficking-Rep
ort-WEB-Spreads_compressed.pdf. Accessed September 19, 2023.

Minnesota Office of Justice Programs and Minnesota Statistical Analysis Center. 2019.
Human Trafficking in Minnesota: A Report to the Minnesota Legislature. https://www.
lrl.mn.gov/docs/2019/mandated/191234.pdf. Accessed July 1, 2023.

National Association of Attorneys General. 2023. "Attorneys General Call on Congress
to Improve Federal-State Cooperation to End Human Trafficking," NAAG, February
27. https://www.naag.org/press-releases/attorneys-general-call-on-congress-to-impr
ove-federal-state-cooperation-to-end-human-trafficking. Accessed July 1, 2023.

National Human Trafficking Hotline. 2023. *2021 National Human Trafficking Hotline
Data Report.* https://humantraffickinghotline.org/sites/default/files/2023-01/Natio
nal%20Report%20For%202021.docx%20%283%29.pdf. Accessed July 1, 2023.

Roe-Sepowitz, Dominique, James Gallagher, Karrie Steving, Lisa Lucchesi. 2020.
Maricopa County Sex Trafficking Collaborative—Analysis of Three-Years of Cases.
https://socialwork.asu.edu/sites/default/files/2022-08/final2_maricopa_county_
child_st_collaborative_report_122020.pdf. Accessed July 1, 2023.

Roe-Sepowitz, Dominique, and Kristen Bracy. 2021. *Youth Experiences Survey:
Exploring the Human Trafficking Experiences of Homeless Young Adults in Arizona,
Year Eight.* Phoenix: Arizona State University School of Social Work, Office of
Sex Trafficking Intervention Research. https://socialwork.asu.edu/sites/default/
files/2022-08/combinedyes2021_report.pdf. Accessed September 19, 2023.

Statewide Council on Human Trafficking Florida. 2022. *Annual Report.* http://legacy.
myfloridalegal.com/webfiles.nsf/WF/MNOS-CKLQYN/$file/2022HumanTrafficki
ngAnnualReportFINAL.pdf. Accessed September 19, 2023.

The New York State Interagency Task Force on Human Trafficking. Reports. https://
otda.ny.gov/programs/bria/. Accessed September 19, 2023.

United States of America: Victims of Trafficking and Violence Protection Act of 2000, October 28, 2000. Public Law 106-386 [H.R. 3244]. https://uscode.house.gov/view. xhtml?path=/prelim@title22/chapter78&edition=prelim. Accessed September 19, 2023.

United States Attorney General's Annual Report to Congress on US Government Activities to Combat Trafficking in Persons, Fiscal Year 2020. https://www.justice. gov/humantrafficking/page/file/1486861/download. Accessed September 19, 2023.

Q3. Does Labor Trafficking Occur in the United States?

Answer: Yes. The HTI analyzes the case law in the United States each year and has drawn up a list of over 2,500 cases of human trafficking that have been prosecuted in the United States from 2001 to 2021. While the HTI list reflects only the cases that have been reported, investigated, and prosecuted, it does give us an indication of how many labor trafficking cases have been documented in the United States over a twenty-year period. It is important to remember that one labor trafficking case can have hundreds of victims. Labor trafficking has been neglected in the United States, partly because of perceptions that it only happens overseas—in Southeast and South Asia, in Africa, in South America. But the truth is, labor trafficking has been uncovered in food services and food production factories, hotel and travel industries, garment and clothing factories, the tech industries, construction, mining, farming and agriculture, security services (guards, etc.), and more across the United States (US Department of Defense, 2023).

The Facts: In early 2023, the US Department of Labor (DOL) found that Packer Sanitation Services, a vendor that provides laborers for thirteen US meat packing companies, hired minority workers ages thirteen to seventeen to work overnight sanitation shifts in meat packing plants around the country. The Labor Department investigation found 102 children between the ages thirteen and seventeen working in hazardous occupations. The investigation showed that Packers' systems flagged the children, but the company ignored the flags. When the Labor Department's Wage and Hour Division arrived with warrants, the adults—who had recruited, hired, and supervised these children—tried to derail the efforts to investigate their employment practices.

The DOL investigation, which spanned across eight states, found that the children were working with hazardous chemicals and cleaning meat processing equipment including back saws, brisket saws, and head splitters. Investigators learned that at least three minors suffered injuries while working for the sanitation service provider. DOL issued a statement saying that "The child labor violations in this case were systemic and clearly indicate a corporate-wide failure by Packers Sanitation Services at all levels. These children should never have been employed in meat packing plants and this can only happen when employers do not take responsibility to prevent child labor violations from occurring in the first place" (US Department of Labor [DOL] 2023).

The meat packing industry is not the only one under investigation for labor trafficking. The DOL also began an investigation of a food processing company that produces a popular brand of granola bars as well as cereals and snack foods for employing migrant children. DOL said that there has been a 69 percent increase in children illegally working at US companies since 2018. It also indicated that it has 600 ongoing child labor investigations and it found 835 companies in the last fiscal year that violated labor laws employing more than 3,800 children (DOL 2023).

According to the HTI's *Federal Human Trafficking Report*, an annual report from the only data collection instrument that collects and analyzes data from federal case law on human trafficking, there have been over 2,250 US cases of human trafficking in which there were almost 9,000 victims and over 3,300 convicted of human trafficking (Lane et al. 2022). Of those cases, 2099 were sex trafficking and 151 were labor trafficking cases. There were 1953 victims of labor trafficking and 445 defendants (labor trafficking perpetrators) (Human Trafficking Institute 2022). However, it is important to remember that these are only the criminal cases. Many, in fact most, of the labor trafficking cases are investigated through the Wage and Hour Division of the DOL. Note that DOL says that it has 600 ongoing investigations of child labor cases alone. To get an accurate computation of the number of labor trafficking cases, number of victims, whether they are adults or children, and how many defendants, one would have to combine the reports from these two sources.

Labor trafficking criminal cases are usually charged using 18 U.S.C. §1589 for forced labor, which is found in Title 18, Chapter 77 of the United States Code (US Code) This statute states that

> Whoever knowingly provides or obtains the labor or services of a person by any one of, or by any combination of, the following means—
>
> 1. by means of force, threats of force, physical restraint, or threats of physical restraint to that person or another person;
> 2. by means of *serious harm* or threats of *serious harm* to that person or another person;

3. by means of the *abuse or threatened abuse of law or legal process*; or

4. by means of any scheme, plan, or pattern intended to cause the person to believe that, if that person did not perform such labor or services, that person or another person would suffer *serious harm* or physical restraint,

shall be punished [as provided under subsection d].

Globally, one of the most notorious industries for labor trafficking is fisheries. From Thailand and Vietnam, to Taiwan, to Ukraine, to a number of countries off the coast of Africa, officials have documented serious cases of human trafficking (Task Force on Human Trafficking in Fishing in International Waters 2021, 50). In the United States, the problem has been uncovered in foreign-owned and foreign-operated vessels off the coasts of Hawaii and other Pacific coast states. To date, the United States has not identified cases of human trafficking aboard US fishing vessels (Task Force 2021, 8).

However, several NGOs have claimed that labor trafficking is taking place on US vessels as well, and many have identified trafficking in the supply chain of fish that is sold and served in the United States. NGOs claim that foreign fishing workers employed on U.S. longline fishing vessels have been subjected to exorbitant recruitment and repatriation fees; prolonged work hours; unsanitary and unsafe living and working conditions; denial of medical care; verbal and mental abuse, including threats of deportation; and inadequate provision of basic necessities, including food, water, clothes, and safety gear (Human Rights Institute 2019). Some industry actors have publicly responded to some of these allegations and announced efforts to further improve labor conditions (White 2016).

In 2016, two Indonesian citizens filed the first-ever human trafficking lawsuit against a US commercial fishing vessel under the TVPA and the Alien Tort Statute. In that case, the fishermen alleged they were subjected to human trafficking on a US commercial fishing vessel called the *Sea Queen II* operating in the Pacific Ocean (Task Force on Human Trafficking in Fishing in International Waters 2021, 50).

According to the complaint, the young men signed what they believed to be a legitimate contract to work as tuna fishermen aboard an American vessel. They needed reliable employment to provide for their families, and under the offered contract, they would have earned more money than they had ever been paid before. To get the contract, the men had to pay large recruitment fees for the chance to work. Only after the men were ready to leave did the agent ask them to sign a second contract, containing a $1,000 penalty in US dollars (the equivalent of approximately 2.5 months' wages) if they failed to complete their two-year term. After taking several flights, the two men boarded the overcrowded vessel where they had contracted to work but were soon forcibly transferred in the middle of the Pacific Ocean to a different vessel, the *Sea Queen II*. Their passports and other important papers were taken to prevent them from leaving or seeking help whenever the vessel docked. The owner of the vessel also told them they could not return to their homes unless they paid him $6,000. According to their complaint, conditions on the US vessel were so bad that they fled when the boat was docked in San Francisco, California. When they were found, they were emaciated and traumatized from their ordeal. This case never reached the courts because the parties reached a settlement for an undisclosed amount. As part of the settlement, the owner agreed to adopt a code of conduct to protect future workers and to distribute a flyer to workers informing them of their protections under the law. However, unless someone is investigating, including conducting spot checks and unannounced audits, it will be hard to discover whether the owner is actually ensuring that there is no labor trafficking on his boat.

Another example of the potential for labor trafficking is found in the DoD. U.S. Central Command (CENTCOM) has thousands of foreign contractors authorized to accompany the force (CAAF) within its area of operation. At the height of the war in Iraq some estimates say over 160,000 private contractors supported US forces in Iraq (Singer 2007; Miller 2007). In Afghanistan at the height of the conflict, there were over 115,000 contractors on US military installations (Congressional Research Service 2021). In 2008, the United States had 187,900 troops in Afghanistan and Iraq, the peak of the US deployment, and 203,660 contractor personnel, with a ratio of more contractors to troops (Miller 2007; Congressional Research Service 2021).

In 2011, New Yorker journalist Sarah Stillman published "The Invisible Army," an article about the foreign workers on US military bases in Iraq and Afghanistan (Stillman 2011). She noted that armed security personnel accounted for only about 16 percent of the overall contracting force. The vast majority—more than 60 percent of the total in Iraq—weren't US military personnel but what she called, "hired hands." The workers were recruited from a dozen nations around the globe, primarily countries in South Asia and Africa, and lived and worked inside the US military bases in barbed-wire compounds. They were called "Third Country Nationals"—TCNs for short. In her investigation, she found that thousands were employed by fly-by-night subcontractors who were unwittingly financed by the American taxpayer.

Stillman claimed that many of these TCNs were being held in indentured servitude—a term that describes a form of labor in which a person is contracted to work without salary for a specific number of years. The contract, called an "indenture," may be entered "voluntarily," or it may be imposed by those doing the hiring. In the case of the workers laboring on US military bases, the prime contracts under which they were hired were held by large US defense contractors such as KBR, Dyncorp, Halliburton, and a dozen more. These prime contractors were headquartered in the United States but often subcontracted with other foreign-owned companies to recruit workers to fill civilian positions at US military bases (Stillman 2011). While the modus operandi of these latter outfits differed slightly, many of them placed ads in newspapers and other publications (and sometimes now online) advertising jobs with pay and benefits far more lucrative than what most workers could hope to earn in their own countries. Workers were interviewed in their own countries and asked to sign contracts, sometimes in languages that they could not read. Some of the contracts were forthright, and only later was there a "bait and switch," where workers were told that they had gotten the job working for the US military, but they had to sign another contract because the original contract was not available (US Department of Defense 2023b). One representative account was provided by Kumar, who was tricked during the recruitment process in his small village in India:

> I come from a small city in the southern state of Tamil Nadu, India. One day I saw an ad in the newspaper for a U.S. company that was recruiting for Army jobs in Afghanistan. They wanted people with training and experience in the food service industry. I had work experience and certifications in food services and preparation, so I thought I would apply. I went to the offices of the U.S. company that was listed in the newspaper ad. It took me 36 hours, over two days of travel by train to get to Delhi. When I arrived, they referred me to a sub-agent [who told me I must pay him] 75,000 Indian rupees ($1,200) to get the job. I told him I could get the money. My mama had some gold I could use as collateral to get a loan. The money amounted to what I would make in seven months wages in my hometown and the interest rate for the loan was 30% rate, but the Army job promised around $1,200 per month, so I figured I could pay off the loan in no time at that salary. Once I [paid] the fee, I received the offer. The written contract promised me $4.25 per hour, twelve hours per day, six days per week. After some in-processing in India, I was sent to Dubai. While in Dubai, I was informed that the contract I signed had to be changed. I would not be a food service worker in the dining facility, I would now be a laborer, making $2.25 per hour. I was told that I could go home, but I had already paid the recruitment fee to get the job so that money would be lost. (US Department of Defense 2023)

The recruitment process was corrupt, with many subcontractors "double dipping"—securing payment from the prime contractor to recruit workers, and then forcing workers to pay just to be hired—that prohibitions on charging recruitment fees to workers were implemented via presidential Executive Order (EO) and a new law passed by Congress (Executive Order 13627, 2012). Six years after the EO and the law, it was still not clear what constituted "recruitment fees." Some said all recruitment fees should be prohibited; others said only "exorbitant" fees should be banned. After years of discussion and debate, on December 20, 2018, a Final Rule was issued, with a full definition of what constitutes "recruitment fees."

The Final Rule said that recruitment fees, as used in the anti-trafficking regulations, are "fees of any type, including charges, costs, assessments, or other financial obligations, that are associated with the recruiting process, regardless of the time, manner, or location of imposition or collection of the fee" (Federal Register 2018). The definition provides specific examples of recruitment fees, which they note are illustrative, rather than exhaustive. The examples include:

- Soliciting, identifying, considering, interviewing, referring, retaining, transferring, selecting, training, providing orientation to, skills testing, recommending, or placing employees or potential employees
- Advertising
- Obtaining permanent or temporary labor certification, including any associated fees
- Processing applications and petitions
- Acquiring visas, including any associated fees
- Acquiring photographs and identity or immigration documents, such as passports, including any associated fees
- Accessing the job opportunity, including required medical examinations and immunizations; background, reference, and security clearance checks and examinations; and additional certifications
- An employer's recruiters, agents or attorneys, or other notary or legal fees
- Language interpretation or translation, arranging for or accompanying on travel, or providing other advice to employees or potential employees
- Government-mandated fees, such as border crossing fees, levies, or worker welfare funds
- Transportation and subsistence costs, both while in transit as well as from the point of debarkation to the worksite
- Security deposits, bonds, and insurance
- Equipment charges.

In addition, the definition clarifies that a recruitment fee is prohibited regardless of the manner in which the fee is imposed, noting that prohibited fees include those that are:

- Paid in property or money
- Deducted from wages
- Paid back in wage or benefit concessions
- Paid back as a kickback, bribe, in kind payment, free labor, tip, or tribute
- Collected by an employer or a third party, including, but not limited to agents, labor brokers, recruiters, staffing firms, subsidiaries/affiliates of an employer, any agent or employee of such entities, and subcontractors at all tiers.

The Final Rule made it clear that the timing of the fee is irrelevant: if a fee is associated with the recruiting process, it is a recruitment fee, regardless of what it is called and when the fee is imposed.

Thus, the relevant inquiry to determine if the prohibition applies is the purpose for which the fee is incurred and whether the fee is imposed upon the employee or potential employee. The final rule makes clear that a recruiting entity is not prohibited from charging for its services, and indeed recruitment costs can be reimbursable to the prime contractor, they just may not be imposed or passed on to the prospective contract and subcontract employees.

In addition to being charged exorbitant types of recruitment fees, there were other slavery and slavery-like practices in which unscrupulous contractors and subcontractors are engaged. For example, many workers told stories of being robbed of wages, injured without compensation, subjected to sexual assault, and held in conditions resembling indentured servitude by their subcontractor bosses (Stillman 2011).

During a yearlong detail in Afghanistan, the head of the Combating Trafficking in Persons (CTIP) Office interviewed hundreds of workers on military bases and found widespread problems that the DoD, and even the prime contractors, were not aware of. Several cases were documented by US government Contracting Officer Representatives (CORs) and Contracting Officers (KOs). They documented cases where workers were working in hazardous jobs such as waste management without proper protective clothing or equipment, where workers were living in unsanitary and unsafe housing conditions, with no clean running water, roofs with large holes in them, and overcrowded living conditions. Previously unreleased contractor memos, hundreds of interviews, and government documents confirm many of these claims and reveal other grounds for concern. In at least two instances there were internal rebellions or a series of food riots in Pentagon subcontractor camps, one involving more than a thousand workers.

The DoD responded by creating a semi-permanent CTIP Program Manager position within CENTCOM (Woods 2020). This position was filled from 2014 to February 2020, when the United States withdrew from Afghanistan. For over five years, the CTIP staffer worked full-time as a kind of ombudsmen, meeting with Command, liaising with private contractors and subcontractors, and talking directly to workers. After the end of the war in Iraq and as the United States was withdrawing from Afghanistan in April of 2020, there were still over 25,000 contractors authorized to accompany the force in support of functions such as food services, private security guards, sanitation, construction, electrical utilities, transportation, logistics, and many others (Congressional Research Service 2021, 8).

The CTIP Program Manager noted

Throughout my time in Afghanistan, the number [of military contractors] fell to 12,000 as the military mission reduced and the corresponding proportions of contractors demobilized. I documented conversations with over 2,000 of these contractors, often through the demobilization process, but also in the midst of 34 detentions, 4 pay-protest demonstrations, and hundreds upon hundreds of pandemic strandings. (Woods 2020)

In March of 2020, Covid-19 exacerbated conditions, with workers being held against their will in camps, warehouses, and other makeshift facilities as contracts were abruptly terminated. Consider the words of Lusambu Karim, who was hired as a security guard for one of the camps in Afghanistan:

My name is Lusambu Karim. I was born in Uganda and grew up in the Eastern part of Uganda in Nalugugu Village in the Sironko District. In my childhood, I helped around our house and village doing home cultivations, digging, and rearing domestic animals such as cows and goats. My life was a good one, and mainly uneventful. I went to school and stopped at Ordinary Level of Education (UCE) (equivalent to two years of high school) [to help earn money for our family]. In 2018, I was recruited to work in Afghanistan by a Ugandan security company. They transferred me to a contractor headquartered in Kenya, and they transferred me to another company where I signed a contract to work for $450/month as a security guard. My job description was to provide security to U.S. Army personnel, civilian contractors, and government properties within the Army base. Twenty-one Ugandans (including myself) were sent to Afghanistan. We were responsible for providing security for the camp including three entry points and five towers.

The working and living accommodations were [terrible]. We had no PX (Post Exchange) in Camp; the dining facility (DFAC) was so small that we [had to] eat outside. There was no medical hospital or clinic for us. If we got sick, we had to be flown to Bagram Airbase for treatment. We were not allowed to have or use phones, so it was difficult to communicate with our families. Most of us had families in rural villages in Uganda where there was little or no Internet access so for all practical purposes, we were not in communication with our families during the time we were there. Many times, we registered complaints with the company about these problems, but they did not respond. We were told we had to operate out in the open, where there was no shelter from the elements. In the winter it was cold and rainy, in the summer it was so hot (up in the high 90s in the summer).

Under duress, we continued to serve even though we were treated badly. Although we registered complaints about hazardous working and living conditions, they went unanswered. It got worse. We were "red-badged" and told that we couldn't leave our compound for any reason. Red-badging is a status they give to foreign workers stuck at the largest U.S. airfield in Afghanistan who have been living in what they describe as jail-like conditions for months after their jobs were cut, but they've been unable to return home. Workers with red badges are confined to temporary lodging quarters where they are constantly monitored by security guards. Those who don't meet certain security criteria are given red badges—as opposed to green badges. Then our contracts ran out and we were required to work for 6 months without a contract. When the Taliban attacked Kunduz City where our camp was located, I went to the boss, representing the 21 Ugandans and told him that we couldn't continue working without contracts. I asked him what would happen if anyone got injured or died while on duty. There would be no way to file a case for compensation without a valid contract. He dismissed me.

When I spoke on behalf of the men to the site manager I said "Sir, we don't have any contract outlining our job responsibilities. If you can't get us a contract, you should book us a flight to Uganda so we can go home." He replied, "I will as soon as I can get one." For sure we were working in captivity at that point.

[At the height of the Covid-19 pandemic, we were being held in] the Transit Area. It had so many different people from different countries and different camps with different cultures. The area was filthy. No one was cleaning it. There were no hand sanitizers or water to wash hands before entering the Area. There were hundreds of people from everywhere all using the same showers, toilets, and sinks. No one was testing us. I suggested that everyone should be tested, but they ignored my suggestion. People were sneezing and coughing, and several were seriously sick but there was no place to take people if they got sick. We had to be escorted to go anywhere. We weren't allowed any other movements. We were literally prisoners like this for months. (US Department of Defense 2023c)

During the war in Iraq and in Afghanistan, the Central Command (CENTCOM) of the DoD had thousands of foreign CAAF within its area of operations. In 2020, in Afghanistan, the Covid-19 pandemic caused a slowdown and then a demobilization of many of these foreign contractors. In the process of being sent back to their countries of origin, thousands become stranded without pay—in many cases for three months or more. During the time, they were confined to their room with no TV, no books, no access to the post exchange, no exercise, no computers, no mobile phones, and no ability to leave their rooms without a contractor employee "escort." Some were in six-per-person rooms, but others were in warehouses with bunk beds holding thirty or more workers. They were stuck in limbo without the benefit of out-processing by their company's human resources element. They could not contact their families back home, could not send money, nor could they work in their home countries to provide for their families.

Restrictions that slow or stop demobilization can be caused by changes in hostility levels in a war zone, drawdowns, or new strategic considerations. In 2020, the demobilization was caused by an unexpected global pandemic. In any demobilization, workers are affected, but with Covid-19, the demobilizations were especially chaotic: pay status was canceled, access to healthcare was withdrawn, base access badges were confiscated and an "escort-only" badge was assigned, access to communication systems and devices were removed, and the demobilized workers were moved to transient living spaces. In other words, all the privileges and many protections of CAAF status were removed. In addition, foreign national workers are guaranteed return (by statute in the National Defense Authorization Act and by contract) to their Home of Record (HOR) when the contract is complete, but during the pandemic, this administrative function collapsed. The DoD then found itself responsible for taking care of former workers stuck in a war zone without CAAF status.

During the latter half of 2020 and early 2021, the United States began working on a set of best practices for treatment of Other Country Nationals to mitigate harms during crisis situations such as Covid-22. They included recommendations to:

1. Forbid contractors from leaving an employee in limbo by initiating a demobilization action the contractor knows cannot be completed. If circumstances arise after initiating demobilization that then cannot be

completed, contractors need a contingency plan. The focus should be on ensuring contractors finish processes in a timely way by having a plan to pay the employees until they are returned to their Home of Record, and taking responsibility for costs associated with housing, feeding, and providing transportation to return employees to their homes of record.

2.   Clearly define what an "escorted" status means. If the US Government means "confine", then we should say "confined." The word "escort" means "to accompany." A person not in confinement, who wishes to go for an exercise walk may leave his or her room and go for a walk. An escort may be required to accompany the walker, but lack of escort should result in a citation to the contractor, not confinement for the walker.

3.   Recommend the demobilizing contractor maintain recreation and communication benefits for demobilized personnel to the same degree available to those employees remaining in CAAF status. If costs are associated with CAAF employees in a pay status (such as "air cards" or television), these same opportunities should be offered by the contractor at no cost to the stranded employees as long as they remain in a no-pay status.

4.   Hold contractors accountable, per the terms of the contract, for "*failing to provide return transportation … upon the end of employment.*" Complexity or cost should not be allowed to become default excuses by contractors for failure to repatriate demobilized employees. Contractors should have the foresight to recognize hindrances to demobilization and plan accordingly before initiating a process that cannot be completed in a reasonable amount of time.

5.   Consider weekly pay by the contractor to demobilized personnel, in the form of a stipend or partial pay. In Afghanistan, there are examples of companies paying their workers during the time they were demobilized and stranded in the country, while other workers went unpaid during the transition to their homes of record. Some companies, through their procurement agencies, are utilizing CARES Act funds to cover these costs.

Further Reading

Congressional Research Service. 2021. *Department of Defense Contractor and Troop Levels in Afghanistan and Iraq: 2007–2020*, February 22, p. 6. https://sgp.fas.org/crs/natsec/R44116.pdf. Accessed September 19, 2023.

Federal Register. 2018. *Federal Acquisition Regulations (FAR): Combating Trafficking in Persons Definition of Recruitment Fees.* https://www.federalregister.gov/docume nts/2018/12/20/2018-27541/federal-acquisition-regulation-combating-traffick ing-in-persons-definition-of-recruitment-fees. Accessed September 19, 2023.

Georgetown Law Human Rights Institute. 2019. *The Price of Paradise: Vulnerability to Forced Labor in the Hawaiian Longline Fishing Industry.* https://www.law.geo rgetown.edu/human-rights-institute/wp-content/uploads/sites/7/2019/05/Geo rgetown-THE-PRICE-OF-PARADISE-5-4-19-WEB-2.pdf. Accessed September 19, 2023.

Human Rights First. 2017. "The Beautiful Shores of Hawaii: A Hub for Slavery?" Human Rights First. March. https://www.humanrightsfirst.org/blog/beautiful-sho res-hawaii-hub-slavery. Accessed September 19, 2023.

Human Trafficking Institute. 2022. "Prosecution of Human Trafficking Cases." https:// data.traffickinginstitute.org/prosecution-of-human-trafficking-cases/. Accessed September 19, 2023.

Lane, Lindsey, Angela Gray, Alicen Rodolph, Brittany Ferrigno. 2022. *2021 Federal Human Trafficking Report.* Human Trafficking Institute. https://traffickinginstitute. org/wp-content/uploads/2022/06/2021-Federal-Human-Trafficking-Report-Web. pdf. Accessed September 19, 2023.

Mendoza, Martha, and Margie Mason. 2016. "Hawaiian Seafood Caught by Foreign Fishermen Confined to American Boats." Associated Press, September 16. https:// leads.ap.org/best-of-the-week/hawaiian-seafood-caught-by-foreign-crews-confi ned-on-boats. Accessed September 19, 2023.

Miller, T. Christian. 2007. "Contractors Outnumber Troops in Iraq." *Los Angeles Times,* July 4. https://www.latimes.com/archives/la-xpm-2007-jul-04-na-private4-story. html. Accessed September 19, 2023.

Obama, Barack, President. 2012. Executive Order 13627, "Strengthening Protections against Trafficking in Persons in Federal Contracts," September 25.

Singer, Peter W. 2007. "The Dark Truth about Blackwater." Brookings Institute, October 2. https://www.brookings.edu/articles/the-dark-truth-about-blackwater/. Accessed September 19, 2023.

Souza, Kim. 2023. "Tyson Foods' Green Forest Plant Implicated in Child Labor Investigation." *Talk Business & Politics,* March 1. https://talkbusiness.net/2023/03/ tyson-foods-green-forest-plant-implicated-in-child-labor-investigation/. Accessed September 19, 2023.

Stillman, Sarah. 2011. "The Invisible Army." *New Yorker,* May 30. https://www. newyorker.com/magazine/2011/06/06/the-invisible-army. Accessed September 19, 2023.

Task Force on Human Trafficking in Fishing in International Waters. 2021. "Appendix to Report to Congress: Select non-governmental and International Organization Reports Related to Forced Labor in Fishing in International Waters," p. 50. https:// www.justice.gov/crt/page/file/1360366/download. Accessed September 19, 2023.

US Code, Title 18, Chapter 78, "Peonage, Slavery, and Trafficking in Persons," §1589. https://uscode.house.gov/view.xhtml?path=/prelim@title18/part1/chapter77&edition=prelim. Accessed September 19, 2023.

US Department of Defense. 2023a. "Trafficking in Persons 101 Fact Sheet." https://ctip.defense.gov/portals/12/Trafficking_in_Persons_101_Fact_Sheet_2020.pdf. Accessed June 25, 2023.

US Department of Defense. 2023b. "Survivor Voices of Human Trafficking: Kumar." Combating Trafficking in Persons Program Management Office. https://ctip.defense.gov/Portals/12/Kumar%20Story_1.pdf. Accessed September 19, 2023.

US Department of Defense. 2023c. Survivor Voices of Human Trafficking: Lusambu Karim. Combating Trafficking in Persons Program Management Office. https://ctip.defense.gov/Portals/12/Lusambu%20Karim%20Full%20Story_Final_1.pdf. Accessed September 19, 2023.

US Department of Labor. 2023a. "Department of Labor, Health and Human Services Announce New Efforts to Combat Exploitative Child Labor." https://www.dol.gov/newsroom/releases/osec/osec20230227. Accessed September 19, 2023.

US Department of Labor. 2023b. "More Than 100 Children Illegally Employed in Hazardous Jobs, Federal Investigation Finds; Food Sanitation Contractor Pays $1.5M in Penalties." https://www.dol.gov/newsroom/releases/whd/whd20230217-1. Accessed June 25, 2023.

US Department of Labor. 2023c. "Nationwide Food Manufacturer Agrees to Companywide Compliance with Child Labor Laws After an Investigation Finds 2 Teens Employed Illegally in Minnesota." July 7. https://www.dol.gov/newsroom/releases/whd/whd20230707#:~:text=%E2%80%9CAs%20we%20made%20clear%20earlier,and%20Hour%20Administrator%20Jessica%20Looman. Accessed June 25, 2023.

White, Cliff. 2016. "Hawaii Seafood Council Responds to Alleged Labor Abuse in Longline Fleet." *Seafood Source*, September 19. Hawaii Seafood Council responds to alleged labor abuse in longline fleet | SeafoodSource. Accessed September 19, 2023.

Woods, Jonathan. 2020. "U.S. Military Contingency Operations: Preventing Exploitative Labor Practices," unpublished paper, available upon request.

Q4. Is There One Internationally Recognized Method Used for Estimating Human Trafficking?

Answer: No there is not. Currently there are dozens of different methods being utilized in the United States and abroad for estimating the scope of the problem. Measuring the prevalence of human trafficking is one of the most discussed issues in the anti-trafficking field, but there are significant variations in the way prevalence estimations are generated. However, most of the intergovernmental organizations and some countries (including the United States) increasingly look to and rely upon collaborative efforts of large intergovernmental and nongovernmental agencies one particular nonprofit organization's methodologies (Walk Free 2022; ILO 2023). As many experts have noted, reliable data about the scale and character of trafficking is difficult to find. This is because no standardized measurement tools or procedures for systematic data collection, retention, and sharing have been developed. In addition, the hidden nature of human trafficking makes it difficult to apply conventional probability-based sampling strategies, without which for reference purposes one cannot easily assess the merits of alternative estimation techniques (Weiner 2008).

The Facts: Interestingly, many prominent trafficking researchers focus much of their efforts on measuring the prevalence of human trafficking. Prevalence is a concept that is primarily used in the public health field. The National Institute of Health defines prevalence as follows:

- Prevalence is the proportion of a population who have a specific characteristic in a given time period. To estimate prevalence, researchers randomly select a sample from the entire population they want to describe. Using random selection methods increases the chances that the characteristics of the sample will be representative of the characteristics of the population.
- For a representative sample, prevalence is the number of people in the sample with the characteristic of interest, divided by the total number of people in the sample.
- To ensure a selected sample is representative of an entire population, statistical "weights" may be applied. Weighting the sample mathematically adjusts the sample characteristics to match with the target population.
- Prevalence may be reported as a percentage (5%, or 5 people out of 100), or as the number of cases per 10,000 or 100,000 people. The way prevalence is reported depends on how common the characteristic is in the population.
- There are several ways to measure and report prevalence depending on the timeframe of the estimate.
  - **Point prevalence** is the proportion of a population that has the characteristic at a specific point in time.
  - **Period prevalence** is the proportion of a population that has the characteristic at any point during a given period of interest. "Past 12 months" is a commonly used period.

□ **Lifetime prevalence** is the proportion of a population who, at some point in life, has ever had the characteristic. (National Institute of Mental Health n.d.)

It is important to keep in mind that measuring prevalence is not the same as counting the number of individuals with a particular characteristic of interest. For example, if researchers wish to know the number of people worldwide who have been trafficked over a twelve-month period, they are essentially attempting to measure the frequency of human trafficking cases (i.e., count the number) over the previous year.

Prevalence is focused on probability and risk. For instance, what percentage of adults worldwide over the last year were at risk of being trafficked into forced labor or commercial sex? To properly measure prevalence a researcher must be confident that they can extract a sample that is representative of the target population. That is, a random or probability sample of the adult population in Thailand should produce a representative sample of adult human trafficking victims. The problem for researchers is that victims of human trafficking are not randomly distributed among the population—they are either hidden by their traffickers or geographically concentrated. Against this backdrop several researchers are attempting to measure human trafficking prevalence. What follows is an analysis of several of these attempts.

Walk Free's Mixed-Method Approach

Walk Free (WF) is an NGO focused on working with national and international governmental organizations to design and implement policies aimed at stemming the growth of human trafficking.

> While measuring the number of people in modern slavery remains a challenge, substantial improvements have been made in this field in recent years. In 2017, the inaugural Global Estimates of Modern Slavery were produced by the International Labor Organization (ILO) and Walk Free in partnership with the International Organization for Migration (IOM). The regional estimates produced through this collaboration form the starting point for the estimation of national level estimates presented here. (Walk Free [WF] 2023)

Here WF seems to be describing their success in measuring the frequency of human trafficking victims not the prevalence of human trafficking. This statement indicates that WF, using a representative population sample. did not attempt to measure the risk that an individual might be a victim of human trafficking.

The Global Estimates were comprised of two sub-estimates: an estimate of forced labor and an estimate of forced marriage. The sub-estimate of forced labor was then further broken down into three categories: forced labor in the private economy, forced sexual exploitation, and state-imposed forced labor. (WF 2023)

This description seems to combine several different types of phenomena—with different challenges in counting or measuring frequency. There also are some definitional issues—what constitutes forced marriage and why is it included in measuring trafficking? For instance, are forced marriages arranged marriages or something else? Arranged marriages are quite widespread among certain cultural groups in Asia, the Middle East, and Africa. Most governments, intergovernmental organizations and NGOs seem to have agreed on a definition of forced marriage as a marriage that takes place without the consent of one or both people in the marriage (US Department of State 2023). The State Department notes that sometimes family members will threaten or use force to make someone consent to marriage. This issue does not just affect female victims; research suggests that 15 percent of the cases involve male victims (US Department of State 2023). One gray area is arranged marriage. WF is arguing that all arranged marriages constitute forced marriages and should be counted as human trafficking. One advantage of this approach is that given how widespread arranged marriages are among certain populations, extracting a representative sample is likely to be much easier than finding a representative sample that includes women forced into commercial sexual slavery.

The US definition of human trafficking does not include forced marriage or organ trafficking, so for worldwide purposes, the differences in the legal definitions of what constitutes human trafficking make global estimates much more difficult.

The problems are further exacerbated once WF presents its methodology in more detail:

As no single source provides data that are suitable for the measurement of all forms of modern slavery, a combined methodological approach was adopted for the Global Estimates of Modern Slavery, drawing on three sources of data to calculate the sub-estimates:

1. The central element of the methodology is the use of 54 specially designed, national probabilistic surveys involving interviews with more than 71,000 respondents across 48 countries. The estimates of forced labor in the private economy (excluding the sex industry) and forced marriage were derived from these surveys. Only cases of modern slavery that occurred between 2012

and 2016 were included in these estimates, and all situations of forced labor were counted in the country where the exploitation took place. In the five-year reference period for the estimates, while surveys were conducted in 48 countries, men, women, and children were reported to have been exploited in 79 countries.

2. Administrative data from IOM's databases of assisted victims of trafficking were used in combination with the 54 datasets to estimate forced sexual exploitation and forced labor of children, as well as the duration of forced labor exploitation. This involved calculating the ratio of adults to children, and of "sexual exploitation" cases to "labor" cases in the IOM dataset, which contained information on 30,000 victims of trafficking around the world who had received assistance from the agency. These ratios were then applied to the estimates taken from the survey data on forced labor of adults to arrive at an estimate of the number of children in forced labor and another estimate of "sexual exploitation."

3. As the surveys focused on the non-institutionalized population, meaning that people in prisons, labor camps or military facilities, and other institutional settings are not sampled, the surveys are not suitable for estimating state-imposed forced labor. Instead, the estimate of state-imposed forced labor was derived from validated secondary sources and a systematic review of comments from the ILO Committee of Experts on the Application of Conventions and Recommendations relating to state-imposed forced labor.

Each sub-estimate was initially calculated as a flow estimate; that is, the total number of persons who were victims of modern slavery during a specified period between 2012 and 2016. The flow estimate was then converted into a stock estimate; that is, the average number of persons in modern slavery at a given point in time during the 2012 to 2016 reference period. The stock estimate is calculated by multiplying the total flow by the average duration (the amount of time in which people were trapped in forced labor) of a spell of modern slavery. The average duration of modern slavery was determined from the database of the IOM, containing records of assisted victims of trafficking who were registered during or after 2012. (WF 2023)

Based on their description of their methodology for estimating the number of trafficking victims, WF used the following data collection instrument to determine if an individual who was trafficked during the study period was not likely to produce a representative population sample of trafficking victims.

- Ever been forced to work by an employer or a recruiter?
- Ever been forced to work to repay a debt with an employer or recruiter and were not allowed to leave?
- Ever been offered one kind of work, but then were forced to do something else and not allowed to leave?
- Including children, ever had to work to help another family member who was forced to work by an employer?
- Including children, ever been forced to work for an employer so that another person would receive a job, land, money or other resources?
- Ever been forced to marry? (WF 2023b)

A review of the questions on WF's data collection instrument underscores the observation that is most likely to capture individuals who are no longer under the control of traffickers, not individuals who continue to be exploited.

A review of the questions also reveals that sex trafficking is not directly included. Instead, it appears that WF may have included sex trafficking as a subset of labor trafficking. For the United States and other countries, which define sex trafficking as a commercial sex act compelled by force, fraud, or coercion, or a commercial sex act involving a minor (no force, fraud, or coercion required), this means that an entire type of trafficking may have essentially been relegated to subordinate position or even eliminated altogether.

While using multiple sources is a clever approach to measuring difficult-to-identify populations, such as trafficking victims, combining multiple sources is no guarantee that the final samples are truly representative of the populations they are measuring. Indeed, each of the sources has flaws in producing representative samples. WF identifies the surveys as central to its methods of estimating the prevalence and frequency of human trafficking. To be representative, though, researchers assert there should be no barriers to trafficking victims being included in a survey. However, this is a questionable assumption when trafficking victims can be restricted by their traffickers from participating in surveys and interviews with researchers. Researchers observe that asking individuals whether they were forced to perform some type of labor without proper remuneration is far more likely to generate "yes" responses from those who are no longer subject to the demands of their traffickers than those who are still being exploited (WF 2023a).

This data is useful for designing and delivering services to trafficking survivors but will primarily identify individuals no longer being exploited and/or have managed to find access to government or NGO services.

The third element in the WF methodology is estimating state imposed forced labor. What constitutes forced state labor? Should mandatory military service be included? What about mandatory universal public service? Moreover, WF admits there is no acceptable strategy to directly measure state-imposed forced labor. As such, they must rely on what amounts to some experts' opinions. Again, producing a representative sample seems challenging at best.

Center on Human Trafficking Research and Outreach

The Center on Human Trafficking Research and Outreach (CHTRO), housed in the School of Social Work at the University of Georgia, is a collaborative effort that aims to identify better ways to measure the prevalence of trafficking while crafting real-world solutions to best equip NGOs and policymakers with the tools and information they need to combat trafficking. The CHTRO has a very similar mission to that of WF.

CHTRO is attempting to measure human trafficking prevalence by employing a multidisciplinary research strategy and by working with researchers in a limited number of regions worldwide. As one of their researchers noted,

> Human trafficking and modern slavery are large, complex problems that require solutions from multiple perspectives to address. Thus, a multidisciplinary center allows a variety of disciplines to work together on these problems. Further, locating this center at the University of Georgia allows access to the broader university community, including many talented and motivated faculty and students, who can contribute to finding solutions to these issues.

> Research, policy, and programming work is being done in Guinea, Sierra Leone and Senegal. In Brazil, Costa Rica, Morocco, Pakistan, Tanzania and Tunisia, the center is collaborating with U.S.-based and local researchers to test and validate the existing methods of human trafficking prevalence estimation through the Prevalence Reduction Innovation Forum program. (McGinty 2021)

Human trafficking researchers at the CHTRO methods are similar to WF's in that they are applying and comparing more than one method to measure human trafficking prevalence on the same population.

Lydia Aletaris, an associate research scientist in the School of Social Work, observed the results from this collaborative effort

> should be able to provide guidelines on which methods work best and why. This will be extremely helpful, not only for research on human trafficking, but for research on other hidden populations as well. (McGinty 2021)

University of Georgia has embraced a similar multidisciplinary, multiple source strategy for measuring human trafficking prevalence and estimating the number of victims employed by WF. However, University of Georgia faces the same challenges as WF in finding a repeatable methodology that can produce a truly representative population sample of human trafficking. In addition, as every country has its own laws on human trafficking, and its own definitions of human trafficking, any comparative analysis across countries may be difficult.

Other Trafficking Prevalence Extrapolation Methods

The US Office on Trafficking in Persons (OTIP) in 2020 conducted a comprehensive review of human trafficking prevalence studies. The focus of the OTIP review was on measuring labor trafficking by targeted industries (Barrick, Kelle, and Rebecca 2021). The OTIP review focused on five industries:

1. *Direct care workers*, including personal care aides, home health aides, and nursing assistants in private homes, communities, and nursing homes
2. *Childcare workers*
3. *Animal husbandry*, including chicken, egg, and dairy farms
4. *Construction*, including roofing, carpentry, welding, electrical work, and debris removal (particularly after natural disasters)
5. *Illicit activities*, particularly through forced labor among juveniles in domestic gang activity.

After reviewing the existing studies, OTIP concluded that targeted prevalence studies should

use traditional probability sampling and link-tracing sampling methodologies to estimate the prevalence of labor trafficking victimization. (Barrick, Kelle, and Rebecca 2021)

And concluded that

future studies include the network scale-up method (NSUM) as a no-cost, tag-along third estimation method that can be added to one of the survey techniques listed above. (Barrick, Kelle, and Rebecca 2021)

The OTIP review included 138 studies.

Prior prevalence studies have used various sampling and estimation strategies, including traditional probability samples (e.g., multistage, stratified, cluster), variants of multiple systems estimation (MSE) and capture-recapture techniques, respondent-driven sampling (RDS) and related link-tracing strategies, and other novel approaches. (Barrick, Kelle, and Rebecca 2021)

OTIP found that

Traditional probability samples were used in 17 studies. Most of these estimated the prevalence of child labor outside of the United States (Atteraya et al., 2018; Bhatia et al., 2020; Gilbert et al., 2018; ICF International, 2012; ICF Macro, 2012a, 2012b; Levison et al., 2007; Levison & Langer, 2010; Pinzon-Rondon et al., 2018; Shabbir et al., 2020; Sommerfelt, 2015). For the most part, these studies were able to conduct a secondary analysis of household survey data that had been collected for other purposes. For example, Pinzon-Rondon and colleagues (2018) analyzed data from the Colombian Demographic and Health Survey to estimate the number of children between the ages of 6 and 17 who worked during the week prior to the survey. (Pinzón-Rondón 2018)

However, OTIP found

that methods used to estimate international child labor were not applicable to estimating the prevalence of human trafficking within a specific, targeted industry in the United States. (Barrick, Kelle, and Rebecca 2021)

Several studies (fourteen) used multisystem estimation (MSE) or some variant to measure human trafficking by analyzing existing data sources on known trafficking victims. These studies examined the extent to which trafficking victims were captured in multiple data sources and then used statistical modeling techniques to produce an estimate of the trafficked population. However, this approach is only truly appropriate when victims are captured in multiple datasets (Barrick, Kelle, and Rebecca 2021).

Finally, six studies used several variations of link tracing such as respondent-driven sampling (RDS) or snowball sampling. Link tracing methods are most useful when it is difficult to find an appropriate sampling frame to conduct probability sampling. OTIP found that link tracing was primarily used when attempting to measure the extent of human trafficking involving sexual exploitation. OTIP found two recent studies that successfully used link tracing methods to estimate the prevalence of child labor and sex trafficking in two different regions in India.

The remaining studies in the OTIP review used a variety of less traditional techniques to arrive at an estimate of trafficking, each of these approaches had key limitations:

One study (Kruse & Mahoney, 2000) used secondary data from multiple sources to estimate the prevalence of illegal child labor in the United States. However, the paper does not describe the methods in adequate detail to replicate the estimate. Kazmirski et al. (2009) collected data from local and national organizations on cases of forced marriage in England to estimate the prevalence of reported cases, but they did not extend the estimate to include unreported victims. Williamson et al. (2010) quantified potential pull factors for trafficking among foreign-born individuals (e.g., demand for foreign-born workers, presence of trafficking in neighboring states) to estimate the number of individuals at risk for trafficking (based on census population data). They next quantified the demand for sex and labor and used those ratings to estimate how many at-risk people had been trafficked. A similar method was used for domestic minors involved in sex trafficking. Steinfatt & Baker (2011) used a geographic-based sampling approach to identify and sample sex venues in Cambodia. They observed workers in the selected venues and counted the number of workers who appeared to be underage or unable to leave. Although the field team spoke with management at some of the venues, they did not interview or survey the workers. They used these observational data to estimate the prevalence of sex trafficking. Busch Armendariz et al. (2016) combined administrative data on individuals identified as known or likely trafficking victims, along with surveys of social service providers, to estimate the prevalence of sex and labor trafficking in high-risk populations. They developed victimization rates from the agency survey and applied those percentages to high-risk populations. Anderson et al. (2019) de-duplicated lists of known sex and labor trafficking victims to identify the number of known victims and then incorporated those numbers with aggregate data to arrive at a prevalence estimate.

OTIP also investigated other approaches that "have never or only rarely been used in published human trafficking prevalence studies," including time-location sampling (TLS) and the network scale-up method (NSUM), both of which are being funded through the US State Department's Prevalence Reduction Innovation Forum (PRIF):

> TLS involves developing a sampling frame of venues days-times where the target population congregates and using a random selection procedure (e.g., every fifth person) to select a representative sample of the population. TLS was pioneered by the Centers for Disease Control and Prevention in 1994 to conduct surveys with men who have sex with men (MacKellar et al., 2007). Zhang and colleagues (2019a) applied TLS in city centers and major transportation hubs to recruit youths for their study on the prevalence of child labor in India. They

worked with community agencies and service providers to identify public locations that child laborers frequent and arrange interviews with children. They supplemented this approach with link tracing in one city. NSUM is unique in that it does not require sampling or surveying the target population. In this method, which relies on a probability sample of the general population, survey questions ask how many people the respondent knows who are in the target populations (e.g., "How many direct care workers do you know who [indicators of trafficking]?"). NSUM has been used for more than 20 years in the study of men who have sex with men, heroin users, people with HIV, and other hidden populations (Ezoe et al., 2012; Kadushin et al., 2006; Killworth et al., 1998). There are, however, concerns over the reliability of this method in estimating prevalence, as inaccurate recalls from respondents tend to significantly inflate the numbers. (Salganik et al., 2011)

The OTIP review suggests that the most successful approach to measuring human trafficking prevalence is to focus on a particular industry or sector in a targeted geographic region. This allows the application of several traditional sampling approaches. However, based on the OTIP findings traditional probability sampling strategies seem most appropriate for measuring abuses in labor trafficking in targeted industries such as construction. Linked tracing method and NSUM appear to be more useful for estimating sex trafficking. These methods appear most useful when applied to estimating human trafficking in distinct geographic locations or regions. Attempts to measure trafficking worldwide seem more challenging because of the need to account for local and industry contextual factors.

Further Reading

Barrick, Kelle, and Rebecca Pfeffer. 2021. *Human Trafficking Policy and Research Analyses Project: Comprehensive Review of Prior Prevalence Studies and Recommendations for Field Testing in the United States.* North Carolina: RTI International. https://www.acf.hhs.gov/sites/default/files/documents/opre/HTP RAP%20Prevalence%20Study%20Review%20and%20Recommendations%20508_0.pdf. Accessed September 19, 2023.
McGinty, Johnathan. 2021. "New UGA Center to Combat Global Human Trafficking." *UGA Today*, April 1. https://news.uga.edu/new-uga-center-to-combat-glo bal-human-trafficking/. Accessed September 19, 2023.
National Institute of Mental Health. n.d. "What Is Prevalence?" https://www.nimh.nih.gov/health/statistics/what-is-prevalence. Accessed September 19, 2023.

Pinzón-Rondón, Á. M., L. B. Cifuentes, C. Zuluaga, J. C. Botero, M. Pinzon-Caicedo. 2018. "Wealth, Social Protection Programs, and Child Labor in Colombia: A Cross-sectional Study." *International Journal of Health Services* 48, no. 3:535–48. Doi:10.1177/0020731417747421.

US Department of State. 2023. "Forced Marriage." https://travel.state.gov/content/tra vel/en/international-travel/emergencies/forced-marriage.html.

Walk Free (WF). 2023a. Global Slavery Index. https://www.walkfree.org/global-slav ery-index/#the-scale. Accessed September 19, 2023.

Walk Free. 2023b. "Understanding Forced and Child Marriage." https://cdn.walkf ree.org/content/uploads/2023/05/23134413/GSI-2023-Forced-Marriage-Spotli ght.pdf. Accessed September 19, 2023.

Weiner, Neil, and Nicole Hala. 2008. *Measuring Human Trafficking: Lessons from New York City*. Document No. 224391. U.S. Department of Justice. Award Number: 2005-IJ-CX-0053. https://www.ojp.gov/pdffiles1/nij/grants/224391.pdf. Accessed September 19, 2023.

Q5. Why Do Campaigns to End Human Trafficking Feature Stories of Former Trafficking Victims?

Answer: New research in learning theory tells us that stories can be particularly helpful to people in learning and retaining information. Organizational psychologist Peg Neuhauser found that learning from a well-told story is remembered more accurately, and for far longer, than learning derived from facts and figures (Neuhauser 1993). Similarly, psychologist Jerome Bruner's research suggests that facts are twenty times more likely to be remembered if they're part of a story (Bruner 2010). Anti-trafficking activists assert that telling the stories of survivors, the traffickers, and the illicit trafficking market help make the harm visible and help people understand why and how human trafficking is best understood as a form of modern-day slavery.

The Facts: In 1995, an environmental organization called Global Survival Network (GSN) was formed to track wildlife poachers to document the illicit trade in endangered species. In particular they were interested in uncovering the modus operandi of poachers, wildlife traders, and helping the public to understand black market wildlife trafficking. As part of an effort to stop the poaching of Siberian tigers, mainly for body parts and bones in great demand in China for their supposedly medicinal properties, GSN began conducting undercover video interviews with the poachers. Posing as buyers, they filmed their interactions with poachers and wildlife traffickers using tie tack cameras

(Kelly 2002). In one of the meetings a trafficker admitted he didn't have tigers for sale, but he did have some Russian and Ukrainian women he was selling. This shocking revelation of a link between animal poachers and human traffickers led to a two-year undercover investigation in which GSN arranged meetings with traffickers and pretended to purchase trafficked women in order to interview them.

In 1997, information and undercover video derived from the investigation was used to create a GSN written report, *Crime & Servitude* and a video documentary, *Bought & Sold* (Caldwell 1997a, 1997b). The film received widespread media coverage in the United States and abroad, including specials on ABC Primetime Live, CNN, and BBC and a 1998 article in the *New York Times* (Specter 1998).

The *New York Times* article included an account of Irina, who had answered a vague employment ad in a small Ukrainian newspaper by taking a boat to Haifa, Israel, where she hoped to make a lot of money working in a bar. But that morning, she was driven to a brothel, where her boss burned her passport before her eyes. "I own you," she recalled him saying. "You are my property, and you will work until you earn your way out. Don't try to leave. You have no papers, and you don't speak Hebrew. You will be arrested and deported. Then we will get you and bring you back" (Specter 1998; Lederer 2018, 121).

The *New York Times* article spurred the formation of an unlikely coalition between feminists, evangelicals, human rights organizations, and others who had been quietly tracking the exploitation of women and children across the globe (Hertzke 2004). They believed that the United States needed a new law to address the global trade in human beings. They enlisted champions in the House and the Senate—Republicans and Democrats, liberals and conservatives— to help draft what would become the TVPA of 2000—the first ever whole of government approach to stopping the trade in human beings.

To convince fellow legislators and the general public, they held a series of hearings. The hearings featured experts who testified about the nature and scope of the problem of human trafficking, but more importantly, the hearing gave survivors an opportunity to be heard. Trafficking survivors from Russia, Ukraine, India, Nepal, and Mexico told their stories in Congress (Lederer 2018). While the details of each story were different, the overarching narrative of being tricked, forced, and coerced into forced labor or commercial sex were strikingly similar. Young women and girls were being offered good jobs in hotels and restaurants in other countries, and then forced into prostitution upon arrival.

One particularly compelling story was told in *U.S. v. Cadena* (Lederer 2018, 177). The Cadena case was the first large sex trafficking case in the United

States. A sophisticated criminal network from Mexico, which included sixteen traffickers who were part of an extended family, was indicted for conspiring to lure women and girls from Mexico to Florida with promises of good jobs and better lives and then forcing them into prostitution and holding them as sex slaves in brothel houses in Florida and the Carolinas (US Department of Justice, 2002). This case was the "wake-up call" for the United States as it demonstrated that there were large-scale trafficking rings operating in the US Rosa's story was read into the record because she was a minor:

Rosa was thirteen and waiting tables in a restaurant in a small village in the state of Vera Cruz, Mexico, when she was approached by an acquaintance of the family who told her, "*You know you can make ten times more money in the U.S. doing what you're doing here.* I know someone who can find you a job in Texas—you can send money home to your family; you can have your own life. If you don't like the job, we'll get you a new one. If you're homesick, we'll bring you back across the border. You can't lose."

Rosa had dropped out of school to help her parents earn enough money to feed the family of nine. She knew that her life in Vera Cruz was a dead end. She asked her parents if she could go, but they had heard terrible things about the coyotes who were taking people across the border, and they forbade her. But she was young and hopeful. She wanted a better life than what she had, and so, against her parents' and friends' warnings, she accepted the offer. She was told to pack a small bag of belongings and go to the only hotel in town on Friday evening.

When she got there, a car was waiting, with several other young girls in it from other neighboring villages. She got in, and they drove north into the desert as far as the road went—toward the US border. When the road ended, they got out. There, clustered around in the middle of nowhere, were dozens and dozens more young women and girls from other towns in Mexico.

On the ground were backpacks and water bottles. One of the coyotes told them to pick up a water bottle and backpack each, and then they began to walk. They walked four days and four nights—through the desert, across the Rio Grande, and into Brownsville, Texas, where they were picked up by a series of white vans with no windows and driven across Texas, across Louisiana, and into Florida. There they were dropped off in a rural town called Avon Park, in front of a series of trailers. They were ordered out and the vans drove away.

A big, burly-looking man came out and told them in Spanish, "Now I own you—you will work for me." It was there that Rosa was told for the first time that she had been purchased for $10,000, and that she would have to buy back her freedom by selling her body.

Rosa was young. She was a virgin. She was Catholic. She knew what she was being told was bad—a sin. She began to cry and begged to be taken to a restaurant to work. But she was told, *"There are no restaurant jobs—only this."* When she refused to do what they said, the burly man brought out three other men who took her into one of the trailers and gang-raped her to induct her into the "business." Then they locked her in the trailer without food and water for three days. Rosa testified later in the US Senate that she knew she would die if she didn't succumb. And so, she did.

For the next six months she was a prisoner. During the week, she was forced to service ten or more men a day. On the weekends it was as many as twenty to thirty men. The customers were mainly migrant workers picking orange and tomato crops, but also some men from the surrounding towns. She was very beautiful and young and so was much in demand.

The men bought a ticket, which was a condom, for $20.00. But they often didn't use it. Rosa was impregnated twice and twice forced to have an abortion and forced back into the brothel the next day. She was beaten if she refused a customer's demands. She was guarded twenty-four hours a day, even when she went to the bathroom. She was passed around at private parties that the traffickers held evenings and weekends. Once she and several others tried to escape. They were caught and pistol-whipped around the head and face in front of the other girls—to deter them all from trying that. Shortly after the second abortion and this beating, Rosa became sick and felt crazy. In order to keep her functioning in the brothel, the traffickers gave her drugs and alcohol to numb her pain.

She was only "rescued" when one of the other young women being held prisoner jumped out of a second-story window at one of the private parties and ran to a neighbor's house. The neighbor called the local police. The police called (what was then) the INS and FBI, and a sting operation was set up. Law enforcement officials sent in officers posing as customers and gathered enough evidence to do a raid. Over forty young women and girls were apprehended, and fourteen traffickers were arrested.

A medical doctor examined Rosa. She had several STDs. She had broken bones that hadn't healed properly from the beatings. She had pelvic inflammatory disease and scar tissue from the forced abortions. She was addicted to drugs and alcohol. She was suffering from post-traumatic stress disorder, including nightmares, flashbacks, depression, and suicidal tendencies. In short, she was physically, mentally, emotionally, and spiritually broken (Lederer 2018). Rosa's testimony about her health issues during and after she was trafficked was the inspiration for the first retrospective domestic study on health and human trafficking that has informed an entire new field of research, policy and program development on healthcare providers as first responders to human trafficking (Lederer and Wetzel 2014).

To make matters worse, when Rosa was discovered, the United States didn't have a trafficking law. Instead of rescuing Rosa, the police arrested her and the other females and locked them up in jail along with the traffickers. We simply didn't have a victim-centered approach to trafficking and did not know how to handle the case.

Later, when police began interviewing those they had apprehended, they realized that they were holding two sets of people: the traffickers, who were committing the crimes, and the women and children, who were victims of the crimes. Then Rosa and the other victims were taken from jail to a battered wives' shelter. But there they were told, "Shh—pretend you are a victim of spousal abuse because that was the shelter's mandate." To make matters worse, Rosa wanted to see a priest, but was instead taken to a psychiatrist because that was the medical model this shelter had for addressing violence against women (Lederer 2018, 177, Rosa's Story 1999).

In another early story, a victim of labor trafficking told how she had been recruited to work in a garment factory in American Samoa. She was one of over 260 workers who were told that they would have steady work and a generous biweekly paycheck that would be enough to support their families back home. In order to get the job, she had to pay a recruitment fee of $3,600, but it seemed worth it because she believed she would be making enough to recoup those costs quickly. But when she arrived at the factory, she found the factory had security guards and barbed wire to keep employees in the compound. She was forced to work sixteen-hour days, seven days a week and was not paid, or paid a pittance. When workers complained, the factory owner beat them, assaulted them, threatened them with arrest, deportation, and other tactics. In testimony in court, workers said they fainted from pain and fear. In 2000, the factory owner ordered his guards to beat or kill any workers who weren't producing clothes fast enough. In an ensuing mass attack, the victim told how one of the guards gouged her eye out with a pipe. Word leaked out about how the workers had been beaten and the FBI launched an investigation that turned into one of the first labor trafficking cases in the United States (*U.S. v. Kil Soo Lee*).

Before the passage of the TVPA in 2000, these stories helped advocates and legislators work together to put a human face on human trafficking and to create the 3P framework—*prevention* of trafficking, *prosecution* of traffickers, and *protection* and assistance for victims of trafficking.

Since that time, survivor stories have helped governmental organizations (GOs), intergovernmental organizations (IOs), and NGOs. Many US government agencies feature the stories of survivors on their websites. For example, the US Department of Health and Human Services Office of Human Trafficking recorded stories of survivors to portray the health and human services needs of survivors, and to feature some of the ways that the HHS services meet the needs of survivors (US Department of Health and Human Services n.d.). The US Department of Justice has woven stories into several of its agency divisions, including its Office of Victims of Crime (OVC) which has a website entitled "Faces of Human Trafficking" and has quotes from survivors on posters as well as recordings of survivors as victims of crimes (US Department of Justice n.d.). Combating Trafficking in Persons Program Management Office (CTIP PMO) of the DoD has stories of "military connected" survivors, including survivors whose parents worked for the DoD, either as active military or civil service, survivors who were purchased by active military, survivors who were trafficked by someone active in the Armed Forces, and survivors who tell how joining the military saved their lives (US Department of Defense n.d.).

Further Reading

Bruner, Jerome. 2010. *Narrative, Culture, and Mind in Telling Stories*, ed. Deborah Schiffrin, Anna De Fina, and Anastasia Nylund. Washington, DC: Georgetown University Press. https://repository.library.georgetown.edu/bitstream/han dle/10822/709194/978-1-58901-629-3.pdf?sequence=1&isAllowed=y. Accessed July 1, 2023.

Caldwell, Gillian. 1997. Bought and Sold: An Investigative Documentary on the International Trade in Women.; Global Survivor Network. YouTube. https://hum antraffickingsearch.org/resource/bought-and-sold/. Accessed July 1, 2023.

Caldwell, Gillian. 1998. "Crime & Servitude: An Expose of the Traffic in Women for Prostitution from the Newly Independent States." *Trends in Organized Crime* 3: 10–18.

Hertzke, Allen. 2004. *Freeing God's Children: The Unlikely Alliance for Global Human Rights*. Boulder, CO: Rowman and Littlefield.

Kelly, Elizabeth. 2002. *Journeys of Jeopardy: A Review of Research on Trafficking in Women and Children in Europe*. International Organization for Migration (IOM).

https://publications.iom.int/system/files/pdf/mrs_11_2002.pdf. Accessed July 1, 2023.

Lederer, Laura J. 2018. *Modern Slavery: A Documentary and Reference Guide.* Santa Barbara, CA: ABC-CLIO/Greenwood, 121, 177.

Lederer, Laura J., and Wetzel, Christopher, 2014. "The Health Consequences of Sex Trafficking and their Implications for Identifying Victims in Healthcare Settings." *Annals of Health Law* 23, no. 1: 61.

Neuhauser, Peg. 1993. *Corporate Legends and Lore: The Power of Storytelling as a Management Tool.* New York: McGraw Hill.

Rosa's Story. Lydia's Story. www.globalcenturion.org, P. 121.

Specter, Michael. 1998. "Contraband Women: Traffickers' New Cargo—Naïve Slavic Women." *New York Times*, January 11. https://www.nytimes.com/1998/01/11/world/contraband-women-a-special-report-traffickers-new-cargo-naive-slavic-women.html. Accessed September 19, 2023.

US Department of Defense, Combating Trafficking in Persons Program Management Office. n.d. "Survivor Voices of Human Trafficking." https://ctip.defense.gov/Survivor-Voices/. Accessed September 19, 2023.

US Department of Health and Human Services, Office on Trafficking in Persons. n.d. "Voices of Freedom: An Oral History of Efforts to Address Human Trafficking." https://www.acf.hhs.gov/otip/partnerships/voices. Accessed June 25, 2023.

US Department of Justice, Office of Victims of Crime. n.d. "Faces of Human Trafficking." https://ovc.ojp.gov/program/human-trafficking/faces-of-human-trafficking. Accessed June 25, 2023.

US Department of Justice. 2002. "Florida Man Part of Mexican Trafficking Ring Please Guilty to Involuntary Servitude Charges," September 13. https://www.justice.gov/archive/opa/pr/2002/September/02_crt_525.htm. Accessed June 25, 2023.

U.S. v. Kil Soo Lee. 2004. "Anatomy of an International Human Trafficking Case." Federal Bureau of Investigations, July 16. https://archives.fbi.gov/archives/news/stories/2004/july/kilsoolee_071604. Accessed June 25, 2023.

2

The 3P Framework: Prevention, Prosecution, and Protection and Assistance

We may not know the full nature and scope of the problem of human trafficking, but one thing that the United States and the international community agree upon is a basic structure for addressing the problem. That structure, almost simultaneously presented in US law in October 2000, and in international law in December of 2000, is the 3P (Prevention, Prosecution, and Protection and Assistance) framework. This chapter explores that framework, looking first at its overarching infrastructure as presented in the US Trafficking Victims Protection Act (TVPA) of 2000, then noting a fourth "P"—Partnership—that was added almost a decade after the first three Ps. The chapter also examines each of the "Ps" in more detail.

Let us begin our discussion with Prosecution, because that is where most countries initiated their anti-trafficking efforts—through simple statutes that prohibit human trafficking, thus giving law enforcement the necessary tools for investigations, arrests, prosecutions, convictions, and sentencing of traffickers. This P is an important one, for as one attorney said, "We're always talking about trafficking—but trafficking doesn't happen by itself—we should be focused on the *traffickers*. They are the bad actors—the criminals—doing the recruiting, transporting, harboring, obtaining of victims—by force, fraud, coercion, and taking advantage of vulnerabilities, to traffic people for forced labor or commercial sex." But even though laws and law enforcement officials play a key role in combating trafficking in persons, experts agree that we can't prosecute our way out of this problem.

That leads to another P—Protection and Assistance—which has proven vitally important in helping thousands, indeed, millions, of victims of trafficking around the globe. Whether trafficked for forced labor or commercial sex, they are physically, mentally, emotionally, and spiritually devastated by the exploitation they have suffered. Globally, we marshaled forces to set up emergency services for victims and to provide food, clothing, shelter, medical aid, legal assistance, and more. Over the past twenty years, countries and international entities have offered an astounding number of resources to set up services for victims and survivors. Law enforcement communities in the United States and around the world have come to realize that assisting victims also assists law enforcement efforts. But helping victims to heal is a labor- and resource-intensive business and is primarily focused on helping people recover from trafficking. The final question in this chapter explores effective prevention programs look like and considers various policies and proposals to move "upstream" and keep trafficking from occurring in the first place.

Q6. What Is the Trafficking Victims Protection Act and the 3P Framework?

Answer: The Trafficking Victims Protection Act (Public Law 106-386), commonly known as the "TVPA," became law in the US Congress on October 28, 2000 (TVPA 2000.). It is Division A of the Victims of Trafficking and Violence Protection Act of 2000. The United States was the first country in the world to draft and pass a comprehensive law to combat the transnational crime of human trafficking, TVPA created a "3P Framework"—prevention, prosecution, and protection and assistance—for preventing trafficking, prosecuting traffickers, and protecting and assisting victims of trafficking. This whole-of-government approach has since been modified and adopted by over a hundred countries around the world.

The Facts: The TVPA is arguably the most effective anti-trafficking law in the world. Why is it so effective? Prior to its passage the main statute used for sex trafficking was the Mann Act (18 US Code § 2421), a federal law passed in 1910 that criminalizes the transportation of "any woman or girl for the purpose of prostitution or debauchery, or for any other immoral purpose." But The Mann Act, also known as the White Slave Traffic Act, was inappropriately weaponized after its passage and used to target anyone whom government officials saw as undesirable. For example, in 1912, the Mann Act was used to target Jack Johnson, an African American boxer, for transporting Lucille Cameron, a white woman who was his girlfriend (and later wife), across state lines. Some scholars postulate that he was targeted, using the Mann Act, because he was a successful Black boxer (Blakemore 2023). Seventy two years after his death, President

Trump posthumously pardoned Johnson in an Oval Office ceremony referring to Johnson's conviction as "racially motivated injustice" (White House 2018). Others targeted by the law were actor Charlie Chaplin and singer Chuck Berry. Some believed that men were selectively targeted depending upon their race and their politics. For example, Charlie Chaplin was widely known to have left-leaning views (Weiner 2008). The Mann Act has been amended several times and is still considered good law. In 1986, it was amended to focus further on the protection of minors. The amendment also deleted the terms "debauchery" and "any other immoral purpose" and replaced them with "any sexual activity for which any person can be charged with a criminal offense." Weiner notes that these changes "allowed the government to get out of the business of 'legislating morality' while retaining the essence of the Mann Act as a weapon in the fight against human trafficking" (Weiner 2008).

Despite its use, however, the Mann Act was widely regarded as flawed for its weak statutory provisions, especially with regard to penalties needed to target egregious crimes of traffickers (TVPA 2000; PL 106-386, Section 102 (b) 14).

For labor trafficking, the main statute used for labor trafficking or forced labor was Section 1584 of the US Criminal Code, which was enacted as a part of the 1948 revision of the Criminal Code. But it had been interpreted in court cases to require physical coercion as an element to prove involuntary servitude. During the drafting and passage of the TVPA, Congress argued that many times involuntary servitude was enforced through threats, intimidation, abuse of the law or through a scheme, plan, or pattern. The TVPA introduced new statutes to address both these issues.

In the Purpose and Findings Section of the TVPA, Congress delineates twenty-four reasons (findings) why the new law was needed. Chief among them was the finding that

> Existing legislation and law enforcement in the United States and other countries are inadequate to deter trafficking and bring traffickers to justice. No comprehensive law exists in the United States that penalizes the range of offenses involved in the trafficking scheme. Instead, even the most brutal instance of trafficking in the sex industry are often punished under laws that also apply to lesser offenses, so that traffickers typically escape deserved punishment. (TVPA 2000)

The bill's architects also found that adequate services and facilities did not exist to meet victims' needs regarding health care, housing, education, and legal assistance. Finally, the TVPA noted that the Declaration of Independence, a founding document of the United States, recognizes the inherent dignity and worth of all people, each of whom is endowed by their Creator with certain unalienable rights. Among those rights, according to the TVPA, is "the right to be free from slavery and involuntary servitude is among those inalienable rights."

The TVPA was unique and innovative in a number of ways:

- It defined sex trafficking as, "The recruitment, harboring, transportation, provision, obtaining, patronizing, or soliciting of a person for the purpose of a commercial sex act, in which that act is induced by force, fraud, or coercion, or in which the person induced to perform such act has not attained 18 years of age;" and labor trafficking (forced labor) as, "The recruitment, harboring, transportation, provision, or obtaining of a person for labor or services, through the use of force, fraud, or coercion for the purpose of subjection to involuntary servitude, peonage, debt bondage, or slavery" (TVPA 2000).

- It created a "3P" framework, which has become the fundamental framework used by governments and intergovernmental agencies around the world to combat human trafficking. Although it created new statutes to address modern-day forms of slavery, it incorporated older slavery, peonage, and involuntary servitude statutes in its approach. But it went further than just prohibitions in the law. It also created new protections and assistance for victims, and it acknowledged the fact that preventing trafficking would be preferable to simply countering it.

- It broadened the definition of trafficking to include a range of suspect activities including recruiting, transporting, harboring, provision, obtaining (and later for sex trafficking—patronizing, soliciting, and advertising) as one element of the law. This is important because it reaches the whole pipeline of activity in sex and labor trafficking.

- It created several new statutes that significantly strengthened the federal prosecution and punishment of traffickers, increasing some penalties from twenty years to life. The strong penalties incorporated into the TVPA sent a message to traffickers that the United States took human trafficking as seriously as sexual assault, drug trafficking, and arms trafficking,—and that sentencing for human trafficking crimes needed to reflect that view.

- It created a "T Visa"—a temporary legal residency status for victims of human trafficking, and a process by which victims could apply for the T

Visa. Once granted, the T visa gives the victim legal residency in the United States and all the rights afforded to those who are legal residents.

- It introduced the concept of a victim-centered approach. Trafficking victims and survivors who are granted temporary or permanent residency or "continued presence" qualify for emergency benefits, including food, clothing and shelter, medical assistance, legal aid, as well as education and employment assistance.

- It mandated the formation of a President's Interagency Task Force (PITF) on Trafficking in Persons (TIP) and an Office to Monitor and Combat Trafficking in Persons. The PITF, a cabinet-level task force, is chaired by the secretary of state, and includes the National Security Council advisor, the attorney general, the CIA director, secretary of Health and Human Services, secretary of Labor, the secretary of Defense, and the US AID administrator and ten other agencies that play a vital role in countering human trafficking. This new inter-agency task force created political will at the highest levels, which streams down into each agency.

- It outlined the development of a clear foreign policy approach for diplomatic and other endeavors to help other countries understand the nature of trafficking internationally and within their own borders, and to encourage countries to take action to stop trafficking within and across their borders. To assist in documenting progress, it created minimum standards for the elimination of trafficking and a three-tiered assessment of each country's progress. It tied their progress—or lack of it—to sanctions that could result in countries losing non-humanitarian, non-trade-related foreign assistance from the United States. Any country found on Tier 3—not making significant efforts to meet the minimum standards—could lose millions of dollars in assistance from the United States.

- To document whether countries were making significant efforts, it required the US State Department's Office to Monitor and Combat Trafficking in Persons, to produce an annual TIP Report. The TIP Report assesses and rates every country's record in making "serious and sustained efforts" to eliminate human trafficking. This report, released every year in June, has become the clear standard bearer for assessing countries' efforts to prevent trafficking, prosecute trafficking, and protect and assist victims. Over 160 countries are assessed and rated each year.

- Finally, it authorized $60 million in resources to implement the TVPA in the first year. This amount has quintupled in reauthorizations of the law over the years, with the 2022 Reauthorization of the TVPA law allocating almost $2 billion in resources to address trafficking.

Seven additional "reauthorizations" of the TVPA (each one called Trafficking Victims Protection Reauthorization Act—TVPRA)—in 2003, 2005, 2008, 2013, 2017, 2019, and 2022—have added substantive law to the original TVPA.

One of the key provisions in the Trafficking Victims Protection Reauthorization Act of 2003, for example, was the creation of a Civil Action for victims. This private right of action makes it possible for any individual who is a victim of sex or labor trafficking to bring a civil action against the trafficker in district courts in the United States to recover damages and reasonable attorney's fees. Another key provision was adding "trafficking in persons" to the definition of racketeering activity. This meant that the federal government could prosecute traffickers for conspiracy, which strengthened prosecutions considerably. The TVPRA 2003 also:

- created enhanced border interdiction and publication information programs to educate border guards to identify traffickers and victims of trafficking;
- strengthened efforts to combat international sex tourism (the opposite of international trafficking, where traffickers bring victims across international borders—in sex tourism, perpetrators travel to other countries, to purchase children for purposes of commercial sex);
- required that the attorney general produce an Annual Report on the progress federal agencies were making in implementing the TVPA in the United States. It required data collection on the number of victims granted "continued presence" in the United States, the number of victims receiving services, the number of people applying for T visas as well as the number denied such visas, and the number of people charged, prosecuted, and convicted of trafficking in the United States;
- noted that if foreign governments did not provide information and data regarding investigations, prosecutions, convictions, and sentences, the United States will presume that it has not vigorously investigated, prosecuted, convicted, or sentenced such acts;
- called for research on trafficking in persons including the economic causes and consequences of trafficking and the effectiveness of programs addressing trafficking.

The 2005 reauthorization of the law is split into two parts. The first part, Title I, focuses on international human trafficking, in particular on post-conflict and humanitarian emergency assistance. It directs the State Department and US AID to conduct a study on human trafficking that is generated by post-conflict and humanitarian emergency situations such as civil wars and natural disasters.

This provision was crafted in direct response to a surge in human trafficking in the aftermath of a December 2004 tsunami in the Indian Ocean. The tsunami was triggered by an underwater earthquake with a magnitude of 9.1. The earthquake generated a series of 30-foot waves along the coastal areas in Indonesia and other areas, killing 225,000 people and leaving tens of thousands others injured or missing. The natural disaster left millions with no clean water, food, shelter, roads, or medical assistance. According to the US Department of State, the chaos created by the tsunami was seized on by traffickers to ply their trade: "[The United States is] horrified that thousands of children orphaned by this disaster are vulnerable to exploitation by criminal elements who seek to profit from their misery," declared one State Department spokesperson (Ereli, 2005). He also said the United States was working to raise awareness about the trafficking risk at camps where displaced and homeless people from the tsunami were being housed and treated. The United States subsequently distributed guidelines to officials and volunteers in the camps recommending enhanced security measures to help prevent abductions or abuse.

Congress codified the concern in the TVPRA 2005, calling for an examination of the vulnerabilities to trafficking created by post-conflict and natural disaster emergencies, and requiring a report collecting best practices in combating trafficking in these situations. It also required a report on best practices for rehabilitation of victims of trafficking in residential facilities in foreign countries.

Importantly, the TVPRA 2005 also established extraterritorial jurisdiction for trafficking in person offenses committed by federal government employees or those accompanying the federal government outside the United States. It basically extended the prohibitions of involuntary servitude, forced labor, sex trafficking, and other trafficking in persons offenses to anyone working for the US government in a foreign country. It covered civilian employees, federal contractors, subcontractors, and dependents of those working for the federal government.

This was the first of what would be many provisions to prevent trafficking in government contracting, or by government employees (TVPRA 2005). It arose out of a number of reports in early 2000 of human trafficking violations committed by federal contractors hired as peacekeepers in the Balkans. In particular, it was alleged by several whistleblowers that US contractors attached to the UN peacekeeping mission as in post-war Bosnia and Herzegovina in 1999–2000 had facilitated sex trafficking and the use and abuse of children and young women in brothels. It is alleged that the contractors purchased females for sex, and in at least one case purchased a young woman to keep in his apartment and sell to others (Mendelson 2005; Bolkovac 2011). So, at the least US contractors were fueling trafficking by purchasing commercial sex; and a few may actually have become traffickers, purchasing human beings and selling them to others. At the time, the United States had no jurisdiction over US employees who committed the crime of human trafficking while in another country, even though they were being paid through federal contracts. This provision provided that jurisdiction.

The second part of the TVPRA 2005, Title II, focuses on combating domestic trafficking in persons. For many years, human trafficking was generally seen as a law enforcement and human rights abuse that took place outside the United States. But during the first five years following the passage of the TVPA, evidence emerged of extensive human trafficking within the United States. The findings section of the TVPRA 2005 noted that a 2001 study by a University of Pennsylvania researcher found that as many 300,000 children in the United States were at risk for commercial sexual exploitation (Estes 2001). It also emphasized that according to the National Runaway Switchboard, between 1.3 and 2.8 million runaway and homeless youth—a population that ranks among the most vulnerable to trafficking exploitation—live on the streets in the United States (TVPRA 2005).

Title II outlined fledgling efforts to establish the nature and scope of human trafficking in the United States. It called for data collection, research and literatures reviews of statistical analysis already available to estimate the number and demographic characteristics of human trafficking in the United States, including the number of investigations, arrests, prosecutions, convictions, and incarcerations of traffickers. It also called on the attorney general to conduct a study of the number of people involved in sex trafficking and commercial sex acts, including purchasers of commercial sex acts, and an estimate of the dollar amount of the "commercial sex economy" including the average annual personal income derived from acts of sex trafficking as well as other information related to the sex industry in the United States (TVPRA 2005). It also established a grant program in the HHS to develop and expand services for victims of human trafficking (whether US citizens or not). In addition, it established a pilot program for residential treatment facilities of juvenile victims of human trafficking to test the benefits of specialized shelters for minors recovering from trafficking. Finally, it established a new grant program for law enforcement to investigate and prosecute human trafficking cases in the United States and included a mention, for the first time, of investigating and prosecuting "person who engage in the purchase of commercial sex acts" (TVPRA 2005).

Further Reading

Bolkovac, Kathryn. 2011. *The Whistleblower: Sex Trafficking, Military Contractors, and One Woman's Fight for Justice*. Stuttgart, Germany: Macmillan.

Ereli, Adam. 2005. U.S. Department of State Briefing. *ReliefWeb*, January 5. https://relief web.int/report/indonesia/south-asia-us-horrified-child-trafficking-tsunami-afterm ath. Accessed September 19, 2023.

Estes, Richard, and Neal Weiner. 2001. "The Commercial Sexual Exploitation of Children in the U.S., Canada, and Mexico," University of Pennsylvania, September 18.

Mendelson, Sarah E. 2005. *Barracks and Brothels: Peacekeepers and Human Trafficking in the Balkans*. Washington, DC: Center for Strategic and International Studies. http://csis.org/files/media/csis/pubs/0502_barracksbrothels.pdf.

Trafficking Victims Protection Reauthorization Act of 2000, Public Law 106-386 (22 U.S.C. § 7102 (11 and 12)).

Trafficking Victims Protection Reauthorization Act of 2003.

Trafficking Victims Protection Reauthorization Act of 2005, Section 2, Findings, (6); Section 201(a).) and Section 204 (B).

The White House. 2018. Presidential Pardon of Jack Johnson. May 24, https://trumpwhi tehouse.archives.gov/briefings-statements/statement-press-secretary-regarding-par don-john-arthur-jack-johnson/. Accessed September 19, 2023.

The White House Archives, Statement of the Press Secretary Regarding the Pardon of John Arthur Jack Johnson, https://trumpwhitehouse.archives.gov/briefings-statements/statement-press-secretary-regarding-pardon-john-arthur-jack-johnson/. Accessed November 13, 2023.

US Code. 2015. Title 18, Part I, Chapter 117 § 2421—Transportation generally, Pub. L. 114–22, title III, § 303, May 29, 129 Stat. 255.

Weiner, Eric. 2008. "The Long Colorful History of the Mann Act." *National Public Radio*, May 11. https://www.npr.org/2008/03/11/88104308/the-long-colorful-hist ory-of-the-mann-act. Accessed September 19, 2023.

Q7. Partnership: What Is the So-Called "Fourth P" in the Trafficking Victims Protection Act?

Answer: The "3P Framework" of the TVPA of 2000 created a comprehensive paradigm for addressing trafficking in persons that included *preventing* trafficking, *prosecuting* traffickers, and *protecting and assisting* victims of trafficking. This whole-of-government approach has since been modified and adopted by the United Nations and over a hundred countries around the world. However, the transnational and multi-various nature of human trafficking meant that a "no wrong door" or "any door" policy was best. First used in health and human services, a "no wrong door" approach ensures a holistic approach to services that any door into the healthcare system will provide a universal gateway to the appropriate set of services needed. This provides a holistic way of assessing and providing services across a wide variety of agencies and prevents people with complex needs from falling through the cracks. This approach has been adopted in human trafficking to address the many aspects of human trafficking that require simultaneous assistance. This has also come to mean that an "all-hands-on-deck" process is necessary to counter human trafficking (Governing 2023).

The Facts: The fourth "P" stands for "Partnership" and it is important. Called "the missing P" by the United Nations Office on Drugs and Crime (UNODC), it was first mentioned by the Secretary of State Hillary Clinton in a speech she gave at the release of the tenth Annual TIP Report on June 14, 2010. She noted that "under the paradigm of the three Ps—prevention, protection, and prosecution—and thanks in part to the facts and focus provided by this annual report, governments, law enforcement agencies, international organizations, and families are working more closely together than ever. Now we call for the fourth P—partnership. And that is making a real difference. More countries are updating their laws and expanding enforcement, more criminals are facing prosecution, and more survivors are being helped back into a life of freedom" (Voices of Democracy: The US Oratory Project n.d.).

In the context of countering human trafficking, partnership can mean many different things. In the broadest sense it means enlisting all segments of society in the fight against human trafficking. According to the US Department of State:

> combating human trafficking requires the expertise, resources and efforts of many individuals and entities. It is a complex, multi-faceted issue requiring a comprehensive response of government and nongovernment entities in such areas as human rights, labor and employment, health and services, and law enforcement. It requires partnerships among all of these entities to have a positive impact. Partnerships augment efforts by bringing together diverse experience, amplifying messages, and leveraging resources, thereby accomplishing more together than any one entity or sector would be able to alone.

The State Department goes on to note that there are many types of partnership such as task forces among law enforcement agencies to share intelligence, work across jurisdictions, and coordinate across borders; public private partnerships between governments and businesses that seek to craft protocols and establish compliance mechanisms for slavery-free supply chains; and, regional partnerships among nations, such as the anti-human trafficking efforts of the Organization of American States (OAS) or the European Union (EU). They also discuss the needs for partnership among nongovernmental organizations (NGOs) for advocacy, service provision, information sharing; and alliances and networks of survivors, whose experiences inform the broader trafficking movement. While there is broad agreement on the purpose and benefits of a partnership approach to human trafficking, there is less agreement on and documentation of proven, successful strategies,—something all should endeavor to create and share in the years ahead. (US Department of State 2013)

Several scholars have been writing about the fourth P. For example, Jennifer Sheldon Sherman emphasized that a theoretical and practical framework for partnership is necessary for working together (Sheldon-Sherman 2012). Her work centers on the debate about which of the Ps—Prevention, Prosecution, or Protection and Assistance—is more important, and which should be prioritized especially since resources to fight human trafficking are scarce. She concludes that it is important to work on all three Ps concurrently, that they are dependent upon one another in many ways, and that partnerships among those prosecuting traffickers and those protecting victims are especially important.

She gives the example of the need for partnership between law enforcement officials and NGOs and notes that law enforcement officials need victims to testify in court in order to have successful prosecutions. However, victims of trafficking have immense needs when they emerge from trafficking. They are often physically, mentally, emotionally, and spiritually devastated (Lederer, Laura, and Christopher 2014) and have many needs that only nonprofit organizations and service providers equipped to help them can meet. A partnership between law enforcement organizations at the federal, state, and local levels and NGOs has been encouraged through grant-making to form coalitions and multidisciplinary task forces. The most successful of these task forces have ample funding to bring together all the entities—governmental, nongovernmental, inter-governmental—on a regular basis.

In 2010, the Department of Justice (DOJ) Office for Victims of Crime and Bureau of Justice Assistance launched a multidisciplinary trafficking task force approach employing the "Enhanced Collaborative Model (ECM)" to Combat

Human Trafficking (National Institute of Justice 2022). ECM Task Forces bring together stakeholders from various sectors including law enforcement, prosecutors, victim services providers, survivors, and others at the local, state, and federal levels. These task forces are based on a three-pronged agreement that they will:

- employ victim-centered approaches to identifying trafficking survivors;
- provide services to victims of all forms of human trafficking;
- investigate and process all forms of trafficking.

They receive federal funds to support the development of these multidisciplinary anti-trafficking task forces.

Some preliminary research has shown that these task forces increased trafficking prosecutions and uncovered new victims. However, the (DOJ) acknowledged that "challenges persist." In 2022 an evaluation of ten of the ECM to Combat Human Trafficking Task Forces found that funding from the federal government greatly improved the Task Forces' ability to work collaboratively to investigate, arrest, and prosecute traffickers and to protect and assist victims, but most of the task forces noted that they still needed more resources and that the resources needed to be sustainable (McCoy et al. 2022). The study, which was conducted by the Urban Institute, found that 99 percent of the cases investigated were sex trafficking cases; 92 percent of closed cases were sex trafficking; only 6 percent were labor trafficking; 2 percent were both sex and labor trafficking cases (McCoy et al. 2022, 14).

Even with the collaborative model in place, obtaining survivor cooperation and testimony was difficult: only 33 percent of the cases were prosecuted using human trafficking charges because survivors were not willing to cooperate (McCoy et al. 2022, 44–5). One of the key findings was that

> while the ECM model was effective at connecting various stakeholders and increasing collaboration across the continuum of interactions that system actors (e.g., law enforcement investigators, prosecutors, and service providers) have with survivors, these benefits have come with challenges, such as the need for improved communication between service providers and law enforcement and better and more meaningful collaboration with federal partners. (McCoy et al. 2022, 44–5)

While it was somewhat afield of the original purpose of the study, the researchers did comment on the fact that nearly all ECM task forces are struggling with their response to labor trafficking. Few task forces are investigating labor trafficking crimes, even though labor trafficking is occurring in their jurisdictions and is being reported by victim service providers. One reason seemed to be that several task forces were not set up to address labor trafficking. They were "not well positioned, organizationally or structurally, to effectively address labor trafficking. Most human trafficking investigators at police departments and prosecutors' offices are situated within sex crimes or vice units, so they tend to focus almost entirely on sex trafficking" (McCoy et al. 2022, 45).

The study also found that twenty years after the passage of the TVPA— which asserted that victims of human trafficking should not be incarcerated, fined, or otherwise penalized solely for unlawful acts they committed while being trafficked (National Institute of Justice 2022)—half the ECM task forces regularly arrested survivors of trafficking as part of the investigation. Task forces that arrest survivors indicated that the practice was used as a strategy to ensure survivors' safety and leverage for cooperation in investigations. Three task forces indicated that there had been a change in practice or state law that had resulted in officers no longer arresting sex trafficking survivors. Yet, survivors may still be arrested for trafficking-related offenses, such as drug possession or probation violations stemming from prostitution charges (McCoy et al. 2022, 44–5).

The report emphasized that nearly every ECM task force agreed that more and better housing options are needed for human trafficking survivors. Adequate and safe housing for survivors (both short- and long-term) was consistently identified as an unmet need of survivors. ECM task forces reported that alternative housing strategies, such as domestic violence shelters or group homes for incarcerated youth, are mostly ineffective for meeting the needs of human trafficking survivors. Some task forces learned that law enforcement arrested and detained human trafficking survivors as a means of keeping them safe (because secure housing options were scarce).

On its website, the DOJ said that while the ECM increased collaboration across agencies, improved awareness about human trafficking, and built system capacity to handle trafficking cases, there were still many challenges. These included "breakdowns in communication and coordination, staff burnout and turnover, personality differences, task forces that are siloed and too large, and differing processes and goals that limit productivity and effectiveness." The recommendations they highlighted included improving collaboration, improving organizational and operational factors, strengthening relationships between task force members, and leading more training and reform activities (White et al. 2022).

This is one of the largest country-wide models for partnership between law enforcement and service providers. In other anti-trafficking arenas, partnership models are also being proposed. For example, health providers familiar with the health issues of human trafficking victims and survivors are proposing new Multidisciplinary Teams (MDTs) to meet the many needs of survivors. Each survivor is unique, and health and other services must be tailored to the survivor's needs. The US Department of Health and Human Services suggests an MDT that includes healthcare, legal aid, law enforcement, behavioral health, survivor mentors and other peer support groups, anti-trafficking organizations, and social services. They divide survivor needs into emergency, medium-, and long-term needs (US Department of Health and Human Services n.d.).

The US Department of State also creates partnerships or "compacts" with governments to combat child trafficking. These "Child Protection Compacts" (or CPCs) are partnerships that span over at least a four-year period (US Department of State n.d.). The goal, modeled on the 3P framework, is to develop plans to prosecute child traffickers, provide protection and comprehensive care for child victims, and prevent child trafficking. As of January 2023, the Department of State's Office to Monitor and Combat Trafficking in Persons (TIP Office), which leads US efforts for the CPCs, had selected and signed partnership documents with seven partner countries: Peru, Ghana, Philippines, Jamaica, Mongolia, Columbia, and Cote D'Ivoire. The United States is funding all the projects, with the hope that countries will eventually build in infrastructure and continue the efforts to combat child trafficking on their own (US Department of State n.d.).

After evaluation issues arose, the US Government Accountability Office (GAO) was asked to review progress of the CPCs (US Government Accountability Office 2023). They found that although the United States and partner countries meet annually to discuss steps taken to address child trafficking, there were no set key discussion guidelines for the meetings or measurable goals to assess countries' progress, no method for tracking each country's plans for sustaining ongoing efforts, and no goals or performance indicators. Until these measures are in place it will be difficult to assess whether the CPCs are effective.

According to the GAO:

> The TIP Office has tools to help monitor CPC progress, but none of them include discussions of key performance indicator data or indicator targets. According to TIP Office officials, the primary monitoring tool is the annual dialogues, meetings between agency officials, partner governments, and project implementers, to share information on CPC efforts. Participants at the dialogues provide examples of various activities, but they do not identify key CPC

performance indicators beforehand to discuss or directly mention any during the dialogues. The TIP Office developed two new tools that include indicators to assist with collecting performance data, a broad CPC framework and a country-specific reporting template, but neither addresses the need for indicator targets. TIP Office officials said they have not focused on indicators or targets because they did not prioritize them, although based on agency guidance, the annual dialogues should include discussions of indicators. By not identifying and discussing key indicators at the dialogues and creating targets, the TIP Office has limited ability to monitor the performance and better understand the progress of the CPCs. (United States Government Accountability Office 2023)

The GAO also noted that the TIP Office does not track partner government contributions or sustainability measures such as a government's contributions to personnel or funding. In addition, sustainability plans were called for in the partnership documents, but the partner governments did not provide such plans nor did the TIP Office follow up on them. Without information on partner government contributions and sustainability measures, the TIP Office lacks knowledge on partner country contributions and plans to sustain progress under the CPCs (United States Government Accountability Office 2023).

In considering the varied approaches to the fourth P of Partnership—the ECM in law enforcement, the MDTs in health care and human trafficking, and the CPCs in the international arena—some common issues emerge:

- **Goals**: It is important to set goals and performance indicators at the outset of the partnership.
- **Sustainability:** How will the partnership continue after the initial influx of funds from the United States (or in the case of US-based partnerships, what will happen when federal funding runs out?)?
- **Communication:** It is important—but how will that communication be set up so that it is ongoing, of high quality, and informs the process on a regular basis?
- **Leadership:** One agency or organization must take the lead in order to ensure cohesiveness of the partnership.

Further Reading

Governing. 2023. "No Wrong Door A Wholistic Approach to Human Services." *Governing*. https://papers.governing.com/No-Wrong-Door-A-Holistic-Appro ach-to-Human-Services-73108.html. Accessed September 19, 2023.

Lederer, Laura J., and Christopher A. Wetzel. 2014. "The Health Consequences of Sex Trafficking and Their Implications for Identifying Victims in Healthcare Facilities." *Annals of Health Law* 23, no. 1: 61–91. https://www.icmec.org/wp-content/uplo ads/2015/10/Health-Consequences-of-Sex-Trafficking-and-Implications-for-Iden tifying-Victims-Lederer.pdf. Accessed September 19, 2023.

McCoy, Evelyn F., Paige S. Thompson, Jeanette Hussemann, William Adams, Krista White, and Roderick Taylor. 2022. *Findings from an Evaluation of the Enhanced Collaborative Model Task Forces to Combat Human Trafficking.* Washington, DC: Urban Institute. https://www.urban.org/sites/default/files/publication/105326/ findings-from-an-evaluation-of-the-enhanced-collaborative-model-task-forces-to- combat-human-trafficking.pdf. Accessed September 19, 2023.

National Institute of Justice. 2022. "Federally Backed Human Trafficking Task Force Model Yields Progress, and Opportunities for Continued Growth." National Institute of Justice. https://nij.ojp.gov/topics/articles/federally-backed-human-traffick ing-task-force-model-yields-progress. Accessed September 19, 2023.

Sheldon-Sherman, Jennifer A. L. 2012. "The Missing 'P': Prosecution, Prevention, Protection, and Partnership in the Trafficking Victims Protection Act." *Penn State Law Review* 117, no. 443: 443–502. https://www.unodc.org/e4j/data/_university_u ni_/the_missing_p_prosecution_prevention_protection_and_partnership_in_the_ trafficking_victims_protection_act.html?lng=en&match=the%20missing. Accessed September 19, 2023.

United States Government Accountability Office. 2023. *Human Trafficking: Department of State Collaborates with Partner Governments on Child Protection Compacts but Should Strengthen Oversight.* United States Government Accountability Office. https://www.gao.gov/assets/gao-23-105390.pdf. Accessed September 19, 2023.

US Department of Health and Human Services, National Human Trafficking Training and Technical Assistance Center. n.d. "Multidisciplinary Treatment and Referral Team." National Human Trafficking Training and Technical Assistance Center. https://nhttac.acf.hhs.gov/soar/eguide/resources/Building_a_Referral_Network. Accessed September 19, 2023.

US Department of State, Office to Monitor and Combat Trafficking In Persons. n.d. "Child Protection Compact Partnerships." US Department of State. https://www. state.gov/child-protection-compact-partnerships/. Accessed September 19, 2023.

US Department of State. 2013. "Four 'Ps': Prevention, Protection, Prosecution, Partnerships." https://ctcwcs.files.wordpress.com/2016/07/four-ps.pdf. Accessed September 19, 2023.

Voices of Democracy: The US Oratory Project. n.d. Hillary Rodham Clinton, "Remarks on the Release of The 10th Annual Trafficking in Persons Report." US Department of State. https://voicesofdemocracy.umd.edu/hillary-rodham-clinton-trafficking-spe ech-text/. Accessed September 19, 2023.

White, Krista, Paige S. Thompson, McCoy, Evelyn F., Jeanette Hussemann, William Adams, and Roderick Taylor. 2022. *Collaboration and Challenges in Antitrafficking*

Task Forces: Lessons Learned from an Evaluation of the Enhanced Collaborative Model Task Forces to Combat Human Trafficking. Washington, DC: Urban Institute. https://www.urban.org/sites/default/files/2022-06/Collaboration%20and%20Cha llenges%20in%20Antitrafficking%20Task%20Forces.pdf. Accessed September 19, 2023.

Q8. Prosecution: Is Law Enforcement an Important Aspect of Combating Human Trafficking?

Answer: Yes, it is. But it is not the only approach that is critical to stopping human trafficking. During the drafting of the TVPA, legislators, policymakers, advocates, and activists identified several aspects of the problem of human trafficking that were important in a holistic approach to combating trafficking in persons. In the process they created what they called the "3P" approach: prevention of trafficking; prosecuting traffickers, and protecting and assisting trafficking victims and survivors.

After the passage of the TVPA, federal law enforcement officials slowly began to prosecute traffickers, and the cases they pursued, usually high-profile and complex cases, helped the public to understand how traffickers exploited vulnerable victims. Federal prosecutors took on cases that often had dozens, even hundreds of victims in one case. These cases increased public awareness of the importance of the third P: protection and assistance, which encompasses a range of emergency and long-term resources for trafficking victims, including food, clothing, shelter, medical assistance, legal assistance, and more. Over the past twenty years a debate has emerged about the role of prosecution in stopping human trafficking. Advocates agree that prosecutions are important, but that it needs to be utilized in conjunction with other anti-trafficking resources, initiatives, and programs to end human trafficking.

The Facts: After the passage of the TVPA, the DOJ began to increase its investigations and prosecutions of human trafficking. Between 2001 and 2005, US attorneys investigated 555 suspects in matters involving violations of federal human trafficking statutes. Over half of the matters (58 percent) opened during this period were for offenses created under the Trafficking in Victims Protection Act (TVPA) of 2000 (US Department of Justice 2006). It is important to note that before the TVPA, there were statutes in the US Criminal Code prohibiting enticement into slavery, peonage, and sale into involuntary servitude. These older statutes were updated by amending the laws to increase penalties to twenty years in prison, and to add aggravated circumstances:

> If death results from the violation of this section, or if the violation includes kidnapping or an attempt to kidnap, aggravated sexual abuse or the attempt to commit aggravated sexual abuse, or an attempt to kill, the defendant shall be fined under this title or imprisoned for any term of years or life, or both (TVPA, §112 (a) and (b)).

In addition, the TVPA created new offenses, including statutes prohibiting

- Forced labor (TVPA §1589);
- Trafficking with respect to peonage, slavery, involuntary servitude, or forced labor (§ 1590);
- Sex trafficking by force, fraud or coercion and sex trafficking of children (TVPA §1591);
- Unlawful conduct with respect to documents in furtherance of trafficking, peonage, slavery, involuntary servitude (meaning tampering with documents such as IDs, passports, visas, and other travel papers in order to traffic someone) (TVPA §1592);
- Mandatory restitution (§1593) (US Department of Justice 2006, 32).

The law enforcement process begins with a report of human trafficking. These reports can come from law enforcement officials, citizens, nonprofit organizations, or other credible sources. Once a report has been filed, law enforcement officials conduct an investigation, gather evidence, and charge the suspects. Of the 555 investigations carried out between 2001 and 2005, federal prosecutors declined to prosecute 222 of the cases due to lack of evidence or other related issues. They investigated a total of 377 cases and of those cases they prosecuted 146 suspects in US district courts (US Department of Justice 2006).

In those first years, almost half of the human trafficking suspects referred to US attorneys were in four states: California, Texas, Florida, and New York (US Department of Justice 2006). These four states are the four most populous states in the United States, so it stands to reason from a purely statistical point of view that these would be the states that had the largest number of human trafficking cases following the passage of the TVPA. These prosecutions were a 360 percent increase in convictions for the fiscal years 2001–07 as compared to the previous seven-year period (US Department of Justice 2006).

Following this report in 2006, advocates were vocal about their concern that human trafficking was occurring in every state in the United States, yet only a few prosecutions per year were taking place. In 2007, the DOJ created the Human Trafficking Prosecution Unit, a specialized prosecution unit within the Criminal Section of the Civil Rights Division. The Unit was created to bring together a group of trial attorneys who had experience in prosecuting complex, multi-jurisdictional human trafficking cases involving forced labor, international sex trafficking, and sex trafficking of adults through force, fraud, or coercion to increase the number of cases and convictions (US Department of Justice n.d. The Unit did not prosecute child sex trafficking. These cases were turned over to the Child Exploitation and Obscenity Section (CEOS), which handles only child exploitation cases. In the attorney general's annual report to Congress, the attorney general gathers information from both these prosecutorial units to report on trafficking of adults and trafficking of children (US Attorney General Report to Congress).

In a new approach, DOJ attorneys collaborated with United States Attorneys' Offices nationwide. In addition to prosecutions, the Human Trafficking Prosecution Unit began to play a leading role in formulating and implementing pathbreaking enforcement initiatives, strengthening strategic partnerships, and developing and delivering capacity-building programs on best practices in survivor-centered human trafficking investigations and prosecutions for federal, state, local, tribal, and international law enforcement, and nongovernmental partners (US Department of Justice n.d.).

Since the creation of the Human Trafficking Prosecution Unit, the DOJ has successfully prosecuted labor trafficking crimes on construction sites, in agricultural fields, in garment worker factories, in suburban mansions, and sex trafficking crimes in brothels, escort services, bars, strip clubs, on the streets, and online. In recent years, the number of investigations and prosecutions of human trafficking cases has increased due to enhanced criminal statutes, victim-protection provisions, and public awareness programs introduced by the TVPA of 2000, as well as sustained efforts to combat human trafficking (US Department of Justice n.d.).

Today, as part of the *Attorney General's Annual Report to Congress on U.S. Government Activities to Combat Trafficking in Persons*, the DOJ reports the yearly number of investigations and arrests, prosecutions and convictions, and length of sentences. For example, in Fiscal Year 2020, the DOJ brought 210 human trafficking prosecutions of which 195 prosecutions involved predominantly sex trafficking and 15 involved predominantly labor trafficking, although some involved both. The DOJ charged 337 defendants, of whom 308 predominantly engaged in sex trafficking and 29 predominantly engaged in labor trafficking. The DOJ secured convictions against 309 traffickers, of whom 297 predominantly engaged in sex trafficking and 12 predominantly engaged in labor trafficking, although several involved both forms of trafficking (US Department of Justice 2020, 32). They also published a comparative analysis of the federal human trafficking prosecutions and convictions from fiscal years 2018–20, noting that the drop in the number of prosecutions and convictions in 2020 is mainly due to Covid-19, which slowed processes in the courts.

The main purpose of law enforcement is to protect communities, hold individuals accountable, and ensure justice. One of the mainstream theories of law enforcement is deterrence law enforcement. The primary objective of deterrence law enforcement is to secure compliance with the law by detecting violations, finding the perpetrators, and penalizing them to inhibit future violations. This has been one of the goals of law enforcement in what they call "pimp-controlled" sex trafficking (IACP— International Association of Chiefs of Police). According to the National Human Trafficking Hotline (NHTH), traffickers in street-based commercial sex are usually individual traffickers, commonly known as "pimps ." A pimp is a criminal who is associated with, exerts control over, and lives off the earnings of one or more women in prostitution. For many years, pimping was prosecuted at the state level and many of the state-generated statutes prohibiting pimping had weak penalties. In the first decades of the twenty-first century, new federal cases of human trafficking targeted pimps who were trafficking minors for sex. Instead of being arrested, charged, prosecuted, convicted, and then sentenced to three months in prison, pimps were tried as sex traffickers and being sentenced to ten- and twenty-year sentences.

One famous case is *U.S. v. Pipkins* in which fifteen pimps were arrested on 265-count charges involving activities that took place over a five-year period (*United States v. Pipkins* 2004). Thirteen of the pimps pleaded guilty. Two of the defendants, Charles Floyd Pipkins and Andrew Moore, went to trial. Up until that time pimps who trafficked women and girls into prostitution rarely got more than three months prison time. The evidence at trial demonstrated that Pipkins and Moore prostituted adult and juvenile females, at least one of whom was as young as twelve years old, from at least 1997 until their arrest in late 2001.

Pipkins and Moore were called "Sir Charles" and "Batman" on the street. They operated in southwest Atlanta in an area around Metropolitan Avenue (formerly called Stewart Avenue) known as the "track." To persuade underage females to prostitute for them, they promised fame and fortune, and supported this myth with their own flamboyant dress, flashy jewelry, and exotic, expensive cars. The court summarized their lifestyle saying that the pimps recognized a hierarchy among their own. "Popcorn pimps," "wanna-bes," and "hustlers" were the least respected, newer pimps. A "guerilla pimp" (as other pimps and prostitutes considered Moore) used violence and intimidation to control his prostitutes. Others were regarded as "finesse pimps," who excelled in the psychological trickery needed to deceive juvenile females and to retain their services. Finally, "players" (apparently, in this case, Pipkins) were successful, established pimps who were well-respected within the pimp brotherhood.

The court recounted the nature of "the game" saying that "the pimp(s) frequently used threats of violence to control his prostitutes or rewarded his prostitutes with drugs for meeting monetary goals. Other times, a pimp dispensed drugs to a prostitute to ensure that she was able to function through the night and into the early morning hours."

The pimping subculture in Atlanta operated under a set of rules, presented in a video called *Really Really Pimpin' in Da South* that was made in Atlanta by Pipkins and Carlos Glover, a business associate. *Really Really Pimpin' in Da South* featured prominent Atlanta pimps, including Pipkins, explaining the rules of the game. This video, along with its companion piece, *Pimps Up Hoes Down*, outlined the pimp code of conduct, and was repeatedly shown to new pimps and prostitutes alike to concisely explain what was expected of a prostitute. In essence, these videos taught that prostitutes were required to perform sexual acts, known as "tricks" or "dates," for money. Women "turned tricks in adult clubs, in parking lots, on mattresses behind local businesses, in cars, in motel rooms, or in rooming houses." They charged $30 to $80 for each trick. Some pimps set "quotas" that the women had to earn each night. The court cites some quotas as being over $1,000 a night. The women were required to turn over all of this money to their pimps.

The court described the violence that was a part of this life:

> The pimps ... brutally enforced these rules. Prostitutes endured beatings with belts, baseball bats, or 'pimp sticks' (two coat hangers wrapped together). The pimps also punished their prostitutes by kicking them, punching them, forcing them to lay naked on the floor and then have sex with another prostitute while others watched, or 'trunking' them by locking them in the trunk of a car to teach them a lesson.

The pimps did not service only the Metropolitan Avenue clientele. Pipkins branched out on the internet, forming a web-based escort service that allowed customers to select a particular prostitute from pictures posted on a website. Also, pimps sometimes sent their prostitutes to Peachtree Street in Midtown Atlanta because patrons paid a premium for prostitutes in that neighborhood. Pipkins entertained members of a municipal police force at his home on at least one occasion, where they engaged in sexual intercourse with his prostitutes.

The jury found Pipkins and Moore guilty on many counts, including conspiring to participate in a juvenile prostitution enterprise affecting interstate commerce through a pattern of racketeering activity, enticing juveniles to engage in prostitution, using interstate facilities to carry on prostitution, extortion, involuntary servitude, transfer of false identification documents, distribution of marijuana and cocaine to minors, and more. Pipkins's total sentence of imprisonment was 30 years (*U.S. v. Pipkins* 2004; Lederer 2018, 242–53).

Pipkins was one of the first federal cases of domestic sex trafficking to be tried following the passage of the TVPA. It demonstrated the political will of the federal government in these cases and sent a clear message to sex traffickers, especially those trafficking minors, that the US government would prosecute to the fullest extent of the law.

Since that time, the federal government has successfully prosecuted over 3,500 cases of human trafficking and shown that although prosecution is not the only way to address human trafficking, it is an effective deterrent and an important method for combating human trafficking.

Further Reading

Lederer, Laura. 2018. *Modern Slavery: A Documentary and Reference Guide.* London: ABC-CLIO, 242–53.

United States v. Pipkins. 2004. https://caselaw.findlaw.com/court/us-11th-circuit/1380 071.html. Accessed June 25, 2023.

US Department of Justice. 2020. *Attorney General's Annual Report to Congress on U.S. Government Activities to Combat Trafficking in Person.* Department of Justice. https://www.justice.gov/d9/pages/attachments/2022/03/24/fy20_ag_ht_rep ort.pdf. Accessed June 25, 2023.

US Department of Justice, Civil Rights Division. n.d. "Human Trafficking Prosecution Unit (HTPU)." Department of Justice. https://www.justice.gov/crt/human-traffick ing-prosecution-unit-htpu. Accessed June 25, 2023.

US Department of Justice, Office of Justice Programs. 2006. *Data Brief: Federal Prosecution of Human Trafficking, 2001–2005.* October. https://bjs.ojp.gov/content/ pub/pdf/fpht05.pdf. Accessed June 25, 2023.

US Department of Justice. n.d. "Department of Justice Components." https://www.just ice.gov/humantrafficking/department-justice-components#:~:text=Human%20Traf ficking%20Prosecution%20Unit%2C%20a,multi%2Djurisdictional%20and%20in ternational%20human. Accessed June 25, 2023.

Q9. Protection: Is Victim Assistance an Important Part of Combating Human Trafficking?

Answer: Yes, it is. We offer victims services for two main reasons: first to help make them whole and second to ensure that victims will assist in key government criminal justice efforts. As the federal Office of Victims of Crime (OVC) emphasizes, all victims deserve to feel safe and supported. When a community provides quality care, compassionate responses, and essential services, not only will victims recover from their victimization more quickly, but they are usually more willing to present evidence and testimony in the prosecution of perpetrators thereby helping to accomplish important justice and restitution goals (Office of Justice Programs n.d.).

When it first opened its Office of TIP, the HHS called these the "4 Rs"— rescue, rehabilitation, restoration, and reintegration into mainstream society. Some advocates have expressed concern about the word "rescue," and prefer the word "recovery." They argue that the term "rescue" implies that the person rescuing is saving a completely helpless person:

> When you say that you "rescued" someone, that statement is about empowering and aggrandizing yourself while disempowering the person you think you rescued. This is because "rescuing" creates an uneven power dynamic where the "rescuer" (read: hero) has all of the power in the relationship and the "rescuee" (read: helpless victim) has no agency or role in the exit of his or her abusive situation. (Owens-Bullard 2014)

Whichever term one prefers, the fact remains that victims who are freed from their traffickers need help—sometimes basic needs such as food, clothing, shelter, medical assistance, and legal advice in the short term, and often other kinds of services such as education and employment opportunities as well as life skills, and peer-support groups. In short, all "3Ps"—prevention of trafficking, prosecution of traffickers and buyers, and protection and assistance of victims and survivors— play an important role in combating human trafficking.

The Facts: For many years, the funds made available from the US government for international anti-trafficking efforts have focused on "return and reintegration" services for victims and survivors. Unlike the United States, which offers temporary residency (and permanent residency for people who qualify) for trafficking victims, most countries automatically repatriate trafficking victims back to their country of origin.

The IOM (International Organization for Migration) has long followed its mission of supporting the orderly and humane management of migration through international cooperation and humanitarian assistance to migrants in need, including refugees and internally displaced people (International Organization for Migration n.d.). As human trafficking emerged as an issue, the IOM developed and managed large-scale efforts to repatriate victims of trafficking back to their own countries and to encourage the countries from which they were trafficked to rehabilitate and reintegrate victims back into society. The US supports the IOM and also gives grants to countries to support shelters and service providers, particularly in countries where large numbers of victims have been identified. Other resource-rich countries have also supported the development of shelters and services for trafficking victims and survivors.

As part of its annual TIP Report, which assesses and rates over 160 countries worldwide on their significant progress in combating trafficking in persons, the US Department of State looks at the shelters and services provided in each country. In the individual country narratives, the TIP Report summarizes a government's efforts to ensure that victims are identified and whether they are provided adequate protection. The report uses the minimum standards outlined in the TVPA. The main standards in the category of protection include whether there are shelters for victims, whether and what kind of services are available, and whether victims are penalized for unlawful acts their traffickers forced them to commit while they were being trafficked. Finally, they also examine whether the country offers provisions to remain in the country following their recovery.

The needs of survivors vary greatly, but whether in the United States or abroad, the following list of emergency and short-term needs is generally agreed upon:

Accommodations and Subsistence

- Housing
- Food assistance
- Clothing and personal care assistance

Medical Assistance and Health Care

- Sexual assault forensic examination
- Substance use treatment
- Malnutrition and/or dehydration
- Short- and long-term medical treatment, depending on the seriousness of the injury or infection
- Long-term physical impact of trauma

Legal Assistance

- Assistance obtaining basic identification, such as birth certificate, driver's license, passport, visa
- Information about legal options and legal advocates
- Applying for "T" or "U" visas, for victims and their families
- Helping with orders of protection
- Representing victims who testify against their traffickers
- Assisting with documentation needed for eviction and housing issues
- Vacatur and expungement relief for victims with a criminal history as a result of their trafficking
- Family court issues

Social Services

- Interpretation/translation assistance
- Childcare
- Benefits (i.e., cash, food, or energy assistance for those with low incomes)
- School-based support

In addition, survivors are beginning to identify other areas where they need assistance in recovery. For example, many survivors were trafficked when they were in middle school or high school and their elementary or secondary schooling was interrupted. Survivors need opportunities to complete their basic education and follow their educational dreams. Tutoring and testing services, general education development (GED) programs, and higher education scholarships and tuition aid can be enormously beneficial to those survivors. Other survivors would benefit more from assistance in the forms of job training, job placement, job mentoring, career guidance counseling, and other employment-related services.

Some private universities are offering scholarships for college to survivors of human trafficking. For example, in 2018, Arizona State University announced five full four-year scholarships for sex trafficking survivors, University of Toledo offers scholarships and support for survivors of human trafficking through its Human Trafficking and Social Justice Institute F.R.E.E. program, and Vanguard University's Global Center for Women and Justice offers a GCWJ Survivors Endowed Scholarship for survivors of human trafficking (ASU 2018; University of Toledo 2023; Vanguard 2018).

In addition, the US government is assisting survivors who want to continue their education. One new program is the Granting Courage Scholarship for Survivors of Human Trafficking, offered by the US Department of Homeland Security (Homeland Security Philanthropy Council n.d.). Administered by the Homeland Security Philanthropy Council, it grants up to ten Granting Courage Scholarships each year for full-time undergraduate, graduate, or vocational study. The scholarship awards up to $25,000. The program helps to offset the fees and expenses associated with educational study and support the continued success of survivors of trafficking and exploitation (Homeland Security Philanthropy Council n.d.).

According to the OVC, Finding stable employment is critical to the recovery of survivors (Department of Justice 2022). While some survivors want to return to school following recovery, other survivors would prefer to find employment where there are opportunities for advancement. In these cases, the need is for job training, job placement, job mentoring, and other services to help them obtain a job and maintain it.

Other survivors benefit from services related to pregnancy, childbirth, parenting, and child rearing. Many survivors have children while they are being trafficked and need maternal health care, pre- and post-natal care, mental health and psychosocial support, parenting classes and early childhood education programs to facilitate the development of healthy parent–child relationships, and assistance with psychosocial programs for their children. One study of forty-three children of survivors of human trafficking notes that they were either with their mother during the period of her exploitation, born as a result of her exploitation, or born after she had escaped exploitation but was still recovering from her trauma (Hestia 2021).

While the children had not been trafficked themselves, they experienced abuse and neglect during the time their mothers were trafficked, witnessed their mothers' abuse, or experienced trauma following her release due to secondary trauma. The study found that the trauma a mother experiences as a result of trafficking can affect their parenting, their daily functioning, and the way they view their children, all of which may transmit trauma to their children. This "intergenerational trauma" is a new area of victim services that is just beginning to be developed (Castaner 2021; Talking Circle 2022; Juabsamai and Taylor 2018).

Across the United States and internationally, service providers have developed specialized services for victims and survivors of human trafficking.

Over the past decade, extensive research has revealed the pervasiveness of human trafficking worldwide (Ecker 2022), the harmful and lasting health effects of human trafficking on victims (Lederer and Wetzel 2014), and the multidisciplinary needs of survivors (2008). The US Department of Justice Office for Victims of Crime's (OVC's) website provides access to an online searchable matrix of 548 entries connecting trafficking victims to various entities and organizations that provide services like legal counsel, housing, and case management. The predominant purpose of these services is to address the immediate needs of victims recently removed from their trafficking situation (e.g., an emergency shelter providing short-term shelter for victims usually capping at a two-week stay). Furthermore, the OVC only lists service providers and task forces that receive funding from them. Another platform connecting survivors to services is the nonprofit organization Polaris's online referral directory. However, many of the organizations are proprietary, and Polaris will not publicize its list of contacts and services available across the United States. The emergency, medical, and legal services provided by these platforms are critical for successfully prosecuting traffickers and providing immediate aftercare to victims and should not be dismissed. But these services are largely confined to short-term essentials. To holistically address their needs, survivors must be able to access long-term, nonemergency services as well.

But we are still in the foothills of consciousness on the development of an infrastructure of sustainable and comprehensive services for victims and survivors, particularly in the field of health care. There currently is no comprehensive and easily accessible platform that connects survivors to trauma-informed service providers, maternal resources, life skills coaches, mentoring programs, and other much needed services. One service provider said:

> As a service provider, I find it confusing trying to figure out what services are available for which clients. Most of my time is spent making calls or running around to agencies. We need a road map that helps explain not only what services our clients are eligible for but how we go about accessing these services. What documentation does my client need? What paperwork do they need to fill out? What would make my client ineligible for services? I can barely navigate through all of these systems myself, so how can we expect our clients to take this on? (Clawson and Dutch 2008)

A survivor recounted this experience with a shelter she was sent to:

> I was told to go to [a] shelter for trafficking victims, but I left as soon as I got
> there, because even though my trafficker had threatened my life, I couldn't stay
> there. They were going to make me give my two-year-old boy to Child Protective
> Services. He is everything to me and I vowed we would not be parted. So, we
> slept in an abandoned car the whole winter. (Lederer 2023)

On the need for long-term services one service provider said:

> When working with a domestic victim, I just need more time. I can't stabilize
> a client with an extensive trauma history within 60 days or transition them to
> permanent housing immediately. Right now, these are the only two choices
> in many parts of the country. Most of my clients struggle to get clean, get an
> education (or GED), learn life skills, obtain employable skills, and get employed.
> This is especially true if they have not begun to work on trauma recovery; it
> takes time. (Clawson and Dutch 2008)

On service provider spoke about the barriers to getting services:

> There is a general lack of knowledge and understanding of human trafficking
> and not enough service providers in the healthcare profession, local Social
> Security Administration offices, Department of Motor Vehicles, and other key
> agencies. We are constantly having to take our clients to appointments because
> they are turned away when they try to get services on their own. (Clawson and
> Dutch 2008)

These personal accounts highlight the obstacles survivors continue to face when
seeking food, clothing, shelter, medical assistance, legal assistance, and other
kinds of basic services necessary during their recovery. Survivors tell of spending
countless hours on the telephone trying to locate a health provider or specialist
who is trauma-informed and trained to treat human trafficking victims.

Further Reading

Arizona State University. 2018. "Five Full Four-Year Scholarships to Arizona State
    University for Sex Trafficking Survivors." *Announced in Dignity* 3, no. 3, Article
    7. https://digitalcommons.uri.edu/cgi/viewcontent.cgi?article=1140&context=dign
    ity. Accessed September 19, 2023.
Castaner, Marti, Rachel Fowler, Cassie Landers, Lori Cohen, and Manuela Orjuela.
    2021. "How Trauma Related to Sex Trafficking Challenges Parenting: Insights

from Mexican and Central American Survivors in the US." National Library of Medicine, June 16. https://www.ncbi.nlm.nih.gov/pmc/articles/PMC 8208566/. Accessed June 25, 2023.

Clawson, Heather J., and Nicole Dutch. 2008. *Addressing the Needs of Victims of Human Trafficking: Challenges, Barriers, and Promising Practices.* US Department of Health and Human Services, July 29. https://rhyclearinghouse.acf.hhs.gov/sites/default/files/ docs/19724-Addressing_the_Needs_of_Victims.pdf. Accessed June 25, 2023.

Department of Justice, Office for Victims of Crime. 2022. "New Resource Helps Connect Trafficking Survivors with Employment Opportunities." https://ovc.ojp.gov/ news/grantee-news/new-resource-helps-connect-trafficking-survivors-employment-opportunities. Accessed June 25, 2023.

Ecker, Emma. 2022. "Breaking Down Global Estimates of Human Trafficking: Human Trafficking Awareness Month 2022." Human Trafficking Institute, January 12. https://traffickinginstitute.org/breaking-down-global-estimates-of-human-traffick ing-human-trafficking-awareness-month-2022/#:~:text=24.9%20million%20vict ims%20of%20human%20trafficking&text=The%2024.9%20million%20figure%20i ncludes,every%20region%20of%20th. Accessed June 25, 2023.

Hestia. 2021. *Forgotten Children: The Intergenerational Impact of Modern Slavery.* https://www.hestia.org/Handlers/Download.ashx?IDMF=9e80d 4ef-5910-470d-b46a-968facba852d. Accessed September 19, 2023.

Homeland Security Philanthropy Council. n.d. "Granting Courage Scholarship Program." https://homelandsecuritycouncil.org/granting-cour age/#:~:text=The%20Granting%20Courage%20Scholarship%20Program,college%20 or%20vocational%20school%20programs. Accessed June 25, 2023.

International Organization for Migration. n.d. "Counter Trafficking." https://www.iom. int/counter-trafficking. Accessed June 25, 2023.

Juabsamai, K., and I. Taylor. 2018. "Family Separation, Reunification, and Intergenerational Trauma in the Aftermath of Human Trafficking in the United States." *Anti-Trafficking Review*, no. 10: 123–38. www.antitraffickingrev iew.org. Accessed June 25, 2023.

Lederer, Laura J., and Christopher A. Wetzel. 2014. "The Health Consequences of Sex Trafficking and Their Implications for Identifying Victims in Healthcare Facilities." *Annals of Health Law* 23, no. 1: 61–91. https://www.icmec.org/wp-content/uplo ads/2015/10/Health-Consequences-of-Sex-Trafficking-and-Implications-for-Iden tifying-Victims-Lederer.pdf. Accessed June 25, 2023.

Office of Justice Programs, Office for Victims of Crime. n.d. "Supporting Victims." https://www.ovcttac.gov/taskforceguide/eguide/4-supporting-vict ims/#:~:text=All%20victims%20deserve%20to%20feel,the%20prosecution%20 of%20perpetrators%2C%20thereby. Accessed June 25, 2023.

Talking Circle. 2022. "Intergenerational and Historical Trauma and Human Trafficking," American Indiana and Alaska Native Practitioners, Office of Justice Programs,

Human Trafficking Capacity Building Center, US Department of Justice, June. https://htcbc.ovc.ojp.gov/trauma-and-human-trafficking. Accessed June 25, 2023.

University of Toledo. 2023. "F.R.E.E. Program." https://www.pointloma.edu/centers-ins titutes/center-justice-reconciliation/our-programs/beauty-ashes-scholarship-fund.

Vanguard University, Global Center for Women and Justice 2018. "Endowed Scholarship Fund for Survivors." https://give.vanguard.edu/giving-priorities/endo wed-scholarship/. Accessed September 19, 2023.

Q10. Prevention: Is "Moving Upstream" the Most Essential Part of Stopping Human Trafficking?

Answer: Yes, it is. Studies show that a person who has been trafficked is physically, mentally, emotionally, and spiritually devastated and that repairing that devastation takes months, years, or even decades (Lederer 2014). Survivors, service providers, and social scientists have developed a list of the emergency, short-term and long-term needs of trafficking survivors. They argue that in addition to food, clothing, shelter, medical assistance, legal assistance, translation services, transportation services, childcare, educational opportunities, and employment opportunities, there are other needs such as vacatur of criminal records associated with human trafficking, long-term physical and mental health needs, and assistance with immigration, voluntary repatriation, or legal residency in the country to which they were trafficked.

Many of these needs are expensive, some are labor intensive, and all require investments of money and resources to help survivors recover and be reintegrated into society. A much better approach, in terms of expenditure of resources, would be to prevent trafficking from occurring in the first place. Yet, until very recently, prevention strategies were largely neglected.

The Facts: Prevention of human trafficking is discussed in only one provision of the TVPA of 2000. The section has only two parts, one international and one domestic. The international intervention is titled, "Economic Alternatives to Prevent and Deter Trafficking." This section directs the President of the United States to establish and carry out international initiatives to enhance economic opportunity for potential victims of trafficking as a method to deter trafficking and outlines several such initiatives such as microcredit lending programs, training in business development, skills training, and job counseling; programs to promote women's participation in economic decision-making; programs to keep children, especially girls, in elementary and secondary schools and to educate persons who have been victims of trafficking; development of educational curricula regarding the dangers of trafficking; and providing grants to NGOs to accelerate and advance the political, economic, social, and educational roles and capacities of women in their countries.

The second part directs the president—acting through the secretary of labor, secretary of health and human services, the attorney general, and the secretary of state—to establish and carry out public awareness and information programs to increase public awareness, particularly among potential victims of trafficking, of the dangers of trafficking, and the protections that are available for victims of trafficking. A third section, meanwhile, requires the president to consult with appropriate NGOs with respect to the establishment and conduct of these initiatives.

For twenty years, prevention consisted mainly of education through awareness campaigns, general awareness trainings, and specialized trainings on human trafficking. At first trainings were developed mainly by a few NGOs and consisted of a global "Trafficking in Persons 101"—that is, the who, what, when, and where of international trafficking, based mainly on anecdotal reporting and nongovernmental and intergovernmental programs around the world. These trainings were uneven in quality, varied widely in their approach to the issue and the content presented, and were not revised to make them more relevant and applicable to circumstances in particular places (Polaris, International Justice Mission, Shared Hope International). Trafficking was generally presented as an international problem largely limited to resource-poor and developing countries. The focus was on the problem, with little to offer as to solutions.

By 2010, many organizations were focused on the problem of human trafficking in the US non-governmental and US governmental interest developed in tandem as cases of human trafficking in the United States were reported, investigated, and successfully prosecuted in the country (Human Trafficking Institute). One early map produced by an NGO and presented at numerous conferences and trainings shows cases of human trafficking in every state in the country (Global Centurion 2023).

Twenty-three years after the passage of the TVPA, the US government finally put forward a National Human Trafficking Prevention Framework (US Department of Health and Human Services [HHS] 2023). The Prevention Framework uses concepts from violence prevention to prevent human trafficking. It contains eight strategies and thirty-two approaches to preventing human trafficking. It divides its approach into actions that can directly prevent human trafficking and those that can "contribute to disrupting indirect pathways to human trafficking" (HHS 2023, 5).

The eight Strategies of the Prevention Framework are:

Strategy 1: Strengthen Skills to Promote Self-Efficacy and Prevent Human Trafficking

Strategy 2: Identify and Support People Who Are at Risk for Human Trafficking or Who Have Experienced Human Trafficking to Increase Safety and Reduce Harm

Strategy 3: Strengthen Economic Supports

Strategy 4: Promote Family Environments That Support Health Development

Strategy 5: Promote Social Connectedness

Strategy 6: Create Protective Environments

Strategy 7: Foster Multidisciplinary Networks and Coalitions

Strategy 8: Promote Social Norms That Protect against Violence

Each of these Strategies is identified as working mainly at the individual level, relationship level, community level, or societal level. For example, Strategies 1, 2, and 3 are focused on the individual. Strategies 4 and 5 are focused on relationships. Strategies 6 and 7 need community involvement, and Strategy 8 requires changes at the societal level.

Each Strategy is described generally and followed with a section on "Approaches" that describes particular programs, methods, or applications of the strategy. Each strategy also has "Resource Highlights" that features a particular program designed or funded by the US government and implemented to support the Prevention Framework.

For example, Strategy 1—Strengthen Skills to Promote Self-Efficacy and Prevent Human Trafficking features two approaches: (1) Skills-Based Prevention Education Programs, and (2) Social, Emotional, and Behavioral Well-Being Programs for children and youth (HHS 2023, 28–9). Two HHS-funded projects are highlighted as Resource Spotlights: The first, a Human Trafficking Youth Education Demonstration Program, funds local education agencies to develop and implement programs to prevent human trafficking victimization through training on human trafficking for school staff and students.

The second, Ready4Life, promotes healthy marriages among young refugees and immigrants. Under "Promoting Family Environments that Support Healthy Development," the Prevention Framework offers two approaches: (1) Early Childhood Home Visitation and (2) Parenting Skill and Family Relationship Approaches. These include early childhood home visitation programs to provide information, caregiver support, and training about child health, development, and care to families in their home to reduce the risk of violence. These home visiting programs can be delivered by health providers such as nurses, therapists, social workers, and other professionals. They also include family preservation, parent and caregiver skills, and family relationship programs to strengthen home environments. The strategy says: "Family support and connectedness is a protective factor against multiple forms of violence including chill maltreatment, teen dating violence, youth violence, bullying" (HHS 2023, 42).

But what if the perpetrator has access to the child either within the home or the neighborhood? When survivors tell their stories, almost all start with a childhood of abuse, violence, and/or sexual exploitation close to home. According to the National Human Trafficking Training and Technical Assistance Center (NHTTAC),

> trafficking is usually not an individual's first experience with trauma. Adverse Childhood Events, or ACEs, are stressful or traumatic events that occur during childhood (0–17 years). ACEs encompass several issues, such as abuse, neglect, and household dysfunction, and are strongly related to the development and prevalence of many risk outcomes throughout a person's lifespan, including health problems and trafficking. (National Human Trafficking Training and Technical Assistance Center [NHTTAC] n.d.)

The original adverse childhood experiences (ACEs) measured childhood trauma exposure across a smaller subset of items. Expanded definitions of ACEs take into consideration experiences such as bullying, discrimination, racial inequity, community violence, parental death, and economic hardships.

The ten expanded ACEs are divided into three categories: Abuse, including physical abuse, emotional abuse, and sexual abuse; Neglect, including physical and emotional neglect; and Household dysfunction which includes mental illness, incarcerated relative, interpersonal violence, substance abuse, and divorce (NHTTAC n.d.). NHTTAC cites a 2015 study that provides evidence that youth with violations related to sex trafficking had higher rates for each ACE as well as number of ACEs, particularly sexual abuse and physical neglect, and state that these findings have implications for identifying adverse experiences in both maltreated and offending youth as well as tailoring services to prevent re-victimization (Naramore et al. 2017).

In a similar study in 2017, ACE composite scores were higher and six ACEs indicative of child maltreatment were more prevalent among youths who had human trafficking abuse reports. Sexual abuse was the strongest predictor of human trafficking: the odds of human trafficking was 2.52 times greater for girls who experienced sexual abuse, and there was an 8.21 times greater risk for boys who had histories of sexual abuse (Reid et al. 2017). This led the researcher to conclude that maltreated youths are more susceptible to exploitation in human trafficking. Sexual abuse in connection with high ACE scores may serve as a key predictor of exploitation in human trafficking for both boys and girls (Reid et al. 2017). Jerome Elam, a survivor of child sex trafficking in the United States noted that when tested, he scored as having all ten ACEs (US Department of Defense 2023b).

We need many more national and international studies to confirm the few studies that have been done that provide evidence that ACEs increase the risk of human trafficking for children. In addition, we need more information on *how* ACEs increase the risk of exploitation, abuse, and trafficking. As we acknowledge this key link between ACEs and human trafficking, designing programs to prevent all ten ACEs becomes critical. This requires a focus on early childhood development, including meeting the physical, mental, and emotional needs of children from all communities. Providing communities with better access to basic needs such as food, clothing, shelter, a loving family, health care, education, job readiness, and life skills are just a few ways to lower the risk of ACEs, but they are one small step toward much-needed societal change.

Under Strategy 4, Promote Family Environments that support Health Development, the Prevention Framework notes that the family environment plays a key role in shaping physical, emotional, social, and behavioral health, and presents two approaches: Home visiting programs for caregivers to provide information, support, and training about child health, development, and care to families in their homes. They suggest that home visiting programs could be developed and delivered through our current health-care system and be provided by nurses, social service providers, and other professionals and paraprofessionals. They also suggest family preservation and family relationship programs to strengthen home environments and build family supports to prevent human trafficking.

Most of the strategies presented in the new Human Trafficking Prevention Framework seem to be drawn from previous prevention strategies developed for sexual violence (SV) and childhood abuse and neglect. While the issue of child sexual abuse (especially child sexual abuse committed by someone in the family, neighborhood, or community) is touched upon, most of the prevention strategies suggested will not adequately reach it.

For example, the Sexual Violence Prevention Strategies of the Centers for Disease Control and Prevention (CDC) states that SV starts early in the lifespan: "Among women reporting a history of completed rape, 40% first experienced it before age 18, with more than 28% indicating they were first raped between the ages of 11 and 17; among men who were made to penetrate someone, 71% first experienced this before the age of 25, and 21.3% experienced this before the age of 18" (Centers for Disease Control 2016). The prevention strategy recommends ways to "Create Protective Environments," but then goes on to discuss improving safety and monitoring in schools, establishing and consistently applying workplace policies, and addressing community-level risks through environmental approaches.

Similarly, strategies in the Childhood Abuse and Neglect Prevention plan of the CDC offer strategies to change societal norms to support parents and positive parenting, provide quality care and education early in life, and enhance parenting skills to promote healthy childhood development. Under the latter, the two "approaches" offered are the same two offered in the new Prevention Framework: Early Childhood Home Visitation and Parenting Skill and Family Relationship Approaches (Centers for Disease Control 2016).

Left largely unexplored in the Prevention Framework is the devastating role that early childhood sexual exploitation by family members plays as a precursor to trafficking. In sex trafficking, survivors reported being victimized by stepfathers, boyfriends, and fiancés (of mother), grandfathers, uncles, brothers, friends of the family, neighbors, and temporary caregivers (such as babysitters). These abusers had easy access to children due to an almost automatic or built-in trust that family members, even those who are not blood relatives, or those who are distant relatives, seem to have. This early childhood abuse has been identified by survivors as a key contributor to being pulled into trafficking when they were in their teens or early twenties. A number of survivors talk about how their childhoods and how their innocence was taken from them by predators in their own families or in the wider community who raped, sexually exploited, and molested them (US Department of Defense 2023a).

A number of survivors have spoken about whether their families knew of the sexual abuse. Some tell of mothers, fathers, relatives who knew what was happening but did nothing. One survivor said, "When I told my mother that her new boyfriend was abusing me, she beat me and threw me out of the house. At 12, I was out on the streets, left to fend for myself. To this day, I have been unable to forgive her for choosing a man over the safety of her own child" (Global Centurion 2023).

Some survivors say they never told loved ones about what was happening to them because of the fear that their abuser would hurt or kill them or their loved ones if they spoke up. Jerome Elam's stepfather ran a pedophile ring in which he trafficked Jerome from the time he was five years old until he was twelve: "My innocence was taken from me and [I became] trapped in a web of psychological blackmail as threats of violence against my mother guaranteed my silence" (US Department of Defense 2023b). Even though his mother was herself dysfunctional and addicted to alcohol, she was his mother and he protected her fiercely at all costs (US Department of Defense 2023b). "It would take seven years for me to escape the grip of those who sold me to the depths of perversion for profit," he recalled. "At the age of twelve, I stood in my mother's rose garden, a bottle of sleeping pills in one hand and a bottle of vodka in the other. As I took the pills with the vodka, I felt a sense of peace wash over me. I was finally escaping the nightmare and I was no longer afraid. I awoke in the emergency room to a group of doctors and a nurse who contacted Child Protective Services (US Department of Defense 2023b).

Although activists and advocates can borrow from Violence Prevention Frameworks to prevent trafficking, other related prevention and intervention efforts should also be utilized to stop ACEs such as child sexual abuse.

Any preventive strategy must take into consideration the fact that many early childhood abusers have easy access to children. These cases of abuse do serious physical, mental, emotional, and spiritual damage to young children. Any framework or program to prevent human trafficking must address precursor events that, according to survivors, were events that deflected them, like a river from its course, from a childhood and adulthood where they could live up to their full potential.

Further Reading

Centers for Disease Control, National Center for Injury Prevention and Control. 2016. *Preventing Child Abuse and Neglect: A Technical Package for Policy, Norm, and Programmatic Activities.* https://www.cdc.gov/violenceprevention/pdf/CAN-Prevent ion-Technical-Package.pdf. Accessed June 25, 2023.

Centers for Disease Control, National Center for Injury Prevention and Control. 2016. *STOP SV: A Technical Package to Prevent Sexual Violence.* https://www.cdc.gov/vio lenceprevention/pdf/SV-Prevention-Technical-Package.pdf. Accessed June 25, 2023.

Global Centurion. 2023. "The Pregnancy Continuum: Domestic Trafficking and Pregnancy." www.globalcenturion.org. Accessed June 25, 2023.

Human Trafficking Institute. 2020. *Federal Human Trafficking Report.* https://trafficki nginstitute.org/federal-human-trafficking-report/. Accessed June 25, 2023.

Human Trafficking Institute. 2021. *Federal Human Trafficking Report*.

Human Trafficking Institute. 2022. *Federal Human Trafficking Report*.

International Justice Mission. n.d. https://www.ijm.org/. Accessed June 25, 2023.

Lederer, Laura, and Christopher Wetzel. 2014. "The Health Consequences of Human Trafficking and Their Implications for Identifying Victims in Healthcare Facilities." *Annals of Health Law* 23, no. 1: 87.

Naramore, Racheal, Melissa A. Bright, Nathan Epps, and Nancy S. Hardt. 2017. "Youth Arrested for Trading Sex Have the Highest Rates of Childhood Adversity: A Statewide Study of Juvenile Offenders." *Sexual Abuse* 29, no. 4: 396–410. https://doi.org/10.1177/1079063215603064.

National Human Trafficking Training and Technical Assistance Center (NHTTAC). n.d. "SOAR Handouts." https://nhttac.acf.hhs.gov/system/files/2022-11/ACEs_35533 _Updating_SOAR_handouts_v02(a)_508.pdf. Accessed June 25, 2023.

Polaris. n.d. https://polarisproject.org/. Accessed June 25, 2023.

Reid, Joan A., Michael T. Baglivio, Alex R. Piquero, Mark A. Greenwald, and Nathan Epps. 2017. "Human Trafficking of Minors and Childhood Adversity in Florida." *American Journal of Public Health* 107, no. 2: 306–11. https://www.ncbi.nlm.nih.gov/ pmc/articles/PMC5227932/. Accessed June 25, 2023.

Shared Hope International. https://sharedhope.org/. Accessed June 25, 2023.

Trafficking Victims Protection Act of 2000, Section 106, "Prevention of Trafficking." PL 196–386. https://www.govinfo.gov/content/pkg/PLAW-106publ386/pdf/PLAW-106 publ386.pdf. Accessed June 25, 2023.

US Department of Defense. 2023a. "Survivor Voices of Human Trafficking." https:// ctip.defense.gov/Survivor-Voices/2023. See also survivor stories of Jerome Elam, Katarina Rosenblatt, Brenda Powell, Marlene Carson, Barbara Amaya, Desiree Trail, and more.

US Department of Defense. 2023b. *Survivor Voices of Human Trafficking: Jerome Elam Transcript. Combating Trafficking in Persons Program Management Office*. https://ctip.defense.gov/Portals/12/Jerome%20Elam%20Story_1.pdf. Accessed June 25, 2023.

US Department of Health and Human Services (HHS), Office of Trafficking in Persons. 2023. "Request for Public Comment: Human Trafficking Prevention Framework (draft)." https://www.acf.hhs.gov/otip/news/request-public-comment-human-traf ficking-prevention-framework#:~:text=The%20Framework%20encourages%20co llaboration%2C%20coordination,and%20non%2Dgovernmental%20organizati ons%3B%20educational. Accessed June 25, 2023.

3

Survivors: Language, Image, Life

"Nothing about Us without Us," said one survivor. The phrase is self-attributed to Barbara Amaya, a survivor and author, but it comes from the Latin, *Nihil de nobis, sine nobis*, and has its origins in European and South African political circles. "Nothing about us without us" was a political slogan in Poland and Hungary as far back as the 1500s, and then over the past decade (1982–92) of an almost 100-year struggle against apartheid in South Africa. The phrase was picked up by disability activists in the 1990s (Chalton 1998) and then, in the first decade after the passage of the TVPA, by Amaya and other survivors.

The "Nothing about Us without Us" philosophy put forward by trafficking survivors and advocates is founded on the conviction that survivors should be involved in every aspect of anti-trafficking work, at every level, to inform process and practice. It emphasizes that survivors have an expertise that cannot be learned from any text, and that this lived experience is valuable and contributes to and strengthens anti-trafficking work.

Theoretical advances are also being made that challenge the traditional emphasis on "distance," "neutrality," and "objectivity" in research as well as services. Some social scientists argue that traditional approach discriminates against survivors and their experiential knowledge. These experts explore the idea that "the shorter the distance between direct experience and its interpretation, the less likely resulting knowledge is to be inaccurate, unreliable, and distorted." In other words, lived experience is critical to countering human trafficking.

What does it mean to have a movement that is survivor-centered and survivor-led? We start in this chapter with the question of language, how it is used, and what it signifies. The TVPA does not mention survivors, nor does the international Protocol to Prevent, Suppress, and Punish Trafficking in Persons. Where did the word originate in a human trafficking context? Why did survivors insist on using that term—and then other terms—to describe themselves? In the first article we examine some of the more contentious debates about language and why those debates matter.

Just as language is important, so too, are images. How we "see" a problem is reflected in the language and the images we choose for our public education and awareness efforts, for the policies and programs we construct, and for the work we do together to eradicate trafficking. In the second article, we show how, over time, many people and organizations engaged in anti-trafficking work became aware of a tendency to stereotype both victims and survivors, and how the projection of those stereotypes in our work could unwittingly damage our efforts. Finally, we look at how some of the barriers to ending trafficking are constructs of the problem itself; others, such as implicit bias on the part of law enforcement or service providers, can be easily addressed once we become aware of our own self-conceived notions of what human trafficking looks like.

Q11. Victim versus Survivor: Does the Language Used in Discussing Human Trafficking Matter?

Answer: Yes, the language used does make a difference. Language is a powerful tool that affects the way people think and act (Youth Collaboratory 2019). New language theory postulates that the function of language is to move people toward a common goal, reality, or identity, and that choice of words and phrases play a role in persuading people to think one way or another. This means that speech is inherently political and can be and is utilized to shape policy perspective (Stanley and Beaver 2023). It explains why over the past thirty years there have been pitched battles about the use of one word or phrase over another. In anti-trafficking work, debates over using "victim" versus "survivor," or "child prostitute" versus "victim of commercial sexual exploitation of children," have been largely resolved. But other debates, such as the debate about whether human trafficking is a modern-day form of slavery, or whether an adult person engaged in commercial sex is a victim of sex trafficking or is a sex worker, continue.

The Facts: The terminology used to describe human trafficking has evolved over the twenty-first century. For example, "victim" was the only term used to describe a person who had been trafficked for the first five years following the passage of the TVPA. The title of the law itself contains the word "victim." By 2005, survivors themselves were using the word "survivor," and most recently, the term "lived experience," has been introduced from the medical research field. Specifically, the term was imported into the anti-trafficking world by professionals and survivors who felt it better described a particular set of insights drawn from direct experience.

A 2015 study looked at "media framing"—how US print and broadcast news media covered sex trafficking over a five-year period between 2008 and 2012. The article analyzed trends and patterns in reporting on human trafficking and found the following:

- From the late 1990s to 2008, the US media reported that trafficking mainly occurred in other regions of the world.
- From 2008 to 2012 sex trafficking was framed mostly as a domestic issue.
- Before 2008, media reports on trafficking used the word "victim" almost exclusively; from 2008 to 2012, the term "survivor " appeared over time.
- The use of the word "prostitute" when talking about children or youth was utilized by reporters from 2000 to 2008; in 2008 media analysis shows reporters taking a more nuanced approach with less labeling that used stigmatizing language and more description of children and youth as runaways who get coerced or forced into the sex trade. (Johnston et.al. 2015)

Human Trafficking versus Modern-Day Slavery

In one of his last speeches as ambassador-at-large on Trafficking in Persons at the US Department of State, John Miller said,

> Language is as important in fighting modern-day slavery, also known as human trafficking, as it was in fighting historic slavery. In earlier centuries to avoid facing up to the suffering of slaves, words such as 'houseboy,' 'field hand,' and 'servant' were used. Today, words such as 'forced laborer,' 'sex worker,' 'child soldier,' and 'child sex worker' are commonly used.

Miller went on to describe the way he saw laborers forced to work on a plantation, or in a factory, as "forced laborers" but also as victims of slavery. Children kidnapped and forced to be killing machines may be "child soldiers," but they are also victims of slavery. While he appreciated the phrases "trafficking in persons," and "human trafficking," he believed that while there is some legal foundation for using those phrases (i.e., the TVPA of 2000 uses the phrase "trafficking in persons") the previous words, although, he believed these phrases "verbally anesthetize the abuse to the victim of slavery" (Miller 2006).

On the other hand, the National Survivor Network has argued that while the phrase " modern- day slavery" is a term that is "eye-grabbing and makes awareness easy, it paints a problematic picture of human trafficking," noting that "Human trafficking and historical slavery in the U.S. have similarities, however, framing like this is troubling as they are not the same" (National Survivor Network 2019). They argue that use of the phrase, "modern-day slavery" minimizes historical enslavement of African people and the multigenerational trauma and resulting impact. It can also be harmful to survivors, as it paints an inaccurate picture of many trafficking experiences.

Victim versus Survivor versus Lived Experience

The answer is each term is useful. According to the DOJ, "The term victim describes a person who has been subjected to a crime. The word 'victim' is also important because under U.S. law, a person who is a victim has a status that provides certain rights. Victim is a legal definition necessary within the criminal justice system. In order to qualify for certain federal assistance through the US Department of Justice Office of Victims of Crime or the US Department of Health and Human Services, a person who has been trafficked must be identified as a victim. However, it is important to note that the word 'victim' does not imply weakness, assume guilt, or assign blame. Investigators and prosecutors use this term to illustrate that a crime has been committed against a person" (US Department of Justice 2021).

The term "survivor," on the other hand, is used as a term of empowerment to convey that a person has started the healing process and may have gained a sense of peace in their life. According to the *Cambridge English Dictionary*, a survivor is "a person who is able to continue living his or her life successfully despite experiencing difficulties." Some survivors of human trafficking have suggested that the word "survivor" is not an accurate description of their lives following escape from trafficking. One survivor prefers an altogether new term, "Surthriver," which better describes the fact that she has not just survived but thrived (Carson 2023). Another survivor proposed the word "Overcomer" to indicate that she has overcome difficulties and challenges of being a victim at the age of eleven of child sex slavery, rape, molestation, and pornography (Bello 2023).

Lived experience is a relatively new term when applied to human trafficking. According to the US Department of Health and Human Services,

> People with lived experience are those directly affected by social, health, public health, or other issues and by the strategies that aim to address those issues. This gives them insights that can inform and improve systems, research, policies, practices, and programs. When we say lived experience, we mean knowledge based on someone's perspective, personal identities, and history, beyond their

professional or educational experience. In the health and human services field this term is becoming the preferred term when talking about including survivors in all aspects of anti-trafficking work.

Community-based advocates have been using the word survivor, but many are changing to the phrase lived experience. Practitioners and individuals working with victims and/or survivors understand that the terms can be used interchangeably in a respectful way. Although practitioners and victims-survivors alike typically have a preferred term, both terms are needed and appropriate based on the context and possible requirement for a legal status. A person who identifies as a survivor may not see themselves as a victim because they have gained strength through their process of healing. Explaining the definition of victim within the criminal justice system will help the individual understand the term as a legal status, not as a label.

Trafficked, Prostitute, Sex Worker

The late Carol Leigh, who called herself "Scarlot Harlot," claimed that she coined the term "sex worker" in the late 1970s in an effort to find an alternative term for the pejorative "prostitute," which has so much stigma attached to it. She said that it best described what she and others were doing: selling sex in a sex work industry (Leigh 2010). Although the term made its way into the lexicon and became the term of choice for those who wanted to legalized prostitution, few laws in the United States and around the world use the term. Instead, almost all states have a body of law prohibiting prostitution, pimping, pandering, procuring, and maintaining a brothel.

The federal TVPA defined the term "sex trafficking" as the recruitment, harboring, transportation, provision, obtaining, patronizing, or soliciting of a person by force, fraud, or coercion for the purpose of a commercial sex act. It defines "commercial sex act" as "any sex act, on account of which anything of value is given to or received by any person" (18 US Code 1591). So, essentially, the 2000 TVPA distinguishes between sex trafficking, which is a commercial sex act or acts compelled by force, fraud, or coercion, from commercial sex acts entered into willingly.

Brenda Myers-Powell, a survivor who serves on the President's US Advisory Council on Trafficking, argues, referring to commercial sex: "It's not work because it's nothing like real work: there is no job description, no benefits, no vacation time, no retirement plan, no long-term disability Those of us who have experienced it know that it is violence against women, nothing more." (Myer-Powell 2021). Building on her statement, several anti-trafficking advocates have argued that selling sex for money would not qualify as a job under current labor laws, citing Occupational Safety and Health Administration (OSHA) regulations for hazardous work would mean that gloves, masks, protective gear, and equipment as well as regular testing for STIs and other serious communicable diseases would have to be in place for every "task"; civil rights law and law prohibiting discrimination would prohibit refusal to perform any act or task with a person; and selling of sex is inconsistent with sexual harassment law" (Watson 2023). In Germany, where prostitution is legal, unemployment law might require persons to work in a brothel if they lose their jobs in other sectors. Some have pointed out that the phrase "sex work" obscures the force, fraud, and coercion inherent in trafficking. New Congressional and media focus on online businesses involved in commercial sex, such as OnlyFans, ensure that this debate is far from over (Stoya 2021). John Miller, the second US ambassador-at-large for Trafficking in Persons, noted that the most egregious use of language is "sex worker" and "child sex worker." In his speech he said,

> People called "sex workers" did not choose prostitution the way most of us choose work occupations … After all, who would freely choose an "occupation" in which the death rate from murder and disease is scores of times the norm? Clinical research shows vast majorities of people in prostitution are subject to trauma, violence, rape, and 89 percent want to escape. These 89 percent are victims of slavery. (Miller 2006)

He concluded that

> What is occurring is the use of language to justify modern-day slavery, to dignify the perpetrators and the industries who enslave. Governments, non-governmental organizations, and citizens who care about fighting human trafficking and want to break the cycle of stigmatization and victimization should not use words such as "sex worker" or "child sex worker." For these reasons, I am directing the Office to Monitor and Combat Trafficking in Persons to encourage grantees and contractors to avoid use of the terms "sex worker" and "child sex worker" and I am advising all U.S. agencies issuing anti-trafficking in person contracts and grants to do the same. To abolish modern-day slavery, we must not be afraid to call slavery by its real, despicable name. (Miller 2006)

Child Prostitute, Child Sex Worker, Prostituted Youth

While many of these debates are ongoing, one place that the field of anti-trafficking advocates, survivors, service-providers, policymakers ,and others purport to agree upon is that the use of the term "child prostitute." Survivors in an OJJDP (Office of Juvenile Justice and Delinquency Prevention)-funded discussion about language noted that, "By law, a 'child prostitute,' 'teen prostitute,' or 'minor engaged in prostitution' does not exist." One NGO put it this way: "There is no such thing as a child prostitute: The word 'prostitute' refers to a person who engages in sexual activity in exchange for money. But under federal law, persons under the age of 18 cannot legally consent to commercial sex, so they are always classified as victim" (Love 146 2023). The same is true for almost every country in the world: under international laws as well as the laws of almost every nation, children are not old enough to consent to or choose prostitution.

Anti-trafficking experts state that child prostitution is

commercial sexual exploitation of children" (CSEC), a term used by the United Nations to refer to a "range of crimes and activities involving the sexual abuse or exploitation of a child for the financial benefit of any person or in exchange for anything of value (including monetary and non-monetary benefits) given or received by any person.

Language helps create policy perspectives and cements mindsets. In anti-trafficking work, the words we choose play an important role in communicating our larger view of the world and situate us on one side or another of some ongoing debates.

Further Reading

Bello. 2023, Brook. https://www.trinet.com/article-transcript-people-matter-campaign. Accessed June 25, 2023.

Carson, Marlene, "Ohio SurThrivers are Reclaiming and Rebuilding Live Once Destroyed by Sex Trafficking." August 2, 2021, https://www.einnews.com/pr_news/547574808/ohio-surthrivers-are-reclaiming-and-rebuilding-lives-once-destroyed-by-sex-trafficking. Accessed September 18, 2023.

Johnston, Anne, Barbara Friedman, and Meghan Sobel. 2015. "Framing an Emerging Issue: How U.S. Print and Broadcast News Media Covered Sex Trafficking from 2008 – 2012." *Journal of Human Trafficking* 1, no. 3: 235–54.

Lederer, Laura. 2023. "Survivor Focus Group," Chicago, June 14.

Leigh, Carol. 2010. "Inventing Sex Work," in *Whores and Other Feminists*, ed. Jill Nagle. Milton Park, Abingdon: Routledge.

Love 146. 2023. "Language & Media Guide." https://love146.org/language-media-guide/. Accessed September 19, 2023.

Miller, John. 2006. "A Statement on Human-Trafficking Related Language." US State Department Archives. https://2001-2009.state.gov/g/tip/rls/rm/78383.htm https://2001-2009.state.gov/g/tip/rls/rm/78383.htm. Accessed June 25, 2023.

Myers-Powell, Brenda. 2021. *Leaving Breezy Street.* New York: Henry Holt.

National Survivor Network, 2019. https://nationalsurvivornetwork.org/about/. Accessed September 19, 2023.

Stanley, Jason, and David Beaver. 2023. *The Politics of Language.* Princeton: Princeton University Press.

Stoya, Jessica, 2021. "What Can We Really Learn from the Only Fans Debacle?" Slate. com, August 25. https://slate.com/human-interest/2021/08/onlyfans-sex-banned-allowed-decision-history.html. Accessed September 19, 2023.

US Department of Justice, Bureau of Justice Assistance. 2021. Grant No. 2015-AK-BX-K021, Section entitled, "Victim or Survivor: Terminology from Investigation through Prosecution." https://sakitta.org/toolkit/docs/Victim-or-Survivor-Terminology-from-Investigation-Through-Prosecution.pdf. Accessed September 19, 2023.

US Department of Health and Human Services. 2022. "Methods and Emerging Strategies to Engage People with Lived Experience," https://aspe.hhs.gov/reports/lived-experience-brief. Accessed September 19, 2023.

Watson, Lori. 2023. "Why Sex Work Isn't Work." *Logos: A Journal of Modern Society and Culture*, Winter. https://logosjournal.com/2023/what-we-owe-the-past-william-macaskill-effective-altruism-and-the-wrong-life/. Accessed September 19, 2023.

Youth Collaboratory. 2019. "The Importance of Language in Anti-Trafficking Work." *Youth Collaboratory*, September 30.

Q12. Is Survivor-Informed, Survivor-Centered Engagement an Important Part of Anti-Trafficking Work?

Answer: Yes. Survivors were always a part of the movement to stop human trafficking. As early as 1992, survivors of sex trafficking had begun to speak out against their exploitation. But for many decades, survivor engagement was token—survivors were invited to tell their stories and then the "experts" took it from there. While there has been professionalization of the anti-trafficking movement, in the past ten years, survivors have not only engaged, but they have also found their voices and begun to emerge as leaders of organizations, as highly qualified and credentialed experts, and as visionaries. One might say that increased professionalism and increased attention to survivor voices are linked. As an understanding of the issue deepened, the anti-trafficking movement became more attuned to the value of listening to the experiences and perspectives of people with firsthand experience of trafficking.

The Facts: Maya Angelou once said, "There is no greater agony than bearing an untold story inside you." But some early anti-trafficking advocates cautioned against having survivors of human trafficking tell their stories. They asserted that telling those stories retraumatized the survivor, contributed to feelings of shame and guilt, put pressure on a victim to disclose details of what happened to them, and brought into the open details of exploitation that, once told, could not be untold.

However, slowly, over a period from 1990 to 2020, it became clear that survivor stories were critical to understanding the nature and scope of the problem of human trafficking and to shaping policies and programs that worked. Survivors also began to understand the potential mental health benefits of sharing their experiences. New research began to show that within a safe space, and with support and positive reactions, voluntary disclosure has therapeutic effects and strengthens recovery for the survivor (Infusino 2014). In addition, it also became clear that because most trafficking is hidden—it happens behind closed doors, in back alley brothels, out in agricultural fields or construction zones or factory sweatshops—the general public does not understand what is happening. Only survivor stories can open that closed door.

Finally, as the movement grew, survivors were able to step into advocacy, and take leadership of the movement. Today there are thousands of survivors in the United States, and tens of thousands around the world who are visible in the forefront of the movement. Survivors have formed national and international networks and alliances and have emerged as a key force in combating trafficking in persons.

One of the earliest survivors to speak out and tell her story was Norma Hotaling. Born in Florida, and sexually abused as a five-year-old child, she was trafficked into prostitution before she was eighteen. During that time, she became addicted to heroin to numb the pain of how she was being used. She spent the next twenty-one years on the streets, passed from one vicious pimp to another, and ended up finally in San Francisco, California, in the Tenderloin District, known at the time (in the late 1980s) for its squalid conditions, homelessness, drug addicts, liquor stores, strip clubs, and prostitution, and generally seedy conditions. There was no such thing as "sex trafficking" then. If you were being purchased for sex, you were a prostitute, and prostitution was illegal. There was no understanding of the background of many of the women and girls on the streets. There was little law enforcement focus on the pimps and traffickers, and no focus at all on the buyers.

As Norma told it, she was arrested and booked over eighteen times, particularly by one police officer, Joe Dutton, who got to know her and befriended her. At first, she said, "He used to arrest me all the time and book me for prostitution, drug sales, possession. I hated him. He scared me—he was everywhere" (Derbaken 2003). But she remembered that each time he arrested her he would tell her,

"You don't deserve this life—your life is worth so much more than this. You have to turn your life around." The last time Hotaling was arrested was after she had been kidnapped, driven to a cemetery outside of San Francisco, brutally beaten, and sexually assaulted. She was left for dead, and the resulting physical injuries required her to have a metal plate placed in her skull. Lying in jail, going cold turkey off heroin, she said she decided to help herself first, and then others like her get out of "the life" (Lederer 2018).

Norma was one of the first to tell her story, and to suggest survivor-led solutions. In 1992 she founded SAGE (Standing Against Global Exploitation) in San Francisco. She envisioned it as a "one-stop and shop" for those who had been trafficked into prostitution. SAGE began as a two-room NGO but grew to become an internationally recognized "agent of change." At its peak, it employed almost forty full-time employees. Most were survivors who had originally come to SAGE for help themselves.

By early 2000, SAGE owned its own building at 127 Mission Street in San Francisco. It was a million-dollar property and offered one of the first "Drop-in Centers" for survivors, where former survivors helped victims escape trafficking, heal physically and mentally, and address everything from substance use disorders. SAGE offered direct services to survivors, peer-support groups, life skills programs, health care (including mainstream and alternative health options such as acupuncture). In addition, it offered the public general awareness training on trafficking and commercial sexual exploitation, education, and awareness programs about specific issues in trafficking such as drug addiction and post-traumatic stress disorder recovery.

SAGE was also involved in local, state, and national policy change. Norma regularly met with San Francisco's chief of police, district attorney, and mayor. She worked with the San Francisco Commission on the Status of Women to connect sex trafficking to other violence against women issues and was an outspoken advocate for changing the law enforcement focus from women and children to the perpetrators. SAGE was an innovative organization. It was the first to use a holistic approach to rehabilitate its clients, and the first to refer to victims as survivors. Perhaps most importantly, Hotaling insisted that "survivors of the sex industry are going to be the leaders" (Lederer 2018). Since that time, her unique social service and social justice programs have been replicated nationally and globally. She won many awards, including the American Innovations in Government Award at the John F. Kennedy School of Government (1998), the Peter F. Drucker Award for Non-Profit Innovation (2000), and the Oprah Angel Network Award (2001). Her visionary approach and charismatic personal appeal were admired by many grassroots advocates, policymakers, and business leaders.

Norma died on December 16, 2008. Unfortunately, by the time she passed away, the early winds that had been at her back had shifted. SAGE was experiencing difficulties; it was under attack on many fronts. There were major policy battles—about legalizing prostitution, about whether sex trafficking of a minor was child abuse, and perhaps, most importantly, about whether survivors could run an organization for other survivors—in which Norma was involved. Norma was a fierce advocate for protecting children from child sexual abuse and commercial sexual exploitation. On other issues, such as whether prostitution should be legalized, she maintained a stance that was not so much neutral as nuanced. While she had her own personal views, she wanted SAGE to be a place free of political battles and she was especially aware that for victims and survivors, the academic and political debates were moot. For or against legalization of prostitution, victims and survivors needed services—food, clothing, shelter, medical assistance, legal assistance, drug addiction rehabilitation services, and more. In addition, SAGE was criticized for its *survivor led* services and lack of professionals, particularly professionals to manage the growing number of services—healthcare providers, therapists, counselors and other mental health providers, credentialed social workers, and case management specialists. Its fledgling infrastructure was not strong enough to withstand the criticism. While it struggled to continue, led by survivors Norma had hand-picked, it closed its doors for lack of funding and other support in 2014. In 2009, following Norma's death, the Board of Directors of SAGE hired a consultant to put together a coalition called the San Francisco Collaborative Against Human Trafficking. It established an infrastructure (still in place fifteen years later) of all the working relationships Norma and others had begun including the Office of the San Francisco Mayor, Office of the San Francisco District Attorney, Office of the San Francisco Supervisor, National Council of Jewish Women San Francisco, San Francisco Department on the Status of Women, San Francisco Human Rights Commission, San Francisco Police Department, San Francisco Department of Public Health, Adult Probation Department, Asian Pacific Islander Legal Outreach, Asian Women's Shelter, Because Justice Matters, Freedom House, Jewish Family and Children's Services, Jewish Community Relations Council, Not For Sale, Prostitution Research and Education, and SAGE Project, Inc. (San Francisco Collaboration 2009).

In 2011, the US Department of Justice funded a final evaluation of two of the key SAGE programs. The key findings in the evaluation reveal some of the internal debates in the community about the effectiveness and sustainability of a survivor-led, survivor-centered organization (US Department of Justice, Cohen et al. 2011). The evaluators found that,

> Referrals to the LIFESKILLS program were problematic throughout the entire study period. They came from the Juvenile Probation Department, the Department of Social Services, the Department of Mental Health, Youth Guidance Center, teachers, other community-based organizations, or self-referrals. These divergent referral sources resulted in a mix of high-risk and CSE–involved girls. The majority of GRACE participants are first-time prostitution offenders and are referred by the San Francisco District Attorney's Office. Clients from the DA's Office are sentenced to complete court-mandated hours at SAGE, rather than going to jail. Referrals have been erratic, but the program was more stable than LIFESKILLS until 2008, when funding was cut by the DA's Office.

Staff articulated the mission of LIFESKILLS as to "improve lives of young girls, identify issues, and keep them from moving to the adult component." The GRACE staff felt their mission was to have clients finish their hours, work with the District Attorney's Office, and provide case management. They felt that the main mission is trauma recovery and empowering women to deal with their problems. Fidelity to the program model was compromised by high staff turnover, although two staff members provided critical continuity over the past 8 years. As a result, staff understanding of program completion differed, especially for LIFESKILLS, which was a much more fluid program.

In 2007, SAGE had forty-two paid staff. Of the forty-two staff, twenty-five (60 percent) had a personal history of victimization. All of the direct care staff have either college degrees in relevant fields, such as social work or psychology, or possess certifications in case management, or as alcohol and drug counselors. Although most staff are highly dedicated, an issue in the organization is frequent turnover, especially since training is mostly in the form of informal apprenticeships, which can lead to dilution of program components. Staff are frustrated with a lack of backup and frequent staff turnover. They feel that more staff are needed as well as more supervisory oversight. They also feel that more structure and a tighter curriculum are needed for the program.

However, when the participants in the program were surveyed, the evaluators found that nearly all (89 percent) of the participants in both groups felt that SAGE had helped them. Participants were very positive about their relationships with the case managers.

Yet survivor leaders emerged and founded organizations that provided services. In 1996, in Minneapolis, Minnesota, survivor Vednita Carter founded Breaking Free, an organization that aids girls and women in exiting prostitution (Lederer 2018). She subsequently became the organization's executive director, and the program expanded to offer more support, including: "emergency services such as food, clothing, shelter, medical assistance, legal assistance to victims of trafficking" (Global Centurion 2010). By 1998, the organization rented an apartment block to permanently re-house women and girls, and by 2010, they owned apartments and three "transitional houses."

Kristy Childs, who founded Veronica's Voice in the year 2000 and still runs it today, offered a drop-in center and later a residential house for sex trafficking survivors. Tina Frundt, who founded Courtney's House in 2008 and still serves as executive director, has a drop-in center in Northeast Washington, DC, that offers counseling and survivor support groups for domestic minor victims of trafficking. The groups are open to boys, girls, and transgender survivors and focus on trauma recovery, education and life skills along with therapeutic activities such as dance, art, and yoga.

However, these are the exceptions for the years from 2000 (after the passage of the TVPA, The organizations that emerged and became the large advocacy organizations were founded and run by advocates with college degrees, including International Justice Mission, Polaris Project (now Polaris), Not For Sale, Shared Hope, End Slavery Now, the Coalition to Abolish Slavery.

Slowly, the professional world caught up with the visionary survivor perspective. Peter Beresford published "Developing the Theoretical Basis for Service User/Survivor-Led Research and Equal Involvement in Research." His article put forward a hypothesis that offered a systematic path forward for the full and equal involvement of health service users/survivors in both the research process and research structures more generally. The hypothesis challenged the traditional emphasis on assumptions about the priority of values of "distance," "neutrality," and "objectivity" in research as well as services. It argued that those ideas discriminate against service users and their experiential knowledge and explored instead the idea that "the shorter the distance between direct experience and its interpretation, the less likely resulting knowledge is to be inaccurate, unreliable, and distorted" (Beresford 2005).

After over a decade of protests about the lack of survivor-informed policymaking and programming, in 2015, the Justice for Victims of Trafficking Act created the United States Advisory Council on Human Trafficking (US Advisory Council 2023). According to the US Department of State, the advisory council provides a formal platform for trafficking survivors to advise and make recommendations on federal anti-trafficking policies to the President's Interagency Task Force to Monitor and Combat Trafficking in Persons. Each member is a survivor of human trafficking, and together they represent a diverse range of backgrounds and experiences. Council members are appointed by the president for two-year terms. The council releases annual reports that include key findings and recommendations for the federal government to strengthen policies and programs.

Today, US government agencies make clear that they value and support survivor voices and initiatives. The 2022 US Department of State Trafficking in Persons Report includes a substantial section entitled, "Survivor Engagement in the Anti-Trafficking Field: History, Lessons Learned, and Looking Forward." This chapter emphasizes survivors play a vital role in combating human trafficking:

> Their perspective and experience should be taken into consideration to better address this crime and to craft a better response to it. They run organizations, advocate before legislatures, train law enforcement officers, conduct public outreach, and collaborate with government officials on local and national levels. They serve the anti-trafficking community and society at large as doctors, lawyers, mental health professionals, and more. Engaging survivors as partners is critical to establishing effective victim-centered, trauma-informed, and culturally competent anti-trafficking polices and strategies that address prevention, protection, and prosecution efforts. Meaningful engagement means collaborating with survivors in all aspects of anti-trafficking efforts such as developing practices, policies, and strategies, as well as prioritizing survivor leadership of those efforts whenever possible. (US Department of State, TIP Report 2022)

The report also provides models for engagement for government organizations (GOs), intergovernmental organizations (IOs), nongovernmental organizations (NGOs), and private sector partnerships that are survivor-led, survivor-informed, and survivor-centered. Finally, it offers some key guidance for involving survivors, including utilizing survivor stories in an ethical manner, including survivors in decision-making, addressing barriers to survivor inclusion and leadership, employing survivors in the same manner we employ other staffers, and establishing a trauma-informed workplace, including in hiring and benefits and compensation.

There are still many gaps in the engagement of survivors in anti-trafficking work. One that was recently identified by a number of survivors is the lack of funding for survivor-led service provision. Recently researchers have identified several "markers" of good engagement (vs. bad engagement) with survivors, including long-term initiatives, direct employment, and incorporation into project teams in sustained ways and for specific purposes. High-quality engagement also makes clear how the time and resources of people with lived experience will be deployed and compensated. All people will be recruited appropriately, paid fairly, fully valued, and offered opportunities for professional development (Balch et al. 2023).

Further Reading

Balch, Alex, Allen Kiconco, and Wendy Asquith. 2023. "Could Survivors Help Fix Anti-Trafficking?" *Open Democracy*, February 13. https://www.opendemocr acy.net/en/beyond-trafficking-and-slavery/could-survivors-help-fix-anti-traf ficking/. Accessed June 25, 2023.

Beresford, Peter. 2005. "Developing the Theoretical Basis for Service User/Survivor-Led Research and Equal Involvement in Research." *National Library of Medicine*. https://pubmed.ncbi.nlm.nih.gov/15792288/. Accessed June 25, 2023.

Derbaken, Jason. 2003. "Internal Investigator Who Ruffled the SFPD." *San Francisco Chronicle*, January 13. https://www.sfgate.com/bayarea/article/Internal-investiga tor-who-ruffled-the-SFPD-Cop-2678691.php. Accessed June 25, 2023.

Global Centurion. 2010. "Norma Hotaling Awards." https://www.globalcenturion.org/archi ved-workpages/normahotalingawards/2010-nha-recipients/. Accessed June 25, 2023.

Infusino, Karen. 2014. "From Survivor to Advocate: The Therapeutic Benefits of Public Disclosure." College of Education Theses and Dissertations. 63. https://via.library. depaul.edu/soe_etd/63. Accessed June 25, 2023.

Lederer, Laura. 2018. *Modern Slavery: A Documentary and Reference Guide*. Santa Barbara, CA: ABC-CLIO.

National Defense Authorization Act of 2013, Title XVII, "Ending Trafficking in Government Contracting," https://www.govinfo.gov/content/pkg/PLAW-112publ239/html/PLAW-112publ239.htm. Accessed June 25, 2023.

US Advisory Council on Trafficking in Persons. 2023. "Survivor Leadership." https://www.state.gov/humantrafficking-survivor-leadership/. Accessed June 25, 2023.

US Department of Justice, Cohen, Marcia, et al. 2011. *Final Report on the Evaluation of the SAGE Project's LIFESKILLS and GRACE Programs*. May, p. xiii. https://www.ojp.gov/pdffiles1/nij/grants/234464.pdf. Accessed June 25, 2023.

US Department of State Trafficking in Persons Report. 2022. *Survivor Engagement*. https://www.state.gov/reports/2022-trafficking-in-persons-report/. Accessed June 25, 2023.

Q13. Can Images Subliminally Reinforce Misconceptions about Human Trafficking?

Answer: Yes, they can. New brain research shows that vision is by far our most dominant sense, taking up half of our brain's resources. If we listen to a presentation with new information in it, three days later we may remember 10 percent of it. However, studies show that if a picture or visual is added, we remember 65 percent (Newell 2020). That is why the images for human trafficking education and awareness campaigns and trainings must be carefully chosen.

An online search for images of "sex trafficking" brings up photos of scantily clad white women in high heels, fishnet stockings, and pole dancing in a bar. Google "child sex trafficking" and the first images that appear are of young white girls with a man's hand over their mouth, or a rope around their wrists, chains on their ankles, and barbed wire fencing them in. The phrase "child trafficking" brings up images of young school-aged girls and boys sitting in a corner of a room with their heads in their hands or folded almost into a fetal position with their arms wrapped around their legs and their heads down. Experts in human trafficking say these stereotypical images do more harm than good because they reinforce misconceptions about human trafficking, especially sex trafficking.

The Facts: The Senior Policy Operating Group (SPOG) of the President's Interagency Task Force (PITF), a federal interagency group that works on policy issues related to human trafficking, has five standing committees. One of them, the Public Awareness and Outreach Subcommittee, created a Guidance for Introductory Level Human Trafficking Awareness Training.

The guidance includes Standards for Course Design, discusses the use of statistics in presentations and trainings, and describes best practices for use of messaging and images. These guidelines for common messaging, standard statistics, and images form a set of core competencies that the US government uses in creation of content for its education and awareness materials (US Department of State n.d.). They recommend that images should be victim-centered and promote an accurate understanding of human trafficking. "Images can draw connections in the audience's mind that are both intended and unintended. They project an understanding of what a victim may look like. If all sex trafficking campaigns depict child victims, for instance, audiences may not realize that adults can be victims of sex trafficking" (US Department of State n.d.). The SPOG advises anti-trafficking advocates to use images that:

- Represent the diverse spectrum of human trafficking victims—individuals of all races, ethnicities, ages, genders, sexual orientation, and socioeconomic backgrounds.

- Show examples of how trafficking might appear in a public encounter or setting. This could include health-care settings, transportation settings, and/ or recruitment settings.
- Encourage appropriate action, such as reporting suspected trafficking to local authorities or the National Human Trafficking Hotline.
- Encourage a person who suspects trafficking to get help rather than take independent action.

The SPOG also has a list of "Don't Do's." These include images that display physical abuse or reinforce misconceptions about human trafficking: ones that use sensationalized depictions of victims of trafficking in chains, behind bars or in handcuffs; and titillating images that focus on nude or nearly nude figures of women.

Another issue that has been raised in the anti-trafficking community is the tendency to typecast certain individuals or communities in certain roles. For example, some government officials noted that in health-care trainings, most of the health-care providers were white and most of the victims were Black. On the other hand, survivors have continuously raised the concern that a large number of victims and survivors in the United States are African American and/or from other communities of color, but education and awareness campaigns of GOs and NGOs depict largely white victims. Fascinatingly, in one government training, this problem was overcorrected to the point that all the health providers were Black and all the victims were white.

One serious concern was the tendency in the media and in service provider organizations to utilize pictures of victims and survivors without their permission, or to display minor victims without redacting their faces. Using these images without permission, or even with permission but without understanding the circumstances surrounding the case can be deleterious. In one case, the early use of a survivor's picture and name negatively affected a court case that was pending.

The problem with these images is more than just it being a poor choice of visual. When viewers see too many images of women and children chained in articles about human trafficking, the take-away is that this is what trafficking looks like. Although the definition of trafficking includes force as a means of controlling a victim, it also lists fraud and coercion as means. When survivors tell their stories, there is often an element of force, but there are other elements used to compel a victim, including threats, intimidation, and emotional abuse.

The problem with having a misconception about what trafficking looks like— thinking for example, that it means survivors are locked in basements or chained to walls—is that such images do not prepare people to recognize real signs and indicators of human trafficking.

In addition, the SPOG Guidance emphasizes that image displays of physical or sexual abuse and/or their aftereffects can be dehumanizing and objectifying, depicting survivors merely as objects of violence.

Another critique of the use of stereotypic images is the young person, usually female, usually white, usually very young, crouched on the street, sidewalk, or in a corner of a room.

More recently, some education and awareness campaigns have focused on the buyer instead of the victim.

The State of Georgia has been a leader in these campaigns. The first campaign, a series of Dear John letters to the "John"—slang for purchaser of sex—featured a series of billboards with images of Mayor Shirley Jackson, a mom and her baby girl, and a coach. Each featured a letter to the sex buyer that children would not be for sale in the city, the neighborhoods, the schools, of Atlanta, Georgia. The bold campaign raised the profile of the anti-trafficking efforts in Atlanta and was a response to a series of particularly vicious cases of pimps trafficking girls as young as ten, eleven, and twelve years old (Pipkins 2004).

The campaign, however, was not universally praised. As one scholar put it:

> Even as Dear John did not use stereotypical images and stories of dark, predatory men and innocent white girls, its emphasis on individual men limited how it defined and addressed commercial sex. Namely, through symbolic images of easily identifiable characters/personas (a mayor, mom, and coach) and direct and consequential text, Dear John reinforced the idea that sex trading is a necessarily heterosexual phenomenon, where (English speaking) men are dominative predators who perpetrate the majority of harms against always victimized girls and young women. (Majic 2017)

Georgia's next attempt at a public awareness campaign addressing the buyer side of human trafficking was its "Georgia's Not Buying It campaign." The campaign played on the word "buyer," and featured a hard-hitting set of public service announcements showing ordinary businessmen in suits and ties who, when looking into a mirror or going through a revolving door morphed into men wearing wolf masks, ostensibly to show that it is your average man on the street who is a sex buyer. It was designed by a leading-for-profit advertising agency in Georgia The original campaign was launched in 2013; then retired; then refashioned and relaunched in 2018 as the "Demand an End" campaign.

Both versions of the campaign were championed by the attorney general of Georgia and Street Grace, an NGO headquartered in Georgia, but working with a dozen other states (Street Grace 2023). It targeted buyers of sex from minors and was, according to then attorney general Sam Olens, the first time a state created a united front to target the demand side of child sex trafficking. According to campaign materials, the campaign focused on aggressively prosecuting those who purchase sex illegally, promoting training for mandated reporters, and incentivizing businesses and civic organizations to get involved (Street Grace 2023).

The new version of the campaign was launched in 2018. According to Attorney General Chris Carr, in conjunction with Street Grace and the Georgia Bureau of Investigation (GBI), Demand an End focuses on education and awareness, aiming to create a united force and stop the growth and proliferation of sex trafficking by targeting the demand side of this issue. "We are focused on bringing an end to Domestic Minor Sex Trafficking in Georgia and around the country by addressing the root of the problem—demand," said Attorney General Chris Carr. "This horrific industry will continue to victimize and exploit children as long as there is a high demand for it. This is why we are asking all cities, counties, businesses, non-profits, houses of worship, law enforcement officials, judicial professionals and concerned citizens to join us in demanding an end."

The campaign used the striking, scary, images to get the word out about the business of child sex trafficking. "As is the case with any business, child sex trafficking operates on the economic principle of supply and demand," added Carr.

> In this case, however, the supply is comprised of children who are frequently abused and exploited at a very young age, and the demand is comprised of the individuals who are seeking to buy children for sex .... To date, responses to child sex trafficking have been focused almost exclusively on the supply side of the equation—providing crucial rescue and rehabilitation services to survivors of child sex trafficking after they have been exploited. These services are greatly needed; however, this approach only addresses half of the equation and does not target the source that perpetrates the industry, demand.

To date there have been few if any education and awareness campaigns using images of traffickers. While there are thousands of mug shots of convicted traffickers available, the focus is on the trafficking and not the actual traffickers who are doing the trafficking.

Most non-governmental organizations are beginning to edit the images in their education and awareness campaigns to reflect these guidelines, and while there is much room for improvement, progress is being made in the representations and images utilized in anti-trafficking work.

One spectacularly successful early public service campaign was the US Department of Health and Human Services public awareness campaign on human trafficking. First launched in April 2004, under the title "Rescue and Restore," the goal of the campaign was to help communities identify victims and respond appropriately, including reporting suspected trafficking to a newly formed National Human Trafficking Hotline. A secondary goal was to help US citizens understand that human trafficking is not just an international problem, it occurs in every state in the United States.

New statistics show that in the first several years, the campaign generated over 200 million media images across the United States. The campaign used the slogan, "Look Beneath the Surface" and featured a series of individuals from every walk of life, in many different settings—on streets, in health provider offices, in factories, in schools—with a saying "Look Beneath the Surface: A victim of trafficking may look like many of the people you see every day." It was simple, broke all stereotypical depictions of trafficking, and ran for almost a decade before it was overhauled and released as Look Beneath the Surface, 2.0. Almost uniformly the campaign gathered praise; it eventually was credited with recruiting more than 1,000 local and 75 national partners and formed coalitions in 19 cities.

One critique of the campaign was the initial title, Rescue and Restore. Some survivors objected to the notion that victims of trafficking can be "rescued" in the same way one would rescue a survivor in a shipwreck. In "Take Off the Cape," an anti-trafficking blogger noted that the term "rescue" would rarely be used in intimate partner violence or most forms of sexual violence. Scholars said the term "rescue" conveyed a romanticized scene in which a helpless victim waited for a strong savior to come and swoop them away (Bullard-Owens 2014).

The second iteration of the campaign was more sophisticated. It removed the words "Rescue and Restore," and focused on the phrase "Look beneath the Surface." It had a strong emphasis on action as opposed to simply education. In the public service announcement videos, the first page, featuring a victim in a common setting, gave way to a second image underneath (literally under the surface of the first image) that exposed what was really happening to the victim behind closed doors, in factories, fields, building construction, and other scenes of both labor and sex trafficking. The images were tailored to the demographics of the target audience (the general public) to ensure that the message was relatable.

Choice of images is important in any social justice campaign, but especially in anti-trafficking campaigns. Human trafficking is a complicated problem that includes sex trafficking and labor trafficking, adults and children, international and domestic cases, traffickers, buyers, and victims from every age, race, nationality, ethnicity, gender, sexual orientation, and socioeconomic background. Ensuring that images reflect the complexity of the crime will ensure that the campaign gets messaging right.

Further Reading

Bullard-Owens, Becky. 2014. "Take Off the Cape: Why Using the Word 'Rescue' is Harmful to Anti-Trafficking Efforts." *Colorado Coalition Against Sexual Assault*, July 24, 2014. https://www.ccasa.org/take-off-the-cape/. Accessed July 1, 2023.

Covington News, "Campaign against Sex Trafficking in Georgia Kicks Off," March 18, 2013. https://www.covnews.com/nationworld/campaign-against-sex-trafficking-in-ga-kicks-off/. Accessed July 1, 2023.

Majic, Samantha. 2017. "Sending a Dear John Letter: Public Information Campaigns and the Movement to 'End Demand' for Prostitution in Atlanta, GA." *Social Sciences* 6, no. 4: 138. https://doi.org/10.3390/socsci6040138.

Newell, Chad. 2020. "Why a Picture Really Is Worth a Thousand Words According to Neuroscience." *MarketingProfs*, May 19. https://www.marketingprofs.com/artic les/2020/42939/why-a-picture-really-is-worth-a-thousand-words-according-to-neuro science. Accessed July 1, 2023.

Street Grace, "Georgia's Not Buying It" Campaign. https://www.streetgrace.org/. The website is no longer active.

United States v. Pipkins. 2004. https://caselaw.findlaw.com/court/us-11th-circuit/1380 071.html. Accessed July 1, 2023.

US Department of State, Senior Policy Operating Group Public Awareness and Operating Committee. n.d. *Guidance for Introductory-Level Human Trafficking Awareness Training*. https://www.state.gov/wp-content/uploads/2023/02/ PAO-Guide-for-Intro-HT-Awareness-Training_FINAL508.pdf. Accessed July 1, 2023.

Q14. What Barriers Do Trafficking Survivors Face to Escape and Obtain Care?

Answer: Victims of human trafficking face a staggering array of physical, social, and economic barriers to escaping their traffickers. Perhaps the most common barrier, though, is violence and physical abuse at the hands of those who profit from their exploitation.

The Facts: In 2020, research published in the US Department of Health and Human Services National Institute of Health identified three types of barriers: extrinsic, intrinsic, and systemic (Garg et al. 2020). Extrinsic barriers included trafficker control, physical confinement, and influence of peers. Intrinsic barriers included discrimination, confidentiality, trust in health-care providers, knowledge of the health-care system, and emotional reluctance. Systemic issues inherent to the health-care system included health-care provider knowledge, complex registration process, language barriers, appointment times, and service coordination.

Most of the barriers can be divided into two columns: victim-created barriers and barriers caused by first responders who often unwittingly make it difficult for victims to seek help. Finally, there are barriers in the systems themselves, whether child welfare, social services, foster care, education, health care, or other systems of care that have inadvertently been designed in ways that make it difficult for victims of trafficking to seek and receive services.

In one study in Detroit, eighty-seven women who were trafficked or engaged in prostitution were asked a series of questions about the barriers to health care and to escaping their trafficker or exiting prostitution. The respondents mentioned five distinct categories of challenges or barriers:

- Challenges with substance drug use and addiction
- Homelessness
- Experience with violence
- Experiences with law enforcement
- Health-care issues.

Others mentioned homelessness and drug addiction on the part of the victim, and alcohol addiction create yet another tie to their exploitative situation and can even bar women from some of the resources that would otherwise be available to them. Furthermore, limited education, few employment opportunities, and homelessness or unstable housing further a cycle of hopelessness that makes escape or an alternative lifestyle seem nearly impossible to achieve (Lederer, Stinson, and Chandler Forthcoming). In its training on human trafficking for health-care professionals entitled "SOAR: Stop, Observe, Ask, Respond," the US Department of Health and Human Services identifies a number of barriers on the part of the victim, which prevent them from obtaining care. These are the "intrinsic" barriers. They include a patient who:

- Lacks awareness of victimization
- Lacks understanding of legal rights
- Lacks I.D. and other records
- Has a language barrier
- Fears deportation or law enforcement
- Has experienced trauma bonding with the trafficker or with other victims
- Fears that reporting could lead to return to an abusive home, jail, or foster care
- Feels complicit in an illegal act
- Fears that traffickers will cause harm to self, family, or loved ones
- Has limited literacy and education that hinders the ability to communicate
- Distrusts the provider or those in authority
- Feels hopeless and helpless
- Feels shame or guilt. (US Department of Health and Human Services [HHS] 2012)

On the service provider side, the training identified a number of barriers too. These are "extrinsic" barriers—barriers beyond the control of the victim. These include a service provider who:

- Lacks knowledge about human trafficking
- Has inadequate understanding of federal, state, and local human trafficking laws
- Fears violating the rules of the Health Insurance Portability and Accountability Act of 1996 (HIPAA)
- Lacks trauma-informed care training
- Misidentifies the case
- Has preconceived notions of attributes of a victim of trafficking
- Lacks access to neutral, professional interpreters
- "Checks off boxes" without seeing the full patient or client situation
- Thinks that asking will be time-consuming or too complex
- Feels the patient is unresponsive or hostile to questioning or tells a rehearsed story
- Lacks information on good referral options
- Attributes behavior(s) to harmful cultural stereotypes
- Does not believe it is his or her role to get involved. (National Human Trafficking Training and Technical Assistance Center [NHTTAC] n.d.)

In the Detroit study, 74 percent sought help from health-care providers and other service providers while they were still being trafficked. Forty-three percent said that the main reason they could not obtain help was that they had no identification papers such as a driver's license, social security card, or other acceptable I.D. forty-two percent said that transportation was a barrier to getting help. Eighteen percent said that they were embarrassed or felt shame or guilt and did not seek help because they blamed themselves for their situation or they thought that service providers would blame them. Four percent said they did not know where to go, and four percent said that they had previously encountered rude or judgmental staff, and this prevented them from seeking help (Lederer, Stinson, and Chandler Forthcoming).

Experts have identified another provider-related barrier to getting victims of trafficking the help they need. That barrier is implicit or unconscious bias. According to the US Department of Health and Human Services, the term "implicit bias" refers to the "attitudes (positive and/or negative) or stereotypes toward a person, thing, or group that affects our understanding, actions, and decisions in an unconscious manner" (NHTTAC n.d.).

The National Institute of Health describes implicit bias as a form of bias that occurs automatically and unintentionally, affecting judgments, decisions, and behaviors (National Institutes of Health [NIH] n.d.). Implicit bias results in subtle but highly impactful behaviors, messages, and other signals that send positive or negative messages. They reveal our unconscious thoughts and send messages of disapproval, dislike, or distaste and slights that cause others to feel devalued, slighted, discouraged, and excluded (NIH n.d.). Throughout our lifetime, a complicated network of experiences shapes our values and beliefs. Factors such as family of origin, education, occupation, socioeconomic status, culture, and gender are some examples of ways implicit bias is cultivated over our lifetime through both direct experiences and indirect messages. We form judgments about individuals, situations, and circumstances based on stereotypes, professions, culture, and a host of other factors (NIH n.d.).

Whether conscious or unconscious, everyone forms judgments about individuals and circumstances that can interfere with their ability to effectively and ethically serve individuals who have experienced trafficking.

Implicit bias includes snap judgments about the experiences and character of individuals who end up as trafficked persons.

This resulted in years of minors being identified as juvenile delinquents or criminals when actually they were being exploited by pimps, pedophiles, and/ or traffickers. Now we have laws that identify children in prostitution as victims, not criminals.

Survivors tell stories about the way implicit bias negatively affected them. Here are some examples:

> I was always labeled the bad kid in school. Teachers couldn't figure out why I was always misbehaving. I seemed angry and violent for no reason, when in actuality I was being raped by my stepfather and passed around at his pedophile gatherings. (Jerome Elam, Survivor)

> I must have run away a dozen times, but no one understood why. They just kept bringing me back home to the abusive situation in the group home. (Barbara Amaya, Survivor)

> I was a preacher's daughter who was trafficked by someone who gained my parents' trust. After it happened people said, "Oh she's just a fast girl." I was *anything but* a fast girl, but no one looked beneath the surface. (Marlene Carson, Survivor)

> I was trafficked from Central America into a box-making factory in the U.S. People assumed I was an illegal alien, but I was a trafficking victim. (Ronny Marty, Survivor)

In a survey published in 2023 on pregnancy and human trafficking, pregnant victims of trafficking were asked if they had sought help from many different kinds of health providers during the time they were trafficked. Ninety percent of victims said that they sought health care; 80 percent sought health care in emergency rooms ("ERs" in hospitals); 58 percent sought care in neighborhood or urgent care clinics; 35 percent sought care from private physicians. Unfortunately, even though most reported interacting with medical professionals, when they were asked to characterize their general interactions with health-care providers, only 9.7 percent reported agreeing with the statement that medical professionals understood what was happening to them. Only 12.9 percent believed the care they received was "excellent." Only 9.7 percent reported that medical professionals were "trauma-informed." Only 6.5 percent reported receiving helpful referrals, and only 9.7 percent reported that the medical professional followed up with them or provided aftercare (Lederer, Flores, and Chandler 2023).

These dismal results have prompted HHS and others to emphasize that service providers have an ethical obligation to be aware of human trafficking, recognize its signs and indicators, and be aware of and reduce the effects of implicit bias on providing a victim with high-quality care. Some states have passed laws requiring specialized trainings tailored for service providers to help them identify victims and respond appropriately. For example, in Texas, a new law, House Bill 2059, requires all health-care providers who have direct contact with patients to take a health and human trafficking training once a year (House Bill (HB) 2059, 86th Legislature, 2019). The law requires the Texas Health and Human Services Commission (HHSC) to approve training courses on human trafficking, including at least one that is free of charge, post the list of approved trainings on the HHSC website, and update the list of approved trainings as necessary. The completion of an approved training course is a condition for registration, permit, or license renewal for certain health-care practitioners. The State of Texas reviews trainings produced by nonprofit and other organizations to ensure that the training covers a list of "core competencies" (Texas Health and Human Services Commission (HHSC) n.d.).

To be approved as a trainer, the Texas HHSC considers five categories. The categories include, first, ensuring the training has appropriate learning objectives, is created in consultation with survivors, excludes sensationalized imagery, and uses content that is evidence-based and free from factual errors; second, ensuring a thorough understanding federal law on trafficking, the main types of trafficking (sex trafficking and labor trafficking), the difference between trafficking and smuggling, and vulnerabilities that lead to victimization; third, ensuring understanding of the health impacts of human trafficking, including acute injuries, chronic medical problems, mental health issues, reproductive and sexual health concerns, and the impact of human trafficking on quality of life, autonomy, and independence; fourth, ensuring understanding of the identification and assessment of victims.

The reviewers have a list of "core competencies" that must be covered in the training itself or in supplemental materials. These include a section on a patient-centered approach, clinical settings in which trafficked persons may be encountered, and challenges and opportunities when interfacing with trafficked persons. In addition, the training needs to address survivor barriers to disclosure and health-care provider barriers to identification and response. It must guide the health-care provider through potential indicators of trafficking in persons, the role of trauma-informed care in trust-building and communication, safety planning to keep victims and providers safe, the importance of the use of professional interpreters, and the importance of and strategies to have private conversations with potential trafficked persons; and finally, it must cover response and follow up, including the importance of referrals within the health care organization and with community partners, a discussion of mandated reporter obligations, a discussion of the implications of law enforcement involvement, and information on how to contact your community, local, and/or state resources for victims and survivors.

Together these five categories ensure that each training is comprehensive, trauma-informed, and upholds survivor-informed principles (HHS n.d.)

A handful of other states have also passed similar laws requiring training for health-care providers, law enforcement officials, educators, foster care administrators and parents, social workers, child protective services, the hospitality industry (Freedberg and Messinger 2022), transportation industry, and other industries, professions, and sectors where there is evidence that human trafficking occurs, and where it is clear that certain professions are first responders to human trafficking, meaning person with specialized training who is among the first to arrive and provide assistance or incident resolution or who may be in the unique position of seeing a human trafficking victim in the course of their work.

As first responders are trained in how to identify victims of human trafficking and how to respond appropriately, within their mission and mandate, many of the current provider-related barriers to helping victims escape human trafficking may disappear.

Further Reading

Freedberg, Eli, and Liran Messinger. 2022. "New York to Require Human Trafficking Recognition Training for Certain Hospitality Employees." *Littler*, November 22. https://www.littler.com/publication-press/publication/new-york-require-human-trafficking-recognition-training-certain. Accessed July 1, 2023.

Garg, Anjali, Preeti Panda, Mandy M. Neudecker, and Sarah Lee. 2020. "Barriers to the Access and Utilization of Healthcare for Trafficked Youth: A Systematic Review." *Child Abuse & Neglect* 100: 104137. https://www.sciencedirect.com/science/article/abs/pii/S014521341930314X?via%3Dihub. Accessed July 1, 2023.

Lederer, Laura, Stanley Stinson, and McKamie Chandler. Forthcoming. "Barriers to Escaping Trafficking or Prostitution."

Lederer, Laura, Theresa Flores, and McKamie Chandler. 2023. "The Pregnancy Continuum in Domestic Sex Trafficking in the United States." *Issues in Law and Medicine* 38, no. 1: 61–89. https://www.globalcenturion.org/the-pregnancy-continuum-in-domestic-sex-trafficking/. Accessed July 1, 2023.

National Human Trafficking Training and Technical Assistance Center. n.d. "Barriers That Prevent Identification." https://nhttac.acf.hhs.gov/soar/eguide/observe/Barriers_to_Screening_and_Responding. Accessed July 1, 2023.

National Human Trafficking Training and Technical Assistance Center n.d. "SOAR Training: SOAR to Health and Wellness." https://www.ssw.umaryland.edu/media/ssw/pari/2018/odapb_UMD_SOAR_TIC_ppt_092018.pdf. Accessed July 1, 2023.

National Institute of Health. n.d. "Implicit Bias." https://diversity.nih.gov/sociocultural-factors/implicit-bias. Accessed July 1, 2023.

Texas Health and Human Services (HHS). n.d. *HHSC Human Trafficking Training Standards*. https://www.hhs.texas.gov/sites/default/files/documents/services/safety/human-trafficking/human-trafficking-training-standards.pdf. Accessed July 1, 2023.

US Department of Health and Human Services, Office on Trafficking in Persons. 2012. "Rescue & Restore Victims of Human Trafficking." https://www.acf.hhs.gov/archive/otip/training-technical-assistance/rescue-restore-victims-human-trafficking. Accessed July 1, 2023.

Q15. Can Trafficking Be Reduced by Targeting Buyers?

Answer: Yes. The demand (from sex buyers) for commercial sex drives sex trafficking. The demand (from businesses and corporations) for free or virtually free labor drives labor trafficking. People and organizations working to combat human trafficking say that to reduce demand for trafficking in human beings, the risk of punishment for purchase of sex and the risk of punishment for exploiting workers for free labor must be increased. According to the 2020 US Department of Justice Attorney General's Report to Congress, there are efforts that can be undertaken within the 3P framework to reduce demand for both labor and sex trafficking (US Department of Justice [DOJ] 2020, 34).

The Facts: Demand reduction for sex trafficking and labor trafficking is a relatively new focus for NGOs, IOs, and governments. In the triangle of activity that occurs in human trafficking (supply, demand, distribution), demand reduction is primarily a prevention strategy. If demand for commercial sex and demand for free or exploitive labor can be reduced, trafficking will be reduced. Most demand reduction efforts focus on either sex trafficking or labor trafficking, which operate very differently and thus require different responses.

Looking first at sex trafficking, one key approach to demand reduction is to prohibit the purchase of commercial sex acts. This is the approach taken first in Sweden in 1998, and then adopted by several other Scandinavian countries in the early 2000s. Sweden waited ten years to publish a study on its approach, which criminalized purchase of sex but decriminalized the sale of sex (prostitution). It concluded the prohibition against purchase of sex reduced sex trafficking, a finding supported in additional studies (Waltman 2011).

There exists a growing international consensus on the need to reduce demand in trafficked humans. The United Nations *Protocol to Prevent, Suppress and Punish Trafficking in Persons, Especially Women and Children, Supplementing the United Nations Convention Against Transnational Organized Crime* of 2000

> expressly addresses the requirement that nations make serious efforts to reduce demand for trafficked persons ... . States Parties shall adopt or strengthen legislative or other measures, such as educational, social or cultural measures, including through bilateral and multilateral cooperation, to discourage the demand that fosters all forms of exploitation of persons, especially women and children, that leads to trafficking.

Other intergovernmental organizations have also called for demand reduction programs. For example, the Europe Convention on Action against Human Trafficking, the 2011 European Union Directive of the European Parliament, and the Council on preventing and combating trafficking in human beings also specifically address the need to prevent human trafficking by reducing demand for trafficking victims.

Anti-trafficking scholars and activists point to research studies that have found a link between legalized prostitution and increased human trafficking. For example, in 2012, researchers Seo-Young Cho, Axel Dreher, and Eric Neumayer reported findings that "the scale effect of legalized prostitution leads to an expansion of the prostitution market, increasing human trafficking ... . On average, countries where prostitution is legal experience larger reported human trafficking inflows" (Cho, Dreher, and Neumayer 2012). Another study focused on eleven European Union countries, sponsored by the European Parliament's Committee on Women's Rights and Gender Equality and performed by Transcrime, found that stricter prostitution laws correlated with fewer human trafficking victims. Finally, case studies published by researchers Niklas Jakobsson and Andreas Kotsadam support the possibility of a causal link between laws prohibiting prostitution and reduced human trafficking. Jakobsson and Kotsadam found that trafficking of persons for commercial sexual exploitation is least prevalent in countries where prostitution is illegal and most prevalent in countries where prostitution is legalized (Jakobsson and Kotsadam 2012).

A Sex Trafficking Demand Reduction Bill was introduced in Congress in 2022. It sought to amend the Trafficking Victims Protection Act of 2000 to require countries to make serious and sustained efforts to prohibit the purchase of commercial sex acts; to educate buyers of commercial sex as to how traffickers exploit prostituted persons for human trafficking; to reduce demand for international sex tourism by increasing investigations, arrests, prosecutions, and convictions of sex tourists; and to ensure that anti-trafficking trainings include codes of conduct for the staffs of all governments.

Although the United States does not clearly prohibit prostitution or the purchase of commercial sex at the federal level, at the state level most states have a body of law prohibiting prostitution, pimping, pandering, procuring, and other related commercial sex activities. After the passage of the Trafficking Victims Protection Act, the US Department of Defense added a statute to the Uniform Code of Military Justice (UCMJ) prohibiting the purchase of sex (patronizing of a prostitute).

In addition to passing laws prohibiting the purchase of sex, other sex trafficking demand reduction programs have included First Offender Programs, colloquially called, "John's Schools." These are rehabilitation programs for men arrested for the first time for soliciting for prostitution. These schools were the brainchild of the late Norma Hotaling, a survivor who recognized that providing services for victims and survivors of trafficking would not be enough to stop trafficking. She partnered with the San Francisco District Attorney's Office to cofound the first-of-its-kind classes for sex buyers. The Department of Justice sponsored an evaluation of these programs, which strongly suggest that the programs led to less reoffending among men arrested for purchasing sex (National Institute of Justice 2016).

Other demand-reduction campaigns include social media and public service campaigns that target frequenters of prostitutes and codes of conduct for government officials, private businesses and nongovernmental organizations to obtain assurances that travelers will not purchase sex while engaging in public or private business (Rosenberg 2011). The US Department of Defense has produced several public service announcements on demand reduction aimed at informing service members and civil service employees about the ways prostitution can fuel human trafficking (Shively et al. 2012).

The script of the PSA reads in part:

> Human trafficking is a crime and a human rights abuse. It victimizes an estimated 49.6 million people worldwide. The number of sex trafficking victims increases with demand, including demand from DoD Service members, contractors, civilians, and dependents. Anyone involved in the purchase of sex, online exploitation of children or other cyber-sex crimes, production of child pornography, or other trafficking or trafficking related activities is a part of the problem. Remember, since 2005 it has been a crime for a US service member to patronize a prostitute. And Federal law prohibits contractors from purchasing sex during the contract performance period. The message DoD is sending is

loud and clear: *Do your part to help stop human trafficking: Don't purchase sex.* (Shively et al. 2012)

Some law enforcement efforts also focus on demand reduction. *The Attorney General's Annual Report to Congress on U.S. Government Activities to Combat Trafficking in Persons* devotes a section of its report each year to demand reduction. In the 2020 report, it noted that the Department of Justice is committed to the mission of reducing demand and developing new strategies and programs to reduce demand. It reported that approximately half of the task forces in which the US Attorneys' Offices (USAO) participate "use tactics and strategies to reduce demand and target buyers (DOJ 2020, 34).

To help address demand, the USAO for the Eastern District of Virginia, for example, focuses on customers on the demand side for potential additional prosecutions. In the District of North Dakota, the local task force uses online platforms to identify and focus on regions where demand for commercial sex is high. The USAO for the Middle District of Louisiana led an effort during FY 2020 to focus on sex buyers, as similar operations in other areas have resulted in significant decreases in commercial sex activities (DOJ 2020, 34). The FBI also conducts "demand-focused operations" across the United States during FY 2020 through partnerships established between the 86 FBI Child Exploitation and Human Trafficking Task Forces and state and local law enforcement agencies (DOJ 2020, 34).

Reducing Demand in Labor Trafficking

Reducing demand in labor trafficking requires strategies and programs that focus on the primary markets of private businesses and corporations in labor-intensive industries. Labor trafficking has been documented in agriculture, mining, fishing, garment factories, childcare, cleaning services, hospitality (hotel and travel) industries, elder care, health-care sectors, manufacturing, food services and food production factories, construction, security services sectors, the tech sectors, and other industries where large numbers of workers are required to produce goods and services. The list is endless, but some high-profile cases of labor trafficking in recent years include:

- Mining for coltan, lithium, and other rare earth minerals in the Democratic Republic of Congo
- Fishing vessels in Thailand and other Southeast Asian countries
- Logging camps in the United States, Central and South America

- Garment worker factories in the United States, South America, and South Asia
- Brick kiln factories in South Asia
- Cocoa bean farming and harvesting in West Africa
- Rug-making factories in South and Southeast Asia
- Meat packing and producing factories in the United States and other countries
- Janitorial, security, and hospitality services on U.S. military bases in foreign countries
- Clothing and shoe factories in China, Southeast Asia, and other countries
- Polysilicon for high-tech products produced in Xinjiang Uyghur Autonomous Region
- Domestic workers trafficked into Gulf Coast countries from South Asia and Africa
- Cotton picking and production in Uzbekistan and China.

Human trafficking experts emphasize that the policy and program focus to end labor trafficking must be multipronged. It should include consumers, industries and businesses, intergovernmental agencies, and governments. Recently, nonprofits have run education and awareness campaigns to inform consumers of slave labor in the supply chains of the products they purchase. Examples of successful efforts include campaigns aimed at:

- Producers of chocolate to force them to develop programs to eliminate child labor from cocoa plantations
- The rug-making industries to provide a certification trademark that assures importers and buyers that carpets have been manufactured by companies with effective surveillance mechanism to eliminate illegal child labor
- Coffee drinkers to promote and to encourage fair-trade practices for coffee growers and farmers
- Footwear companies to ensure that high-end running shoes are not tainted by trafficking in their supply chain.

These grassroots campaigns have resulted in the development of many third-party independent companies that monitor the supply chains in various sectors.

Governments also have a role to play in ensuring that supply chains are free of slave labor. The United States has been one of the leaders in drafting, passing, and implementing laws to prevent trafficking in production of services and goods. One law, the National Defense Authorization Act of 2013, title XVII, is entitled "Ending Trafficking in Government Contracting" and sets out a list of prohibited activities for contractors supplying labor to the U.S. government (NDAA 2013). A new Forced Labor Enforcement Task Force, which is led by the US Department of Homeland Security, is a task force of interagency partners that are dedicated to monitoring the enforcement of the prohibition on importing goods made wholly or in part with forced labor into the United States. Forced labor includes the use of forced, convict, and indentured labor, including forced or indentured child labor (US Department of Homeland Security n.d.).

Another law, the Uyghur Forced Labor Prevention Act (UFLPA), directs the US government to develop a strategy for supporting enforcement of the prohibition on the importation of goods into the United States manufactured wholly or in part with forced labor in the People's Republic of China, especially from the Xinjiang Uyghur Autonomous Region, or Xinjiang (Uyghur Act 2021). The act puts the burden on China to prove that the goods produced in the Xinjiang region are not produced with slave labor.

In other words, goods mined, manufactured, or produced wholly or in part in that region are assumed to be produced with slave labor unless proven otherwise (rebuttable presumption) by US Customs and Border Protection (CBP) (US Department of Homeland Security, CBP, WROs 2023).

CBP is the agency responsible for preventing the entry of products made with forced labor into the US market. They act on any allegations of forced labor in supply chains (US Customs and Border Protection n.d.).

With these and other laws, the United States created a policy and legal framework for monitoring and combating trafficking in supply chains of goods and services produced around the world but coming into the country.

While government law and policy and grassroots consumer campaigns are important, the burden of the work to prevent slave labor in supply chains must come from the industries themselves. Industries and businesses must set up monitoring and surveillance programs to ensure that goods are not made from forced or exploited labor and that workers they hire are not recruited, transported, harbored, or obtained using force, fraud, or coercion. Pressure from governments, intergovernmental organizations, and nonprofits can help industries to adopt codes of conduct, develop supply chain audit practices, and eliminate unethical recruiters and other bad actors exploiting workers in the production of goods and services.

Further Reading

Cho, Seo-Young, Axel Dreher, and Eric Neumayer. 2012. "Does Legalized Prostitution Increase Human Trafficking?" *World Development* 41: 67–82. https://doi.org/10.1016/j.worlddev.2012.05.023. Accessed June 25, 2023.

Jakobsson, Nicklas, and Andreas Kotsadam. 2012. "The Law and Economics of International Sex Slavery: Prostitution Laws and Trafficking for Sexual Exploitation. *European Journal Law and Economics* 35: 87–107. https://doi.org/10.1007/s10657-011-9232-0.

National Institute of Justice. 2016. "Reducing Demand for Prostitution in San Francisco With a 'John School' Program." https://nij.ojp.gov/topics/articles/reducing-demand-prostitution-san-francisco-john-school-program. Accessed June 25, 2023.

Rosenberg, Ruth. 2011. *Tackling the Demand That Fosters Human Trafficking: Final Report.* https://pdf.usaid.gov/pdf_docs/pnadz753.pdf. Accessed June 25, 2023.

Sex Trafficking Demand Reduction Act. HR. 6420, 117th Congress, 2020–2021. https://www.congress.gov/bill/117th-congress/house-bill/6420?s=1&r=9. Accessed June 25, 2023.

Shively, Michael, Kristina Kliorys, Kristin Wheeler, and Dana Hunt. 2012. *A National Overview of Prostitution and Sex Trafficking Demand Reduction Efforts*, Final Report. https://www.ojp.gov/pdffiles1/nij/grants/238796.pdf. Accessed June 25, 2023.

US Customs and Border Protection. n.d. "Uyghur Forced Labor Prevention Act." https://www.cbp.gov/trade/forced-labor/UFLPA. Accessed June 25, 2023.

US Department of Homeland Security. n.d. Forced Labor Enforcement Task Force. https://www.dhs.gov/forced-labor-enforcement-task-force. Accessed June 25, 2023.

US Department of Homeland Security. 2023. "Withhold Release Orders (WROs)." https://www.cbp.gov/trade/forced-labor/withhold-release-orders-and-findings). Accessed June 25, 2023.

US Department of Justice. 2020. *Attorney General's Annual Report to Congress on U.S. Government Activities to Combat Trafficking in Person.* https://www.justice.gov/d9/pages/attachments/2022/03/24/fy20_ag_ht_report.pdf. Accessed June 25, 2023.

Uyghur Forced Labor Prevention Act. 2021. PL 117–78, December 23. https://www.govinfo.gov/content/pkg/PLAW-117publ78/pdf/PLAW-117publ78.pdf. Accessed June 25, 2023.

Waltman, Max. 2011. "Sweden's Prohibition of Purchase of Sex: The Law's Reasons, Impact, and Potential." *Women's Studies International Forum* 34, no. 5: 449–74. https://papers.ssrn.com/sol3/papers.cfm?abstract_id=1910657. Accessed June 25, 2023.

Q16. Has Production of Electric Vehicles Been Linked to Forced Labor?

Answer: Yes. The demand for cobalt is increasing dramatically because of its critical role in clean energy technologies globally. For example, cobalt is a key component of lithium-ion batteries, the batteries used in all electric cars. Human rights organizations report that this mineral and other rare earth are being mined using illegal child laborers and forced labor. This human trafficking is taking place in cobalt mines in the Democratic Republic of Congo (DRC), which produces around two-thirds of the world's cobalt and has over half of the world's cobalt reserves . In 2021, the demand for cobalt rose by 21 percent from the year before (Cobalt Report 2021). Due to rising demand of electric vehicles (EVs), the price of cobalt nearly quadrupled between 2016 and early 2018 (S & P Global 2019). Eighteen experts predict that EVs will account for most of the annual demand. In 2022 alone, 86 percent of annual demand growth was from EVs (The Cobalt Market Report 2022). In its 2016 report, *This Is What We Die For*, Amnesty International sounded an early alarm, noting that "people around the world will increasingly rely on rechargeable batteries to power their mobile phones, tablets, laptop computers and other portable electronic devices," and further asserted that in 2016 between 110,000 and 150,000 artisanal miners, 40,000 of them children, were working in these small mines in hazardous and unsafe conditions. Seven years later, that figure had risen to over 225,000 artisanal miners, and tens of thousands more children (Kara 2023).

The Facts: In 2022 more than 10 million electric cars were sold worldwide. In 2023, projected sales are expected to grow by another 35 percent to reach 14 million. Electric car sales are increasing in the overall car market, going from 4 percent in 2020 to 14 percent in 2022 and to 18 percent in 2023 (International Energy Agency 2023). That's nearly one-fifth of the overall car market. Most of the market for electric car sales is in Europe, China, and the United States.

As part of a wider slate of policies designed to combat climate change by reducing production of greenhouse gases, in April 2023, President Joe Biden signed an Executive Order stating that by 2030 the United States will work toward having 50 percent of all new vehicle sales be electric (The White House 2021). Meanwhile, the US Army announced that it would install a microgrid on all of its military bases and have a fully electric non-tactical vehicle fleet by 2035 (Department of the Army 2022). The navy has similar plans but is aiming for 2025 (Luckenbaugh 2023). It is one of the most ambitious plans for "going green" in the US government.

However, anti-trafficking experts and activists as well as some legislators caution that in this instance, going green may have unintended consequences, including increasing forced labor and child labor, if anti-trafficking measures are not factored into the plans (Amnesty International 2016; Kara 2023; Rubio 2023).

Each year the US Department of Labor produces a List of Goods Produced by Child Labor and Forced Labor (US Department of Labor [DOL] n.d.). The 2022 edition of the list includes 159 goods from 78 countries, as of September 28, 2022. The DOL identifies the DRC as a country where child labor, forced labor, and human trafficking are used in the mines that produce more than 70 percent of the global total of cobalt needed for the batteries for electric cars. While China supplies over two-thirds of the refined cobalt, the raw mineral comes mainly from the DRC (DOL n.d.).

The US Department of Labor has documented the nature and scope of the cobalt problem in the DRC. The department reported that "in 2019, the DRC made no advancement in efforts to eliminate the worst forms of child labor." Research conducted by the department's Bureau of International Labor Affairs (ILAB) indicates that government labor inspectors in the DRC "failed to conduct any worksite inspections for the fourth year in a row." Over the past two years, a few corporate supply chain audit companies have helped monitor DRC mining sites for slavery in cobalt mining (DOL n.d.). Other minerals listed as being mined in the DRC with child labor or forced labor include cobalt, copper, diamonds, gold, tin, and tungsten (DOL n.d.).

One emerging issue has been the mining of rare earth and other minerals used to produce electric cars. According to one mining trade newsletter, a typical EV battery weighs one thousand pounds and is about the size of a travel trunk (Stein 2022). It contains 25 lbs. of lithium, 60 lbs. of nickel, 44 lbs. of manganese, 30 lbs. of cobalt, 200 lbs. of copper, and 400 lbs. of aluminum, steel, and plastic. Inside are over 6,000 individual lithium-ion cells (Stein 2022). To manufacture each EV auto battery, 25,000 lbs. of brine are processed for the lithium, 30,000 lbs. of ore for the cobalt, 5,000 lbs. of ore for the nickel, and 25,000 lbs. of ore for the copper. All told, 500,000 lbs. of the earth's crust are mined for one battery.

Large-scale purchasers of cobalt are taking some steps to keep their supply chains free of forced labor. Some are helping DRC villages dependent on cobalt mining to combat trafficking. In the twenty-first century, however, cobalt mining has been a free-for-all—anyone with a pickaxe who can dig can become a cobalt miner. Villages where cobalt had been discovered were seeing thousands of amateur miners flock to their sites, and literally dig holes and tunnels under streets, in backyards, and around parks. When these tunnels began to collapse, houses started to crumble, and streets damaged by unplanned tunnels, the village took action. With the help of the local government, they evacuated the people (600 households, according to one source) living in the parts of the village that were damaged, built a wall around the mining site with a security gate and checked for miners. Then they helped miners organize into cooperatives.

In addition to providing some small political voice for the miners, the cooperatives help with medical expenses, bargain for better conditions and better price for the raw cobalt for the miners, and organize the sale of the cobalt. The process means the miners have some assistance after digging up the cobalt with the mineral being crushed, weighed, graded on site and then authenticated and sold to local traders who are in touch with big refining companies in China, Switzerland, and other countries. There are still serious issues with the process such as who controls the cooperatives. Recently miners have been reverting back to what is euphemistically called "informal mining" because they don't make enough money if they participate in the cooperatives (Sanderson 2019).

In the UK, where several nonprofits have taken the lead in preventing trafficking in supply chains, for-profit audit companies have been hired to assist with onsite monitoring of the cobalt mining process. One company created and distributed a smartphone app to miners in 2018 that could be used to report accidents, deaths, child labor, forced labor of any sort, including threats, intimidation, nonpayment or withholding of payment for cobalt produced. In the three months after the app was introduced, there were five reports of child labor (Sanderson 2019).

Buyers of cobalt have become increasingly reluctant to buy from informal mining sites. They are signing long-term contracts with mining in companies and sites that guarantee no slavery, child labor, forced labor, or human trafficking in the mining process. But these companies are struggling. One company said that about 2,000 "informal miners" a day trespass on mining sites near a DRC city of 250,000 people.

The 2021 US State Department Trafficking in Persons Report mentions trafficking in cobalt mining in their Trafficking Profile of DRC. They noted:

> Decades-long instability in eastern DRC ... continued, resulting in armed groups and criminal networks engaging in unlawful child soldier recruitment and use, forced labor in artisanal mining, as well as in sex trafficking and slavery-like practices. Traffickers—including mining bosses, other miners, family members, government officials, and armed groups—force or coerce some adults and children to work in artisanal mines in eastern DRC, including through debt-based coercion. Individuals associated with the extractive sector abuse some children in forced labor in the illegal mining of diamonds, copper, gold, cobalt, tungsten ore, tantalum ore, and tin, as well as the smuggling of minerals to Uganda, Burundi, Rwanda, the United Arab Emirates, and Tanzania.

The action items focused on improving measures to identify victims in artisanal mining and refer them for services.

The 2023 Trafficking in Persons Report notes NGO reports of child trafficking and forced labor in mining in the DRC and makes particular mention of trafficking-related activities in cobalt mining. It also mentions a heretofore unspoken geopolitical issue: China is investing millions of dollars in the DRC and is positioning itself to own and operate many of the metal mines, including cobalt:

> Labor trafficking in the DRC is most prevalent in provinces with mining activity (Haut Katanga, Haut Uele, Kasai, Lualaba, North Kivu, South Kivu, and Ituri). Traffickers—including mining bosses, other miners, family members, government officials, and armed groups—force or coerce some adults and children to work in artisanal mines in eastern DRC, including through debt-based coercion. Individuals associated with the extractive sector abuse some children in forced labor in the illegal mining of diamonds, copper, gold, cobalt, tungsten ore, tantalum ore, and tin, as well as the smuggling of minerals to Uganda, Burundi, Rwanda, the United Arab Emirates, and Tanzania. ... Children travel long distances to smuggle minerals are vulnerable to trafficking and recruitment by armed groups. Observers noted children in mining areas are vulnerable to sexual violence, including sex trafficking, in part due to traditional and religious beliefs correlating harming children and sex with protection against death or successful mining.
>
> Congolese workers in People's Republic of China national-owned cobalt mines may be exploited in forced labor; observers reported workers faced wage violations, physical abuse, employment without contracts, and restricted movement – all potential indicators of forced labor. (US Department of State [DOS]. n.d.)

In 2019, a US-based NGO filed a federal class action lawsuit against Apple, Google, Alphabet, Microsoft, Dell, and Tesla. The lawsuit was filed on behalf of fourteen plaintiffs who are either guardians of children killed in tunnel or wall collapses while mining cobalt in the DRC or are children who were maimed in such accidents. All plaintiffs are representative of a larger class of unnamed children who have faced similar injuries from mining hazards. All defendants make up a large portion of buyers in the cobalt market. The plaintiffs assert claims for forced child labor in violation of the Trafficking Victims Protection Reauthorization Act. They also seek relief based on common law claims of unjust enrichment, negligent supervision, and intentional infliction of emotional distress. They request that the court order the defendants to create a fund to contribute to the appropriate medical care of the plaintiffs and other unnamed children who were injured while mining cobalt.

The lawsuit alleges that "the young children mining defendants' cobalt are not merely being forced to work full-time, extremely dangerous mining jobs at the expense of their education and futures; they are also being regularly maimed and killed by tunnel collapses and other known hazards common to cobalt mining in the DRC." It also alleged that electric car and big tech companies

> "are knowingly benefiting from and providing substantial support to this "artisanal" mining system in the DRC. Defendants know and have known for a significant period of time the reality that DRC's cobalt mining sector is dependent upon children, with males performing the most hazardous work in the primitive cobalt mines, including tunnel digging. These boys are working under Stone Age conditions for paltry wages and at immense personal risk to provide cobalt that is essential to the so-called "high tech" sector, dominated by Defendants and other companies.

The State Department TIP Report placed the Democratic Republic of Congo on Tier 2, meaning it has assessed the country as "not fully compliant, but making significant efforts to be compliant with minimum standards for the elimination of trafficking." The report notes that the DRC is making some progress in addressing trafficking in the mining of cobalt and other minerals:

> The Ministry of Labor, in partnership with an international organization, trained labor inspectors on topics such as child labor trafficking and referral mechanisms. The Minister of Human Rights continued implementing an August 2020 decree to increase oversight of mining communities, including a zero-tolerance policy for forced child labor in the mining sector. As part of this ongoing effort, the government, in cooperation with an international organization, certified nine artisanal mining sites in eastern DRC as conflict-free and child labor-free. As part of the certification process, the government, in collaboration with civil society, screened for child labor and child trafficking victims, and when victims were identified, referred them to care. The government did not report how many trafficking victims, if any, it identified and referred to care as a result of the inspections. Observers reported limited administrative capacity and funding hindered provincial departments' ability to monitor mining sites. In October 2022, the government, in partnership with an international organization, relaunched the inter-ministerial committee in charge of monitoring child labor in artisanal mining (CISTEMA) and began creating a database to track child labor cases in artisanal mines. (DOS n.d.)

Although a few NGOs, IOs, and GOs and agencies have begun to take action, the key actors in the fight to stop human trafficking in the supply chain of EVs and high-tech products are international and multinational private corporations who need these metals to produce their products. They must build in measures to prevent child labor, forced labor, and other forms of trafficking in mining in the DRC.

Further Reading

Department of the Army, Office of the Assistant Secretary of the Army for Installations, Energy and Environment. 2022. *United States Army Climate Strategy*. Washington, DC. https://www.army.mil/e2/downloads/rv7/about/2022_army_climate_strat egy.pdf. Accessed July 1, 2023.

International Energy Agency. 2023. "Demand for Electric Cars Is Booming, with Sales Expected to Leap 35% This Year after a Record-Breaking 2022." April 26. https://www.iea.org/news/demand-for-electric-cars-is-booming-with-sales-expec ted-to-leap-35-this-year-after-a-record-breaking-2022. Accessed July 1, 2023.

Kara, Siddharth. 2023. *Cobalt Red: How the Blood of the Congo Powers Our Lives*, New York: Macmillan.

Luckenbaugh, Josh. 2023. "Power-Hungry Navy Ships Require New Engine Tech." *National Defense*, March 3. https://www.nationaldefensemagazine.org/articles/2023/3/3/power-hungry-navy-ships-require--new-engine-tech. Accessed July 1, 2023.

Rubio, Marco. 2023. "U.S. Senate, Letter to Secretary of Defense Lloyd Austin." May 4. https://www.rubio.senate.gov/public/_cache/files/b90a319d-2dbc-4788-ae06-336bd113a882/F7A280ABB251AF4F0F91A977488DFDC1.05.04.23-rubio-letter-to-secdef-re-electric-vehicles.pdf. Accessed July 1, 2023.

Sanderson, Henry. 2019. "Congo, Child Labour and Your Electric Car." *Financial Times*, July 7. https://www.ft.com/content/c6909812-9ce4-11e9-9c06-a4640 c9feebb. Accessed July 1, 2023.

S & P Global Market Intelligence. 2019. "Volatile Prices Leave Cobalt Miners No Quick Fix for Supply-Demand Conundrum." April 26.

Stein, Ronald. 2022. "Is It Unethical to Buy a Vehicle Powered by a Lithium Battery?" *Issues & Insights*, June 13. https://issuesinsights.com/2022/06/13/is-it-unethi cal-to-buy-a-vehicle-powered-by-a-lithium-battery/. Accessed July 1, 2023.

The Cobalt Institute. 2022. *The Cobalt Market Report, 2021*. May. https://www.cobaltin stitute.org/wp-content/uploads/2022/05/FINAL_Cobalt-Market-Report-2021_Cob alt-Institute-1.pdf. Accessed July 1, 2023.

The Cobalt Institute. 2023. *The Cobalt Market Report, 2022*. May. https://www.cobaltin stitute.org/wp-content/uploads/2023/05/Cobalt-Market-Report-2022_final-1.pdf.

The White House. 2021. "Fact Sheet: President Biden Announces Steps to Drive American Leadership Forward on Clean Cars and Trucks." https://www.whiteho use.gov/briefing-room/statements-releases/2021/08/05/fact-sheet-president-biden-announces-steps-to-drive-american-leadership-forward-on-clean-cars-and-trucks/. Accessed July 1, 2023.

US Department of Labor. n.d. "List of Goods Produced by Child Labor or Forced Labor." https://www.dol.gov/agencies/ilab/reports/child-labor/list-of-goods#:~:text=The%20most%20common%20agricultural%20goods,and%20d iamonds%20are%20most%20common. Accessed July 1, 2023.

US Department of State, Office to Monitor and Combat Trafficking In Persons. n.d. 2023 *Trafficking in Persons Report: Democratic Republic of the Congo.* https://www. google.com/url?q=https://www.state.gov/reports/2023-trafficking-in-persons-rep ort/the-democratic-republic-of-the-congo&sa=D&source=docs&ust=168990382 6513754&usg=AOvVaw1SQJ3dMT9a6svxxft8GMAJ. Accessed July 1, 2023.

4

Countering Trafficking in Persons

Twenty years into the battle to prevent, suppress, and punish trafficking in persons, it is becoming clear that some of the anti-trafficking programs, measures, organizations, and initiatives created have been successful and others less so. Albert Einstein famously said, "Don't listen to the person who has the answers; listen to the person who has the questions." In this chapter we ask some of the hard questions in human trafficking:

> What are some of the emerging issues? Where are we falling down, fooling ourselves, failing? How and what should we troubleshoot? Beginning with one of the most important tools we have created—the National Human Trafficking Hotline, created in 2007, and now 15 years-old, we ask: Is it working? What is its mission and purpose, and is it fulfilling its raison d'etre?

Even more troubling are some of the scandals that have emerged over the years in some of the larger international relief and development and humanitarian aid organizations. In the second article, we examine what happens when "helpers hurt," and the struggle for accountability, transparency, and reform in these organizations.

The next essay explores how to reduce demand for trafficked persons. There has been much rhetoric about demand reduction, both in sex trafficking (reducing the number of sex buyers) and in labor trafficking (reducing the demand for products that have forced labor in their supply chains, finding ways to hold companies responsible for ensuring that there is no forced labor in their supply chains). It also explores ways to help consumers understand how some purchasing choices perpetuate trafficking. Can we effectively target purchasers to reduce demand?

In the last question in this chapter, we use international demand for cobalt, a metal key to production in electric vehicles and other parts of the high-tech industry, as an example of the very hard work that will need to be done to eliminate forced labor and child labor in some parts of the world. There are no easy answers to these hard questions, but they do shed light on where our next efforts must be focused.

Q17. Have Some Anti-Trafficking and Law Enforcement Entities Been Rocked by Trafficking Scandals Themselves?

Answer: Yes. Over the past twenty years, thousands of intragovernmental organizations (IOs) and nongovernmental organizations (NGOs) have been formed to address human trafficking. Most of them do excellent work, with the support they obtain from governments, religious institutions, private philanthropic foundations, generous individuals, and other funders to counter trafficking. Currently the majority of the resources are used to provide protection and assistance for victims and survivors, including food, clothing, shelter, medical assistance, legal aid, and other emergency needs. Recently more NGOs are providing longer-term services such as educational and employment opportunities for survivors. Finally, some NGOs are also beginning to focus on preventing trafficking altogether. Yet over the years, victims registered complaints that often in the most horrific situations—in the wake of natural disasters, or during or directly after civil war, or other economic or political instability—the very organizations that were there to help them hurt them. For years the IOs and NGOs involved suppressed the complaints, but when patterns began emerging, some victims, with the help of investigative journalists and other allies, began a whistleblowing process. Today some of the larger organizations involved, such as the United Nations, have set up databases to track complaints, procedures for investigating complaints, and a process for accountability.

The Facts: Oxfam is one of the largest relief and development organizations in Europe with an annual budget of £300 million, which it receives largely from donations made by citizens in Britain and around the world. In 2011 Oxfam fired four workers and accepted the resignation of three others after an investigation found that, following the devastating 2010 earthquake in Haiti, where Oxfam had sent employees to help a recovery effort, they sexually exploited victims of the earthquake at weekend parties. One of the employees who resigned was Oxfam's country director of Haiti, the highest Oxfam official in Haiti. He admitted to participating in the sex parties and to purchasing females for sex at Oxfam's rented villa, Eagle's Nest, only a year after a terrible earthquake hit Haiti and devastated the country. This was not an isolated incident; a subsequent investigation found that groups of young women, who were earthquake victims and in need of food, clothing, and shelter, were taken to sex parties at homes and guesthouses paid for by Oxfam. "They used us like trinkets," one victim said (*Guardian* 2018). In all, twenty-six separate incidents were reported (Oxfam 2018).

This investigation into allegations of sexual misconduct and other unacceptable behavior by Oxfam employees during Oxfam's humanitarian response to the 2010 earthquake in Haiti was not released to the public until 2018. During that seven-year gap, the Oxfam director in Haiti moved on to work for a French charity, Action Against Hunger, in Bangladesh, ostensibly after receiving a reference from Oxfam. Ultimately, Oxfam lost over 7,000 donors as a result of the sexual exploitation scandal (*Guardian*, February 12, 2018).

This egregious case, which came to light ten years after the passage of the TVPA and the UN Protocol to Prevent, Suppress, and Punish Trafficking in Persons, is unfortunately not an isolated example (UN Comprehensive Database SEA 2023; UN Secretary General Reports, SEA 2003, 2016, 2017).

- In 2015, a UN report interviewed over 200 Haitian women—a third of whom were minors—who claimed they were forced to have sex with UN soldiers in exchange for material aid
- 700 cases of sexual exploitation and child sexual abuse were reported by the UN (2016)
- Four UN workers were dismissed for storing and trading child pornography on UN computers (September 2015)
- 134 Sri Lankan peacekeepers exploited nine children in a sex ring from 2004 to 2007, according to an internal UN report. In the wake of the report, 114 peacekeepers were sent home.
- United States and other peacekeepers in Bosnia/Herzegovina were accused of child sex trafficking and child sexual exploitation while stationed as peacekeepers (September 2004)
- A 2002 UN report documents 67 cases across 40 international humanitarian agencies of sex trafficking, child sexual abuse, rape, and other reprehensible or criminal behaviors such as trading sex for food or other exploitation
- A high-level Canadian UN official was arrested in Nepal on sex trafficking charges, accused of raping boys twelve and fourteen years old (April 2018)

- Police arrested four charity workers from several European countries and accused them of child sexual abuse (February 2018)
- Police arrested a director of a German charity in Kathmandu who gave free lunches to children in exchange for sex and charged him with child sexual abuse (February 2018)
- The UN and international charities are accused of abusing displaced women in Syria by trading food for sex (UN Comprehensive Database SEA 2023; UN Secretary General Reports, SEA 2003, 2016, 2017).

In 2002, 2004, 2007, 2008, 2012, and 2017, the UN and other coalitions issued major reports with recommendations for addressing what is now called SEA (Sexual Exploitation and Abuse). One of the documents, "Building Safer Organizations Handbook" is a 395-page guide, compiled by a coalition of twelve of the largest international aid organizations in the world. It is a guide for taking, investigating, and judging the veracity of SEA reports of misconduct by workers in the field.

Another article on issues of sexual exploitation and abuse in the UN, entitled, "UN Secretary General Guterres' Biggest Challenge," asks how the UN can end the suffering of vulnerable populations when its own female employees face hostile work environments—and documents what happens when they attempt to raise issues of sexual abuse and exploitation by UN staff (Handrahan 2017). Based on these reports, over the past decade IOs and NGOs have made changes and put new rules and regulations in place after each scandal. These have included:

- Setting up prevention programs
- Instituting codes of conduct for IOs and NGOs
- Creating new policy-level committees to review allegations
- Adopting minimum operating standards for prevention, investigation, and action
- Dismissing staff following allegations and investigations
- Launching a new E-learning on sexual abuse and exploitation
- Setting up a new UN Trust Fund for victims of SEA. (2016)

However, the problem continues, with the latest scandal a suspected twenty years of abuse by Canadian, German, Dutch and other aid workers (Reuters Survey 2017). One recommendation is that large funding organizations such as the Millennium Challenge Corporation (MCC) should not wait for the UN and other large international IOs and NGOs to solve the problem. They should be instituting their own policies, programs, and procedures for addressing sexual abuse and exploitation, including commercial sexual exploitation of children, child rape, sex trafficking, and other forms of abusive and criminal behavior in IOs and NGOs around the world, including loss of funds. This is especially important since it gives the majority of the support to agencies in a number of countries where helper organizations have had employees who have committed the most egregious acts (Reuters 2017).

Almost all of the serious abuses occurred in resource-poor countries or regions torn apart by civil war or natural disasters. These conditions typically result in large numbers of people being displaced from their homes, disruption of work and living rhythms, and inability to obtain basic necessities such as food, clothing, and shelter. These vulnerabilities were exploited not just by criminals but also by some who were sent to help. The situation is so dire that, following numerous reports by human rights organizations, the United Nations has begun to keep a database of allegations of sexual exploitations by peacekeepers (United Nations Database on SEA 2023). Since 2006, almost 2,000 allegations of abuse and exploitation have been reported (Petesch 2019). Some investigations have taken over a decade to conclude. The UN tried to re-create some of the data back to 2007 but only began taking full reports in 2015.

The data can be examined by type of allegation received, perpetrator (including nationality of the perpetrator, whether they were uniformed personnel or civilians, and how many victims), victims (particularly whether they were adults or children), the year the allegation took place and year reported, and the actions taken when allegations were substantiated (sanctions including repatriation of perpetrator to his country, dismissal, action taken by perpetrator's home country).

The UN Department of Peacekeeping Operations (formerly known as DPKO, now DPO) was created in 1992. Its mission has been "to help countries torn by conflict to create the conditions for lasting peace." At its height, over 100,000 peacekeepers from over 120 countries were on peacekeeping missions in countries around the world. Almost immediately after its formation, allegations of abuse were reported, but they were not addressed.

In 1996, though, abuse and exploitation allegations burst into view with a landmark report entitled, "The Impact of Armed Conflict on Children," by Graca Machel, the former first lady of Mozambique (Machel 1996). The UN appointed her in 1994 to investigate the effects of armed conflict on children, and one of her key findings was that some children were vulnerable to sexual exploitation by the international organization that was sent to help—in Mozambique's case, the DPO (Essa 2017).

In 2003, then secretary general of the UN, Kofi Annan, issued a "zero tolerance" policy on sexual exploitation and abuse for all UN personnel. The UN created a special mechanism for reporting it. But though reports came in, there was no procedure for punishing even those egregious offenders who exploited children as young as ten or twelve, trading sex for food or shelter.

Since 2015, however, the UN has worked to strengthen the actions it can take to punish perpetrators. These actions can be taken by the UN itself, and/ or by the country that sent the perpetrator and include dismissal, termination, separation from service, and financial sanctions.

In 2015, the United Nations began publishing the nationalities of peacekeeping soldiers alleged to have sexually exploited and abused women and girls. In March 2016, the secretary-general created a "Trust Fund in Support of Victims of Sexual Exploitation and Abuse." The fund provides support for physical and mental health care, job training and other services for victims, including children fathered by peacekeepers. In 2017, following a report from the secretary-general's office entitled, "Special Measures for Protection from Sexual Exploitation and Abuse: A New Approach," the UN established a global "Victim Rights Advocate Program" and began embedding victim witness advocates within peacekeeping missions (United Nations 2017).

One model is a US government agency: the US Department of Defense (DoD). In 2008, DoD created specialized programs for its 3 million military men and women to help them understand human trafficking. A key part of these programs was the military-centric approach designed to make military members, from top to bottom, understand that human trafficking is an issue that affects them, to show them how they may encounter it in military settings, and to teach them how to approach highly specialized training relevant to the military. Such training uses real-life scenarios, case studies, and current newsworthy issues, relating material to everyday applications on the job, to help members of the armed forces understand how they may encounter trafficking in their day-to-day work.

But training alone is not enough. This should be evident from the fact that the UN instituted anti-trafficking training for peacekeepers and UN workers over fifteen years ago, and revised it half a dozen times (UN Peacekeeping Resources Hub 2023). Yet as recently as 2018, dozens of high-level aid workers have been arrested on charges of abusing the children with whom they are entrusted care (UN Database on SEA 2023; Secretary General Reports 2017).

The US military also found that training was not enough. For human trafficking, it instituted unique monitoring programs in key "hot spots" such as Iraq and Afghanistan, where as many as 100,000 US troops were stationed. The DoD created specialized trainings on human trafficking, especially labor trafficking in government contracting (Department of Defense Acquisition Personnel Training). In addition, the DoD stationed a Program Manager (PM) on-the-ground in Afghanistan., The PM instituted incoming troop and contractor trainings, and conducted unannounced audits, spot-checks, surveys, and interviews. Over a six-year period, until the United States pulled out of Afghanistan, these proactive measures uncovered potential human trafficking, examined allegations of human trafficking, and crated an ombudsman process for workers that prevented human trafficking in many cases and intervened in other ongoing incidents. The fact that the audits, spot-checks, and interviews were conducted by a third party, independent entity has been cited as an essential factor in for the success of the intervention (US Department of Defense CTIP 2023).

This proactive approach is critical to identifying and addressing sexual exploitation in IOs and NGOs, given the record that some international aid agencies have suppressing reports of abuse or exploitation. Independent assessments and complete transparency have also been urged by experts because of the vast imbalance of power between the IO/NGO relief and development organizations and the people who are dependent upon organizational personnel for food, clothing, shelter, medical assistance, and other kinds of aid.

To date there is no place to report abuse in nonprofit organizations. NGOs and faith-based organizations should take note: Trafficking experts believe that to put an end to helpers who hurt, a similar database and program to combat exploitation and abuse in the nonprofit world should be created to include nongovernmental, nonprofit, and religious organizations and missions at work around the world.

Further Reading

Ahlenbeck, Veronica. 2023. "Analysis of Sexual Exploitation and Abuse Risk Overview." Violence Against Women and Children Helpdesk. July 21. https://safeguardin gsupporthub.org/documents/analysis-sexual-exploitation-and-abuse-risk-overview. Accessed June 25, 2023.

"Child Sexual Exploitation and Abuse by Peacekeepers and Humanitarian Aid Workers: A Critical Analysis of the Humanitarian Aid Structure," University of Glasgow, August 2, 2021. https://dspace.cuni.cz/bitstream/handle/20.500.11956/150 383/120399838.pdf?sequence=1&isAllowed=y. Accessed June 25, 2023.

Elgot, Jessica, McVeigh, Karen, "Oxfam Loses 7,000 Donors Since Sexual Exploitation Scandal," The Guardian, February 12, 2018, https://www.theguardian.com/world/2018/feb/20/oxfam-boss-mark-goldring-apologises-over-abuse-of-haiti-quake-victims. Accessed November 13, 2023.

Essa, Azad. 2017. "Why Do Some Peacekeepers Rape? The Full Report." *Al Jazeera*, August 10. https://www.aljazeera.com/features/2017/8/10/why-do-some-peacekeepers-rape-the-full-report. Accessed June 25, 2023.

Handrahan, Lori. 2017. "UN Secretary General Guterres' Biggest Challenge." *Forbes*, February 3. https://www.forbes.com/sites/realspin/2017/02/03/un-secretary-general-guterres-biggest-challenge-a-culture-of-impunity/?sh=782f4696561c. Accessed June 25, 2023.

Machel, Graça. 1996. "Impact of Armed Conflict on Children." United Nations, Office of the Special Representative of the Secretary-General for Children and Armed Conflict. https://childrenandarmedconflict.un.org/1996/08/1996-graca-machel-report-impact-armed-conflict-children/. Accessed June 25, 2023.

Oxfam. 2018. *Haiti Investigation Final Report*, February. https://d1tn3vj7xz9fdh.cloudfront.net/s3fs-public/haiti_investigation_report_2011.pdf https://www.oxfamamerica.org/press/oxfam-releases-report-into-allegations-of-sexual-misconduct-in-haiti/. Accessed June 25, 2023.

Petesch, Carley. 2019. "Leaked UN Report Shows Failed Investigation on Sexual Abuse." *Associated Press*, October 31. https://apnews.com/article/671330c575b44272bbabe69e43740ac9. Accessed June 25, 2023.

Thompson-Reuters. 2017. "Survey on Sexual Misconduct by Aid Workers Staff." February 7. https://safeguardingsupporthub.org/news/exclusive-more-120-aid-workers-sacked-lost-jobs-over-sexual-misconduct-2017-survey. Accessed June 25, 2023.

United Nations, Conduct in UN Field Missions. n.d. "Comprehensive Database of Misconduct in U.N. Field Missions: 'Sexual Exploitation and Abuse.'" Conduct in UN Field Missions. https://conduct.unmissions.org/sea-data-introduction. Accessed June 25, 2023.

United Nations. n.d. Office of the Secretary-General. *Special Measures for Protection from Sexual Exploitation and Abuse: All Reports.* February 16, 2016. June 23, 2016./ June 17, 2016. January 20, 2017, October 9, 2003. https://www.un.org/preventing-sexual-exploitation-and-abuse/content/documents. Accessed June 25, 2023.

United Nations. Office of the Secretary-General. 2017. *Special Measures for Protection from Sexual Exploitation and Abuse: A New Approach. Report of the Secretary General—Addendum.* In 6 languages. t. https://digitallibrary.un.org/record/861704?ln=en. Accessed in English, July 2023.

United Nations Peacekeeping Resources Hub. 2023. "Pre-Deployment Training Materials." https://peacekeepingresourcehub.un.org/en/training/pre-deployment. Accessed June 25, 2023.

United Nations, Preventing Sexual Exploitation and Abuse Database, https://www.un.org/preventing-sexual-exploitation-and-abuse/content/data-allegations-un-system-wide. Accessed November 13, 2023.

U.S. Department of Defense, Combating Trafficking in Persons Program Management Office, CTIP Newsletter, January 2018, Volume 1 and Volume 4, October 2020, https://ctip.defense.gov/portals/12/Quarterly%20CTIP%20Newsletter%20Oct%202020_vol%204_v2_1.pdf

Q18. Is the National Human Trafficking Hotline an Effective Tool for Combating Human Trafficking?

Answer: Yes and no. While a Hotline is critical for human trafficking victims, survivors, and concerned citizens, considerable debate has arisen as to whether the National Human Trafficking Hotline (NHTH) is primarily a line to report crimes and catalyze law enforcement action—or a resource for victims and survivors to obtain help, guidance, support, and referrals for resources. Until recently the Hotline had been attempting to do both and there is ongoing discussion and debate about whether it should be collecting information for and making reports to law enforcement or whether that should be done separately. A related debate is whether the Hotline should be centralized, and if it is, how much federal support and resources does it need to set up the overarching network of referrals for action across the country at the local level, where services will inevitably be provided. Looking to the way other Hotlines operate, including the sexual assault hotline maintained by RAINN and 988, the new national suicide prevention hotline, can be helpful in answering these questions.

The Facts: The NHTH (the Hotline) is a federally funded 24/7, confidential, toll-free, multilingual hotline for victims, survivors, and witnesses of human trafficking. It has live Bi-lingual Spanish-speaking Anti-Trafficking Hotline Advocates and can also communicate with callers in more than 200 languages through a twenty-four-hour tele-interpreting service. Bi-lingual Spanish-speaking Anti-Trafficking Hotline Advocates are also available. Hearing- and speech-impaired individuals can contact the Hotline by dialing 711, the free national access number that connects to Telecommunications Relay Services (TRS).

The main purpose of the Hotline is to provide a centralized place for reporting human trafficking and related issues. The Hotline is designed to provide access to critical emergency, transitional and long-term social services for victims and survivors of human trafficking, and to connect individuals with training and technical assistance and opportunities to get involved in their communities. Frequently requested service referrals include case management, shelter, transportation, legal services, mental health and counseling services, and much more. The website for the Hotline states: "We'll listen. We'll help. If you or someone you know is a victim of human trafficking, we're here to provide the support you need" (National Human Trafficking Hotline [NHTH] n.d). On the landing page of the website, a user can contact the Hotline, Report a Tip, Obtain Safety Planning information, and Learn the Statistics. Flyers and posters for the Hotline instruct users to call the Hotline to (1) Get help, (2) Report a tip, (3) Find services, and (4) Learn about your options.

The Hotline was first established on December 7, 2007, and has been operated by a nonprofit organization called Polaris (formally Polaris Project). Polaris is not a law enforcement or immigration agency. Instead, funding is provided by the US Department of Health and Human Services (HHS) through a yearly $4.5 million grant, and by other private donors and supporters (NHTH n.d.).

The Hotline's main *raison d'etre* is to provide trafficking victims and survivors with access to critical support and services to get help and stay safe, and to equip the anti-trafficking community with tools to effectively combat human trafficking (NHTH n.d). It offers confidential round-the-clock access to a safe space to report tips, seek services, and ask for help. The National Hotline also provides innovative trainings, technical assistance, and capacity-building support to organizations and individuals. The National Hotline serves all victims and survivors of sex and labor trafficking (NHTH n.d.).

Prior to 2007, no centralized system existed for reporting human trafficking allegations or for finding out where to obtain assistance for a victim of human trafficking. The NHTH was designed to address that void. It set up an infrastructure for reporting suspected human trafficking anywhere in the United States, and for identifying places that provided victim assistance including emergency needs such as food, clothing, shelter, medical assistance, translation services, and legal assistance.

During its first years operating the Hotline, Polaris developed contacts with local law enforcement officials, service providers, and other agencies that aided victims of human trafficking. Calls came in from all over the country to the central Hotline number, and callers were then referred back out to local law enforcement and/or to service providers close to the geographic area where the case was located. By 2020 Polaris had a network of over 4,000 service provider contacts across the United States (Polaris n.d.a).

The Hotline process includes taking basic information for every call, and then ascertaining appropriate next steps, including reporting to law enforcement authorities or referral to a local agency to help with services. This is done, according to Polaris, by a careful trafficking assessment to determine next steps. These might include but are not necessarily limited to:

- Follow-up call with the caller for additional information or to coordinate next steps (with caller's consent);
- Report to our designated law enforcement partners for investigation;
- Coordinate with law enforcement and/or service provider partners for emergency assistance; and/or
- Referral or live transfer to our service provider partners to ensure victim service needs are met. (NHTH n.d.)

In cases of an emergency, the Hotline staff is trained to provide crisis counseling, safety planning, and immediate connections to local emergency services. The Trafficking Hotline supports victims' right to choose what those next steps might be, including whether or not to access services or report information to law enforcement. Frequently requested service referrals include case management, shelter, transportation, legal services, mental health and counseling services, and much more. Referrals and assistance are available to all survivors of human trafficking regardless of whether or not the need is urgent. One note in the description of services has been the subject of discussion and debate: "Except in situations involving potential abuse of a minor or if we believe a person is in imminent danger, the Trafficking Hotline will not take action without the consent of the person in the situation."

This position has generated debate and discussion in the NGO community, among service providers, policymakers, and even legislators. Prior to adopting this position, Polaris was criticized for allegedly reporting adults who voluntarily engaged in commercial sex. Since adopting this position, Polaris has been harshly criticized in some quarters. A letter signed by thirty-six state attorneys general (AGs), for example, charged that "Polaris only forwards tips to state law enforcement about adult victims in limited circumstances. This practice is contrary to what Polaris advertises, to what states and organizations have come to expect from this partnership, and, the attorneys general believe, to what Congress expects from its funding. Additionally, in some cases, states have discovered a delay of even several months before the Hotline shared tips with states."(AG Letter 2023). It appears that the main concern of the AGs is that Polaris is sorting through tips that come in and only forwarding those that are, in their assessment, emergencies or mandatory reporting cases, such as child sex trafficking.

The letter also registered concern that tips to the Hotline are delayed sometimes a month, sometimes two months, after a tip of suspected trafficking is reported to Polaris and notes,

> If the Hotline is not promptly sharing tips with law enforcement, law enforcement cannot act to help victims of trafficking. Timely information is necessary for a quick recovery of victims of human trafficking and is paramount to the entire purpose of the Hotline. Polaris's current system of reporting is hurting the very victims Polaris purports to be central to their approach. (AG Letter 2023)

Some service providers started to ask whether a system that requires a call to Washington, DC, and then calls back out to the city or town where the trafficking actually occurred was efficient. Service providers noted that they received calls in the middle of the night when the DOJ or Department of Homeland Security—or their own local law enforcement officials—had apprehended a ring of traffickers and needed to find shelter for twenty-five victims of trafficking. The funding was going to Polaris to make the initial contact, but no funds were available for those doing the work in the middle of the night to take care of the needs of these victims. One provider pointed out that there is

> a multi-faceted gap in our current solutions for victims of human trafficking. Even with advancements to increase access to services through various directories, regional private inventory systems, and central referring centers like the National Human Trafficking Hotline and the BeFree text-line, still there is no simple way to determine if a victim service provider has an opening without calling them. Additionally, on the ground level, advocates and entities that provide referrals to services for victims of trafficking often lack the ability to search for services based on matching criteria for eligibility (let alone preferences), which further belabors the effort to find appropriate services that go beyond having an opening to being a true match with a victim's needs and preferences. (TIRA 2023)

During the first ten years of operation, callers to the Hotline reported wait times as long as seventy-two hours for referrals to local agencies. Following that, one NGO, the National Trafficking Sheltered Alliance (NTSA), noted that it takes an average of 14 days from referral to intake into a residential shelter (NTSA 2023). On the other hand, having a centralized Hotline allowed for a national mechanism to gather information from across the United States. The Hotline website claims that it has handled 82,301 situations of human trafficking since Polaris began operating it in 2007 (Polaris n.d.b). The organization says this comprises the largest known data set on human trafficking in the United States. In 2015, the Hotline began publishing annual statistics gathered from calls to the Hotline, writing an annual report, and highlighting key findings. For example, in 2021 (published in 2023) the Hotline took:

- 32,709 Phone Calls
- 1,256 Texts
- 3,490 Online Tips
- 2,802 Emails
- 816 Webchats (Online chat feature on website). (NHTH n.d.)

According to the Hotline, in 2021, a total of 10,360 unique cases (incidents) of potential human trafficking were reported to the Hotline in 2021. The Report breaks down the contacts to show that the main calls came from victims themselves (26 percent) and community members (19 percent). It also provides information on where the contacts were coming from, by state, showing that California, Florida, New York, and Texas made the highest number of contacts. It also reported on why the call was being made, with the following reasons for calling:

- Report a Trafficking Tip—6,546 (63 percent)
- Access Service Referrals—3,284 (32 percent)
- Request Crisis Assistance—528 (5 percent)
- Request General Information—2 (0 percent)

Finally, it noted that a single human trafficking situation may involve a single potential victim and broke down how many cases were:

- labor trafficking versus sex trafficking
- adult versus minors
- domestic versus foreign national victims
- male versus female versus other gender identity.

In 2017, Polaris issued a report that took over 32,000 cases from a ten-year period and analyzed them to draw up a "typology of trafficking" in the United States consisting of twenty-five distinct "business models" of trafficking, each with their own specific and distinct operational models, depending on the industry in question. These were:

1. Escort Services
2. Illicit Massage, Health, & Beauty

 3. Outdoor Solicitation
 4. Residential
 5. Domestic Work
 6. Bars, Strip Clubs, & Cantinas
 7. Pornography
 8. Traveling Sales Crews
 9. Restaurants & Food Service
10. Peddling & Begging
11. Agriculture & Animal Husbandry
12. Personal Sexual Servitude
13. Health & Beauty Services
14. Construction
15. Hotels & Hospitality
16. Landscaping
17. Remote Interactive Sexual Acts
18. Illicit Activities
19. Carnivals
20. Arts & Entertainment
21. Forestry & Logging
22. Commercial Cleaning Services
23. Health Care
24. Factories & Manufacturing
25. Recreational Facilities.

A number of issues have arisen over the years about the operation of the Hotline:

1. Does a centralized Hotline work if responses must come from the local level?
2. How effective is the Hotline in fielding reports, tips, and queries for help?
3. Who decides what tips should be forwarded to law enforcement officials and service providers and on the basis of what criteria?
4. What improvements or changes need to be made to make the Hotline more effective?

The question about whether a centralized Hotline works if law enforcement and service provider responders must come from the local level is ongoing in a number of other issue areas, most notably suicide prevention. In 2022, the federal government launched a new centralized number (988) to call for suicide prevention and related mental health crisis issues. When they call 988, callers are connected to counselors at about 180 crisis centers in the United States. While some who study suicide are hailing the new centralized number as the most efficient method to aggregate calls for help to prevent suicide, the criticism of the hotline is similar to the critique of the NHTH.

One scholar noted that the new national hotline does not solve the suicide problem in the United States because we still don't really have effective local access for most people who call in with suicidal thoughts. "We have a nicely painted and landscaped front door," the scholar said, "We have signs pointing at the front door. The problem is once people walk through that front door, it's not clear what happens next. We don't really have the rest of the house built. We just have a very nice front door" (Wehrwein 2022, 60). This is very similar to the infrastructure that Polaris has set up for the NHTH. The Hotline is funded, but the services needed at the local level are uneven, unfunded, under-resourced, and unstable.

This may explain why some tips are not immediately forwarded to local authorities and service providers. The Hotline resources say, "Decisions to report tips to law enforcement are handled on a case-by-case basis with priority on safety and the consent of the individual involved."

Who makes those decisions? How are they made? What are the criteria for safety and consent of the individual? In some interviews survivors of human trafficking have said that they did not disclose what was happening to them to those they came in contact with, such as health-care providers, or law enforcement authorities, when they were arrested, or if they did disclose, they did not want action taken because they feared for their lives and the lives of their loved ones. Traffickers use physical force and physical and psychological coercion such as threats and intimidation to compel victims to engage in commercial sex or forced labor. In a meeting with the state AGs, the head of Polaris said that Polaris uses a victim centered approach that takes into consideration the potential adverse consequences to victims (National Association of Attorneys General 2023). However, given the nature of the crime, and the on-going long-term danger to the victim who is trapped in the trafficking situation, some observers believe that the Hotline's policy of not taking action without the consent of the person in the situation should be re-thought. These critics assert that since the Hotline is located sometimes as much as 3,000 miles away from the place where the trafficking is taking place, bringing local authorities and local service providers in as quickly as possible might be a better and more efficient approach to getting trafficking victims the help they need. One compromise might be a proactive question on the part of the Hotline asking specifically if the caller wants law enforcement called in. Another possible solution would be two lines—one for law enforcement tips and action and the other for guidance, support, and service provision.

To make the NHTH truly effective, proper resourcing is necessary to fund an infrastructure of emergency shelters, service providers, and anti-trafficking advocates and experts in every state in the country. Particular attention needs to be paid to those states that have had the highest numbers of calls to the Hotline each year. Some experts say that a truly effective infrastructure would ensure that every county has an ability to respond to human trafficking reports, both on the law enforcement side and on the victim services side.

A good example of a national infrastructure can be found in VAWA, the Violence Against Women Act. Every year, Congress authorizes and appropriates funds for Violence Against Women programs in every state in the United States. In 2022 more than $4 billion was appropriated for shelters and services for domestic violence (The White House 2022). In comparison, pilot programs for anti-trafficking shelters and services in the United States received only a few million dollars. Another example is the newly formed 988 Hotline for suicide prevention. It is partnering with states, counties, and localities to create an infrastructure locally to support the 988 national crisis line. Following the creation of 988, new resources were distributed to each locality and state, including Virginia:

> Before 988, access to Virginia's behavioral health system often started with an emergency 911 call. Sometimes those 911 calls, for concerns such as suicide or threats to self or others, resulted in law enforcement responding to situations that did not truly require police involvement. But now with 988, it's never been easier to get help.
>
> What can you expect if you contact 988?
>
> You can call or text 988. When you call, an automated greeting invites you to choose specialized options, like if you are a veteran or military service member. Most callers simply remain on the line to be routed to a call center crisis worker. No matter whether you call or text, you will be connected to a compassionate counselor who is trained to listen to your concerns and link you to helpful services. In Virginia, the call wait time averages about 20 seconds, which makes us a national leader.
>
> When a 988 call is received, the crisis worker provides support and conducts an assessment. National models show that through listening and helping the caller navigate a web of services, the crisis worker can resolve a resounding 80%

of calls. The crisis worker has options for the remainder of the calls that need additional assistance:

- If an in-person response is needed, Virginia is building a network of mobile crisis teams that can race to the location of the emergency. The national model shows 70% of calls referred to mobile crisis can be resolved by those teams.
- If there is an immediate life-threatening emergency or if backup is needed, the crisis worker can involve 911.
- If services such as short-term crisis and stabilization services are needed, Virginia is building crisis centers and other community crisis services. (Office of the Governor, Virginia, 2023)

This is a model that, with the right resources, could be helpful for creating a holistic response where the national hotline and states, cities, and counties are linked to respond appropriately.

Further Reading

"Coming Home: a secure interactive app with included online case management system that provides human and sex trafficking victims a reliable means of finding and receiving resources." https://apps.apple.com/us/app/cominghome-app/id1488844596. Accessed June 25, 2023.

Commonwealth of Virginia, Office of the Governor. 2023. 988 Press Release, https://richmond.com/opinion/columnists/column-for-those-in-crisis-988-is-making-a-difference/article_415cc508-20b1-11ee-8a04-1b777e25e1e3.html. Accessed June 25, 2023.

Commonwealth of Virginia, Office of the Governor. 2023. "What They Are Saying [About 988]." https://www.governor.virginia.gov/newsroom/news-releases/2022/december/name-948106-en.html. Accessed June 25, 2023.

National Association of Attorneys General, February 28, 2023, Letter to Congressional Leaders re National Human Trafficking Hotline, https://www.naag.org/press-releases/attorneys-general-call-on-congress-to-improve-federal-state-cooperation-to-end-human-trafficking/. Accessed June 25, 2023.

National Association of Attorneys General. 2023. "National Association of Attorneys General to Congress, February 27, in National Human Trafficking Hotline Reports." https://www.tn.gov/content/dam/tn/attorneygeneral/documents/pr/2023/ma23-10-letter.pdf. Accessed June 25, 2023.

National Human Trafficking Hotline. n.d. https://humantraffickinghotline.org/en. Accessed June 25, 2023.

National Human Trafficking Hotline. n.d. *Data Reports: 1/1/2021–12/31/2021.* https://humantraffickinghotline.org/sites/default/files/2023-01/National%20Report%20For%202021.docx%20%283%29.pdf. Accessed June 25, 2023.

National Human Trafficking Hotline. n.d. National Human Trafficking Hotline At-A-Glance.

National Human Trafficking Hotline. n.d. "When You Reach Us." https://humantraffic kinghotline.org/en/when-you-reach-us. Accessed June 25, 2023.

National Trafficking Sheltered Alliance. 2023 *Annual Submission to the U.S. Department of State Trafficking in Persons Report.* https://shelteredalliance.org/reports/. Accessed June 25, 2023.

Polaris. n.d.a. "Responding to Human Trafficking." https://polarisproject.org/respond ing-to-human-trafficking/. Accessed June 25, 2023.

Polaris. n.d.b. "U.S. National Human Trafficking Hotline Statistics." https://polarisproject. org/resources/us-national-human-trafficking-hotline-statistics/. Accessed June 25, 2023.

Trafficking Interruption Resource Agent (TIRA). 2023. "Innovative technology solution where victims and survivors of trafficking can quickly find the services they need." https://www.tira.live/. Accessed June 25, 2023.

Wehrwein, Peter. 2022. "Suicide Prevention: A New Number, Old Problems." *Managed Healthcare Executive*, September 26. https://cdn.sanity.io/files/0vv8m oc6/mhe/f81dd854575d6d321659c897eb7492c2f83d2561.pdf/MHE0922_Ez ine.pdf. Accessed June 25, 2023.

The White House. 2022. "Fact Sheet: Reauthorization of the Violence Against Women Act (VAWA)." https://www.whitehouse.gov/briefing-room/stateme nts-releases/2022/03/16/fact-sheet-reauthorization-of-the-violence-agai nst-women-act-vawa/. Accessed June 25, 2023.

Q19. Are the Experiences of Trafficking Survivors Being Incorporated into Anti-Trafficking Work?

Answer: Yes, although this is a relatively recent trend. For many years, survivors were not heard at all. Early anti-trafficking NGOs and others in the fledgling anti-trafficking movement had no survivor leaders or even speakers. Experts and advocates ran roundtables and discussion groups, held meetings, proposed policy and programs, and drafted legislation, usually without meaningful input from survivors.

As time passed, however, survivor leaders emerged. At first, survivors were given a platform on panels, then as guest speakers, or keynote speakers. Survivors also began writing their stories and finding publishers for them or self- publishing them. Some survivors set up their own nonprofits and found success designing education and awareness campaigns, providing services to other survivors, and advising at the local, state, and federal level on law, policy, and program changes. At the same time, experts and advocates began exploring ways to bring collective survivor information and exchanges to the fore. Early examples include this author's focus groups and surveys on health and human trafficking as well as case law analysis for the purpose of better understanding the nature and scope of trafficking (Lederer 2014, 2018, 2023).

Analyzing information from survivor interviews, focus groups, surveys, and case law are now the most popular ways of aggregating data about survivors. In 2015, the US Advisory Council on Human Trafficking was established. It provides a formal platform for trafficking survivors to advise and make recommendations on federal anti-trafficking policies to the President's Interagency Task Force (PITF) to Monitor and Combat Trafficking in Persons. Each member is a survivor of human trafficking, and together they represent a diverse range of backgrounds and experiences.

The Facts: One pioneer in giving a voice to trafficking survivors was a woman who had endured trafficking herself: Norma Hotaling, founder of SAGE (Standing Against Global Exploitation) (May 2008). Speaking before the First World Congress Against Commercial Sexual Exploitation of Children in Sweden in 1996, Hotaling talked about the need for survivor involvement in any movement to combat commercial sexual exploitation (Hotaling 1996). Shortly after, she instituted courses for survivors to learn how to work in the field and coined the terms, "survivor-centered" and "survivor-informed." At a graduation ceremony for her first set of survivors, a speaker noted that survivors need to be at the center of the anti-trafficking work because "they know the hell of it" (Lederer 2023).

A few survivor leaders emerged during the years before and after the passage of the Trafficking Victims Protection Act (TVPA) in 2000. Early testimony from survivors helped to pass the TVPA, but those survivors were mostly brought from South Asia, Russia, former states of the USSR, Mexico, and Central America when the focus was on international trafficking in persons (US Congress 1999). Other survivors testified at briefings and hearings after the passage of the TVPA, but they were all foreign national victims.

Slowly, though, survivors began to publish their own stories without intermediaries or formal invitations. In 2007, Theresa Flores published *The Sacred Bath* and then *The Slave across the Street* in 2010. At the time an unusual story, she told how, as a fifteen-year-old average All American teenager, she was trafficked while living in an upper-middle class suburb of Detroit. She described the modus operandi of a well-organized criminal network used "lover boy" techniques to lure a young unsuspecting girl into a room where the traffickers raped her, took pictures, and used those pictures to blackmail her and force her into commercial sex (Flores 2010). Traditionally, a loverboy seduces young, vulnerable girls and boys over a lengthy period of time, in order to exploit them sexually later on. This practice is being used less and less. Nowadays, loverboys resort more quickly and frequently to threatening their victims, using blackmail and violence (Government of Netherlands 2023).

In 2012, Carissa Phelps published *Runaway Girl: Escaping Life on the Streets*, which told her story of running away in Southern California from a dysfunctional family of eleven children when she was twelve and being picked up by "Icey," a vicious pimp who trafficked her (Phelps and Warren 2013). In 2014, Katariina Rosenblatt published her story of how she was lured into trafficking while staying with her family at a hotel in Miami Beach. Already lonely and a victim of abuse, Rosenblatt fell into the hands of a confident young woman who pretended friendship but slowly lured her into a child prostitution ring. For years afterward, a cycle of false friendship, threats, drugs, and violence kept her trapped (Rosenblatt and Murphey 2014).

In 2012, with a donation from a private foundation, one anti-trafficking organization developed a method for collecting stories and aggregating data from retrospective firsthand interviews and reports of survivors. Set up as a national survey to gather for the first time information on the health issues of victims and survivors of human trafficking, the process involved sets of focus groups in which survivors had a chance to tell some of what happened to them in childhood, how they were recruited, their experiences while being trafficked, especially as related to health issues such as illnesses, injuries from violence, and impairments such as drug use, drug addiction, and drug overdose (Lederer and Wetzel 2014). Over 150 stories of survivors were collected and a survey administered. The survey results were published in a peer-reviewed journal, but the collected stories have a wealth of information that is still being tabulated. Some of the issues embedded in these stories include information about precursor events to trafficking such as child sexual abuse and Adverse Childhood Experiences (ACEs), recruitment techniques of traffickers in domestic trafficking, and modus operandi of the traffickers. For example, out of 108 interviews with survivors in focus groups, 80 were victims of child sexual abuse before they fell victim to traffickers. Many of these survivors were molested by family members such as fathers, stepfathers, uncles, or brothers. Only 28 of the 108 trafficking survivors said that they had relatively normal childhoods (Lederer 2023). One survivor said,

> I was born to a drug addicted mother who gave me to my grandparents to raise. My grandfather was an alcoholic who molested me when I was very young. I

went back to my mother when I was twelve, but she had a boyfriend who was violent. He was very abusive. He would lock me in closets, kick me, hit me. I wanted to get away from him, so I ran away from home. On the street I met a pimp who was a leader in one of the local gangs. He owned a series of trailers in which he kept everybody who was his family. He was a really powerful guy and had a lot of money and … fancy cars. At first it seemed like I had found the family I never had, but after a short time he started to pimp me out. He was a cruel slavedriver. I had to bring in $1000 a day. If something bad happened, we were told to clean up and get back out there.

Another survivor said,

I was molested by my Mom's brothers (my uncles) when I was 8 years old. They took my innocence away from me. She tried to protect me, but she wasn't strong enough. She died soon after and I was sent to live with her sister and her husband. He was also a perpetrator. He would make me have sex with him and then try to bribe me with beer or cigarettes. My aunt did nothing about the abuse. I ran away a lot, but nobody knew why. Eventually they figured out that something bad was going on at that home and they took me away from my aunt and put me in a group home.

Another survivor said,

I grew up in a country town. I was a self-professed tomboy and avid softball player. My father was a surveyor, and my mother was a housewife and member of the PTA. We had the appearance of an All-American family, but behind closed doors it was a different story. My Dad molested me at 9 pm almost every night. He would come upstairs and cover my mouth with duct tape so my cries couldn't be heard.

The interviews also determined that 72 of the 108 survivors were trafficked by someone they met, usually when they were looking for a place to stay, food to eat, or the love that didn't exist at home. Of those seventy-two, two married their trafficker. In addition to those who were trafficked by boyfriends who turned out to be pimps, twenty-two were trafficked by a family member, including fifteen trafficked by their biological parent, four trafficked by their adopted parent or foster parent, and three trafficked by their stepparent (stepfather in this case); ten were trafficked by a female friend, two were trafficked by kidnapping, and 1onewas trafficked by a high school coach (Lederer 2023). One survivor said,

I was always looking for love in all the wrong places. I just wanted the men I was with to love me. Instead, it seems like I was always in some kind of bad relationship. It was with this one boyfriend who really seemed to like me that I was trafficked. I didn't understand what was happening. He brought me presents, took me out for dinner, said all the right things, really treated me nice. Then one day he started taking pictures of me and he told me he had a business that was going to really make us a lot of money. Before I knew what was going on he posted the pictures on the Internet and then he started to get calls and sold me for $10 – $500. He beat me so badly if I didn't perform for him.

Another survivor said,

I met my trafficker when I was young – in my early teens. He was at a gas station near where I lived. We started talking and I was enamored… I spent a few weeks with him, and it was nonstop glamor. He took me to so many nice places, bought me nice things. He would go into a store and get me anything I wanted. That first two weeks was a whirlwind of fun. Around the end of the two weeks, he said I couldn't stay with him unless I could contribute. I didn't want to lose hm, I really thought I loved him, so, I agreed. He set me up with a couple of "dates," and he gave me [drugs]. Until then I didn't know anything about prostitution, drugs, this whole kind of life. But I should say that I was sexually abused by a neighbor when I was 6 and felt after that like I always had something that set me apart from normal people.

Some were trafficked first inside their family. For example, one survivor said,

My grandmother and aunt pimped me out to men when I was in my early teens. They were selling my body to customers and also taking me to a strip club at night where they had fake paperwork that said I was 18.

Another survivor said,

My Dad was my first pimp. He molested me when I was 8 years old and then started selling me to other men, mostly friends of his. When I was 16 I turned him in and testified against him and he went to jail, but the damage was done. By the time I was 19 I was with another pimp fully in the life, forced to turn 20 tricks a day.

Another survivor said,

I was trafficked when I was 11 years old by my foster mother, who let her boyfriend use the six kids she fostered in order to get money for her drug addiction. He sold us to other men. No one in the foster system knew what was going on. We all used to run away together and the police would return us to the foster home where we were being abused.

These harrowing stories helped advocates to better understand the nature and scope of the problem of human trafficking. They were especially valuable in raising awareness that human trafficking is taking place in the United States as well as in other countries, and that the victims were not just foreign nationals trafficked in from other countries, but children and teens born and raised in the United States. Their experiences also helped anti-trafficking organizations better understand how preventing childhood sexual abuse was essential in reducing trafficking.

Labor trafficking victims shared similar stories of betrayal and bondage in the United States:

I was invited to the United States of America in the year 2003 on an H-1B visa. I was promised a salary of $75,000. In India that is a lot of money. The average Indian with an education may earn $3,600 per year. A salary like that would improve my situation and make a huge difference in the life of my kids. So, I accepted the job.. Little did I know that I was walking straight into a trap.. I brought my wife and two small children with me to the U.S. thinking we were starting a new and good life. My trafficker met me at the airport and asked me, "Harold, do you have any cash?" I was carrying a thousand dollars in cash from India. It was all the money I had. He said, "Oh it is not safe for you to carry around all that cash, give it to me." I believed him [and] gave him the cash, thinking it would be in safe custody. Then he drove me to a small apartment over a restaurant and told me that my wife and I would have to work there. I tried to tell him that I came as a business development manager on a $75,000 salary, everything in black and white on an H-1B visa. He didn't care. We landed at 7 in the evening and starting the next day both my wife and I were working.

I still remember the first day, coming back to the apartment from the restaurant. ...My older son was [sleeping] on the floor in his underwear. We had no mattresses, no furniture, no clothes, nothing. That... was the way we lived for over a year, and the owner of the restaurant never paid us that whole time. How does it happen? It happens because of fear. The trafficker [told me] that we were criminals and that I would be arrested if I didn't do what he said. I wanted to protect my family so I just kept working for free... Hee also forced me to sign some documents which turned out to be a bank... loan in my name, and I was thinking, "Where in the world am I going to get $40,000 to pay this loan?"... When I look back, I realize now that I was actually in debt bondage. Before I could digest what was happening to me, he gave me a pat on the back and said, "Harold, this is nothing: you owe me much more." I said, "Oh my God, this was not the final bill, so there is much more. I thought, We will be working like slaves for him forever." (Combating Trafficking in Persons. US Department of Defense, n.d.)

In 2013, a federal interagency group drafted and released a *Federal Strategic Action Plan on Services for Victims of Human Trafficking in the United States*. It identified the importance of engaging with survivors in decision-making processes as anti-trafficking leaders (US Department of Justice, 2013–2017). It required federal agencies to share their plans to apply a survivor-informed approach for human trafficking.

In 2015, Congress passed a law mandating the creation of a US Advisory Council on Human Trafficking to advise federal agencies on their anti-trafficking policies and programs, including on the application of this approach to their efforts. The president (through The White House) appoints the survivors, and the Council, composed of victims of sex trafficking and labor trafficking, males and females, those who were trafficked when they were children, and those who were trafficked when they were adults, as well as foreign national victims trafficked into the United States, and US citizens who were trafficked here is one of the most diverse groups of survivors in government. The appointees serve a two-year term that can be renewed for another two years. They bring survivor voices to the fore at the highest level of government by publishing an annual report that reviews the efforts of each federal agency and makes recommendations on how each agency can improve (US Department of State n.d.).

In 2017, in addition to its Voices of Freedom website, the Department of Health and Human Trafficking organized a Human Trafficking Leadership Academy. The program provides a set of seminars to twelve leaders each year in order to expand survivor-informed services while also providing leadership development opportunities to survivor leaders and allied professionals. The academy defined a survivor-informed practice as the "meaningful input from a diverse community of survivors at all stages of a program or project, including development, implementation and evaluation." Fellows work collaboratively to provide substantive recommendations that will inform research, policies, and programs that improve awareness, understanding, and assistance to survivors of human trafficking or those at risk of human trafficking (Office on Trafficking in Persons 2020). The academy

> provides leadership training at monthly seminars that is applicable to the fellows' current work and helps them grow in their chosen career. As they collaborate through a combination of in-person and virtual work, they also establish a trusted network among all the fellows that could last a lifetime. The

final seminar includes a graduation ceremony and a presentation to federal stakeholders on findings and recommendations related to the project question. (Office on Trafficking in Persons 2020a)

In 2021 the US Department of State's Annual Trafficking in Persons Report included a section that focused on the vital role that survivors of human trafficking play in developing and implementing survivor-led, trauma-informed, and comprehensive victim-centered approaches to human trafficking:

> The Department of State continues to prioritize the integration of survivor expertise into our work. Here, the U.S. Advisory Council on Human Trafficking has been a vital component in our ability to ensure that the strategies we put in place are victim-centered and trauma-informed. Council members come from diverse backgrounds with distinctive experiences. Their contributions and recommendations are invaluable. It is critical that survivor leaders have a seat at the table, but we need to do more. We also rely on our work with the Human Trafficking Expert Consultant Network—which consists of experts with lived experience of human trafficking. Their assistance has helped us develop survivor-informed programs, policies, and resources for our government and beyond, including the introductory essay of this report. As a movement, we must engage survivors early and often in the development of our policies and programs and learn from stakeholders who prioritize meaningful consultation with those with lived experience, to share best practices globally. (US Department of State 2021)

Survivors have a wealth of expertise to offer. A number of high-profile survivors have gone back to schools and earned college, masters, and even doctorate degrees. This makes the integration of survivor leaders into anti-trafficking work more doable than ever. As the State Department noted, "Organizations can set themselves up for success in a manner that is adaptive—not stagnant—to meet the evolving challenges of anti-trafficking efforts by mindfully weaving together survivor-leadership and trauma-informed approaches for the collective good of all who engage in anti-trafficking spaces."

Today, a number of government agencies have a section of their website devoted to survivors' voices: DOJ has a Faces of Human Trafficking Videos and Posters, a series developed for service providers, law enforcement, prosecutors, and others to raise awareness about human trafficking (Office of Victims of Crime n.d.). The series includes information about sex and labor trafficking, multidisciplinary approaches to serving victims of human trafficking, effective victim services, victims' legal needs, and voices of survivors.

The HHS supports Voices of Freedom, an oral history project done in collaboration with several other US government agencies. The program records, preserves, and shares the stories of survivors of trafficking and allied professionals. It is an archive of nearly 100 recorded discussions with those who have informed, shaped, and contributed to the successes of anti-trafficking efforts over the past two decades, including survivors (Office on Trafficking in Persons n.d.b). The Department of Labor has a blog that features the voices of labor trafficking survivors (United States Department of Labor Blog n.d.). The DoD has its Survivor Voices of Human Trafficking, which has 15–20 minute video stories of survivors, and a transcript of their stories, most of which have a military connection, such as survivors who were trafficked in and around military installations, survivors who were trafficked by active military, survivors whose parents or relatives were in the military (Combating Trafficking in Persons, US Department of Defense n.d.). It includes stories of survivors who were victims of labor trafficking while working under contract to the military, sex trafficking survivors, and survivors of child soldiering (Combating Trafficking in Persons, US Department of Defense n.d.).

Still gaps remain. Survivors point out that funding and resources still seem to flow to well-established organizations that provide victim services (especially for foreign national victims) such as Catholic Charities and the US Committee for Refugees and Immigrants (Office on Trafficking in Persons n.d.). For domestic survivors there is still a patchwork of funding, available for short periods of time, to serve domestic victims. For example, as of 2023, currently there are only eleven states funded by the federal government to provide shelter and services for domestic victims.

Further Reading

Amaya, Barbara. 2015. *Nobody's Girl: A Memoir of Lost Innocence, Modern Day Slavery & Transformation*. Pittsburgh, PA: Animal Media Group.

Charlton, James. 1998. *Nothing about Us without Us: Disability Oppression and Empowerment*. University of California Press. https://books.google.com/books?id=ohqff8DBt9gC&pg=PA3#v=onepage&q&f=false. Accessed June 25, 2023.

Combating Trafficking in Persons. US Department of Defense. n.d. "Survivor Voices of Human Trafficking." https://ctip.defense.gov/Survivor-Voices/. Accessed July 17, 2023.

Flores, Theresa L. 2010. *The Slave across the Street*. Garden City, ID: Ampelon Publishing.

Government of the Netherlands. 2023. "Loverboys," Human Trafficking and Human Smuggling. https://www.government.nl/topics/human-trafficking/romeo-pimps-loverboys#:~:text=Traditionally%2C%20a%20loverboy%20seduces%20young,victims%2C%20using%20blackmail%20and%20violence. Accessed June 25, 2023.

Hotaling, Norma. 1996. "Caring for Orchids," Speech, First World Congress Against Commercial Sexual Exploitation of Children, Stockholm, September 20, 1996, mentioned in Lederer, Modern Slavery, 2018, p. 132.

Lederer, Laura J. 2004. "Survivor-Led Anti Trafficking Efforts: The Future of the Movement." Speech, SAGE First Class LIFESKILLS Graduation Ceremony, San Francisco, CA, December 12. www.globalcenturion.org.

Lederer, Laura J., and Christopher G. Wetzel. 2014. "The Health Consequences of Sex Trafficking and Their Implications for Identifying Victims in Healthcare Facilities." *Annals of Health Law* 23, no. 1: 61. https://www.icmec.org/wp-content/uploads/2015/10/Health-Consequences-of-Sex-Trafficking-and-Implications-for-Identifying-Victims-Lederer.pdf. Accessed June 25, 2023.

Lederer, Laura. 2018. *Modern Slavery: A Documentary and Reference Guide. London:* ABC-CIO, Greenwood Publishing.

Lederer, Laura, Theresa Flores, and McKamie Chandler. 2023. "The Pregnancy Continuum in Domestic Sex Trafficking." *Issues in Law and Medicine* 38, no. 1.

May, Meredith. 2008. "Norma Hotaling Dies – Fought Prostitution." *SFGATE,* December 20. https://www.sfgate.com/bayarea/article/Norma-Hotaling-dies-fought-prostitution-3180057.php. Accessed June 25, 2023.

Office of Victims of Crime. n.d. "Faces of Human Trafficking." https://ovc.ojp.gov/program/human-trafficking/faces-of-human-trafficking. Accessed July 17, 2023.

Office on Trafficking in Persons. 2020. "Human Trafficking Leadership Academy." Last updated March 2, 2020. https://www.acf.hhs.gov/otip/training/nhttac/human-trafficking-leadership-academy. Accessed September 19, 2023.

Office on Trafficking in Persons. n.d.a. "Trafficking Victim Assistance Program." https://www.acf.hhs.gov/otip/map/trafficking-victim-assistance-program. Accessed July 17, 2023.

Office on Trafficking in Persons. n.d.b. "Voices of Freedom." https://www.acf.hhs.gov/otip/partnerships/voices. Accessed July 17, 2023.

Phelps, Carissa, and Larkin Warren. 2013. *Runaway Girl: Escaping Life on the Streets.* New York: Penguin Books.

Rosenblatt, Katariina, and Cecil Murphey. 2014. *Stolen: The True Story of a Sex Trafficking Survivor.* Grand Rapids, MI: Revell.

US Congress. 1999. House of Representatives. Committee on International Relations. *Trafficking of Women and Children in the International Sex Trade: Hearing Before the Subcommittee on International Operations and Human Rights of the Committee on International Relations.* 106th Cong., 1st sess., September 14.

US Department of State. 2021. *Trafficking in Persons Report.* https://www.state.gov/reports/2021-trafficking-in-persons-report/. Accessed June 25, 2023.

US Department of Justice, Federal Strategic Action Plan on Services for Victims of
    Human Trafficking in the United States., 2013–2017, Office of Victims of Crime,
    https://ovc.ojp.gov/sites/g/files/xyckuh226/files/media/document/FederalHumanTra
    fickingStrategicPlan.pdf.

5

Learning from Lived Experience: What Survivors Are Telling Us

In this chapter, we examine some additional ways to gather information from survivors to inform anti-trafficking and trafficking recovery efforts. One way, developed in 2012 by the author for the first national survey on health and human trafficking, is now being utilized by researchers, academics, and practitioners across the United States. It relies on a mixed-methods approach consisting of a series of focus groups, with guided questions on a topic, to gather qualitative information, and then the administration of a data collection instrument such as a survey or questionnaire to obtain quantitative data. This methodology is providing rich results on a number of topics, from the health issues of human trafficking survivors to transportation methods used by traffickers, to services most needed by survivors, and more.

The first article in this chapter explores how the experiences of trafficking survivors can inform and improve anti-trafficking efforts. It explains the numerous ways we can listen and learn from those with lived experience. The next three articles explore these new methodologies in greater depth: if we can aggregate survivor experience, we obtain powerful evidence-based data that can and should guide our work on prevention of trafficking, prosecution of traffickers, and protection and assistance of victims.

Q20. Have Researchers Found Links between Trafficking, Homelessness, and Drug Addiction?

Answer: Yes. As part of the largest study conducted on trafficking and homeless youth, researchers conducted interviews with close to 1,000 youth in thirteen cities across the United States and Canada. According to the survey results, nearly 20 percent of the homeless youth were victims of human trafficking, with

15 percent reporting sex trafficking, 7.4 percent labor trafficking, and 3 percent experiencing both (Murphy 2016).

Many runaway and homeless youth have said that their first encounters with their traffickers were when they were homeless and were picked up on the street and offered a place to stay. Numerous studies have also shown a link between substance use and abuse and trafficking. For example, one study surveying 107 individuals who had experienced human trafficking found that 84.3 percent of participants said they used alcohol, drugs, or a combination during their trafficking experience—often as a coping mechanism. Another 27.9 percent of the youth reported substance use was forced on them by their trafficker (Lederer and Wetzel 2014). From January 1, 2015, through June 30, 2017, Polaris recorded 2,238 potential victims of human trafficking whose drug use was either induced or exploited as a means of control in their trafficking situation (Polaris Project n.d.). In addition, some NGOs working in other countries are also reporting that traffickers are coercing people into commercial sex or forced labor using drugs (Kelly 2018).

The Facts: Studies and survivors tell us that victims of sex- and labor trafficking experience a knot of problems that leave them vulnerable to trafficking. In a study conducted by Loyola University New Orleans, youth reported that their fear of sleeping on the streets left them vulnerable to sex- and labor traffickers and to survival sex. Survival sex is defined as the "exchange of sex for food, money, shelter, drugs, and other needs and wants" (NIH 2020). Securing housing was a primary concern for the vast majority of the youth we interviewed. Sixty-eight percent of the youth who had either been trafficked or engaged in survival sex or commercial sex had done so while homeless. One survivor said,

> My family was so violent, especially my Dad. He beat my mother so bad that she had seizures. He beat me too. I took it as long as I could and then I ran away. I met my trafficker on the street when I was trying to figure out what I was going to do, and I was looking for a place to stay.

Another survivor said,

> I was raped by my uncle when I was 4 years old, and he continued to abuse me until I was 9. I ran away from home as soon as I could. On the street it was even rougher, I went from house to house, hotel to hotel, sleeping wherever I could find a roof, including at dope dealer crack houses. I was staying alive any way I could. My goal was to get a hotel room for the night and some chips and a candy

bar to eat. That's when I hooked up with a trafficker who called himself Shack. He was a scary son-of-a-gun. He gave us drugs to keep us under his thumb. I got addicted to crack cocaine and I used any other drug I could find too.

In the Loyola study, 19 percent of all youth interviewed had engaged in survival sex solely so that they could access housing or food. This problem is even starker among those who are not sheltered. The incidence of trafficking among youth who were homeless and living on the street was higher than for those living in a shelter: 24 percent were trafficked for sex, 13 percent for labor. Forty-one percent of the trafficked youth said they saw the shelters as safe havens from their traffickers (Murphy 2016). One survivor said,

> I was a runaway. I ran from severe abuse in the home (my stepfather) when I was 12. When I was hungry and tired and scared, I was "befriended" by men who gave me food, clothing, and shelter in exchange for sex. It was then I met my first [trafficker]. Before that, I did almost anything for almost nothing. I remember having sex in the alley for a can of soup.

Similarly, in a Street Outreach Program study conducted by the University of Nebraska for the US Department of Health and Human Services found that of the 873 "street youth" aged fourteen to twenty-one surveyed, nearly a quarter of them had traded sex with at least one person for money, more than a quarter of them had traded sex for a place to stay for the night, more than 18 percent had traded sex for food, 12 percent for protection, and 11 percent for drugs (Whitbeck et al. 2014). One survivor said,

> Once I was addicted, that led me to being trafficked by my drug dealers. I became so addicted; I was willing to do anything to get my next hit. I had two dealers and they started pimping me out to their friends – not out on the street but in apartments. I was literally being sold for drugs. (Trail n.d.)

In a number of trafficking cases the trafficker has used addiction as a tool of coercion. For example, in 2014, in one of the earliest cases with a clear link between substance use disorder and trafficking, a federal judge ruled that several women had been coerced into sex trafficking using illegal prescription drugs after finding that the trafficker gave them drugs and then withheld them to exploit withdrawal symptoms to force them into commercial sex (Johnston 2014).

In another similar case, the trafficker sold heroin to young women and minors. According to the US Department of Justice,

Witnesses described how the defendant used their addictions to force them to
prostitute for his profit. The defendant would often front heroin to the women
and then arrange prostitution "dates" for them. The women were required to
give the defendant half of the proceeds and then purchase heroin from him
with the remainder. On other occasions, the defendant withheld heroin from
the women, causing them to suffer painful withdrawal symptoms, and then
instructed them to prostitute to earn money to purchase heroin from him. The
defendant's scheme guaranteed that he had a steady source of drug customers
and money. Some of the women were required to help the defendant sell his
heroin and received heroin in exchange. The defendant used violence and
threats to maintain control of the women. (Office of Public Affairs 2019)

In these cases, perpetrators entrapped victims with existing substance use
issues, or they initiate dependency in victims with no prior addiction history
(Office to Monitor and Combat Trafficking in Persons 2020). They then used the
threat of withdrawal—which causes extreme pain and suffering and can be fatal
without medical supervision—to control the victims and coerce them to engage
in commercial sex, compounding the victims' trauma.

There are also cases of substance use disorder and labor trafficking. In
one case, the owner of a chain of sober living facilities was convicted of sex
trafficking individuals in such facilities (FBI 2018). In a labor trafficking case,
traffickers allegedly targeted people with substance use issues who were court-
mandated to recovery facilities in lieu of prison sentences and forced them to
work in chicken processing, sheet metal fabrication, and other dangerous work
(Harris 2017).

A total of 2,238 potential victims of trafficking mentioned drug use as a means
of control to force them into trafficking. That figure represents nearly 15 percent of
all the potential victims for whom there were enough details available about their
trafficking situation to make a determination that drugs were involved (Polaris
Project n.d.). According to Polaris, which runs the National Hotline where these
calls were recorded, the information was only recorded when drug use was
proactively disclosed by a caller. In the same time frame, Polaris recorded 926
potential victims of human trafficking who had a substance abuse issue prior to
the potential trafficking, many of whom had this vulnerability exploited by their
traffickers. Twenty-six of those were recruited into their trafficking situation
directly from drug rehabilitation centers. In addition, of the 2,238 potential
victims for whom drugs played a role in their exploitation 543 were minors at
the time their situations were reported to Polaris; an additional 135 were minors
at the start of their trafficking situation. The vast majority—1,972 individuals or

88 percent—were victims of sex trafficking—as compared to labor trafficking or situations where both sex and labor trafficking were present. Finally, 1,822 of the sex trafficking victims were identified as female (Polaris Project n.d.). A 2018 report from the Salvation Army in the UK corroborate that traffickers are using alcohol and drugs to control and coerce victims into commercial sex and forced labor, with victims being forced to take drugs and sometimes being "paid" in drugs and alcohol (Parkes 2018).

A forthcoming study conducted in Detroit by a Street Medicine Outreach team revealed a complex intertwining of problems linking trafficking to homelessness, violence, and substance use disorder (Lederer et al. forthcoming). It found that women who want to exit the sex trade industry, including sex trafficking, "sex work," and other forms of commercial sex and commercial sexual exploitation, face a staggering array of interconnected challenges. These challenges include increased vulnerability to violence and physical abuse, drug and alcohol addiction, homelessness, and inability to access health care.

Based on how they identified themselves, survivors were placed into three categories (Figure 2): trafficked (in commercial sex by force, fraud, or coercion), engaged in "sex work" (in commercial sex voluntarily), and neither (not currently trafficked or engaged in commercial sex). In all three categories, a majority of respondents reported being homeless, or experiencing housing instability. The trafficking survivors had the highest rates of housing instability,

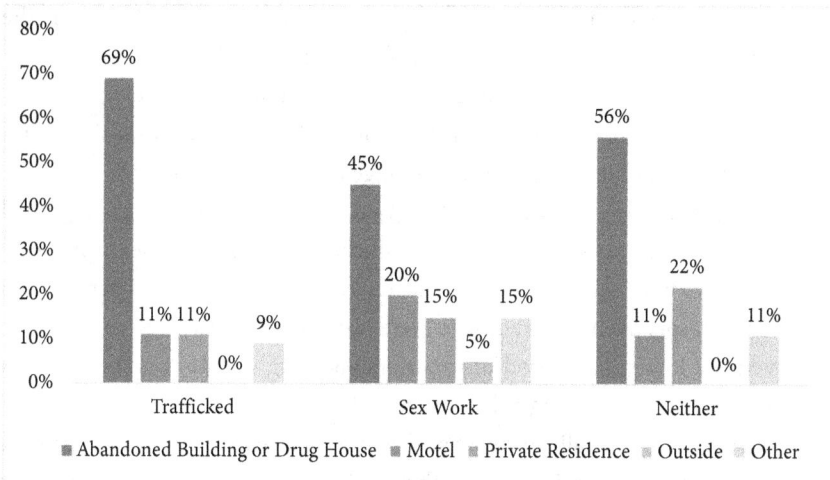

Figure 2 Housing circumstances by status

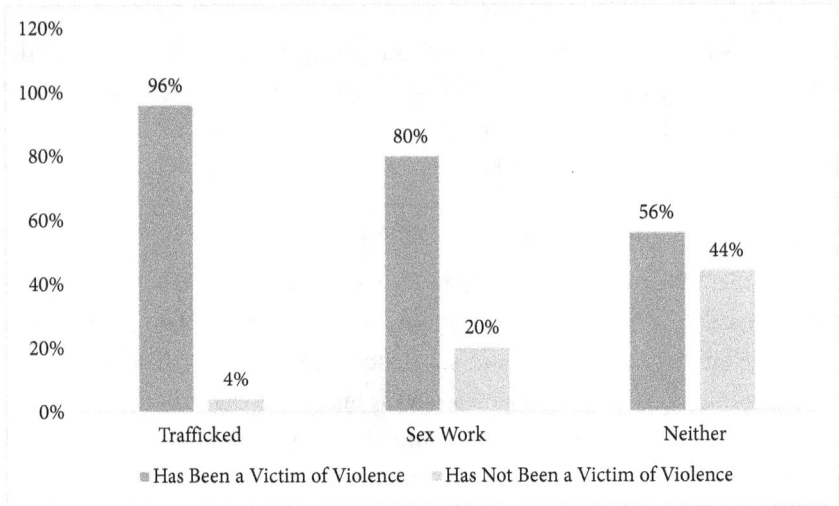

Figure 3 Victim of violence by status

but all three categories of respondents showed high levels of homelessness or housing instability.

The prevalence of violence among victims of trafficking is strikingly high, as evidenced by Figure 3. A staggering 96 percent of respondents who were trafficked reported experiencing violence. The rates of violence exhibited a slight decline among individuals involved in sex work with 80 percent reporting violence.

Substance use and abuse is also very high for all three types of respondents. Cocaine emerged as the most frequently reported drug overall. Heroin is the second most used drug. Among those who were trafficked, cocaine and heroin use stood out with rates of 100 percent and 87 percent, respectively.

Although respondents did report using other drugs, there was a significant decline in the rate of usage compared to usage of cocaine and heroin.

Respondents in the study also discussed overdosing on drugs. Figure 4 illustrates that women who were either trafficked or involved in sex work were highly likely to have experienced at least 1 overdose, with rates of 69 percent and 75 percent, respectively. Women who were currently not involved in sex work displayed the lowest likelihood of experiencing drug overdose, but still had a 44 percent rate of overdosing at least once.

In this study, almost all survivors said that in five years they wanted to be off the street, out of commercial sex (whether trafficked or engaged in voluntary sex work), and no longer addicted to drugs and/or alcohol.

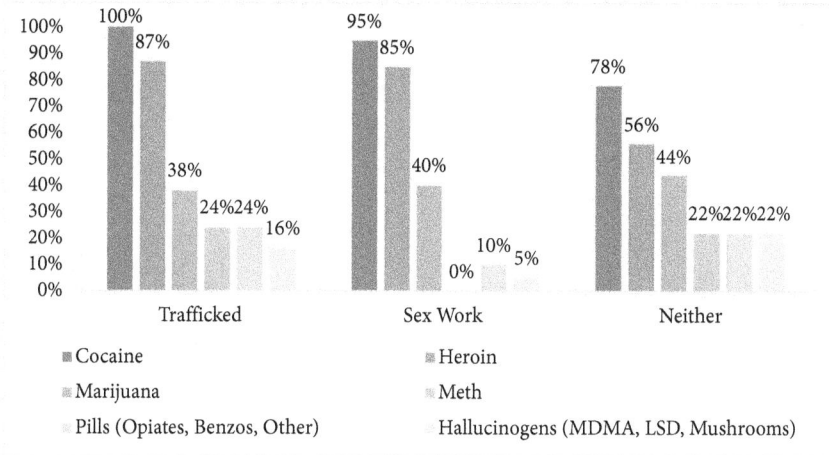

Figure 4 Drugs used by status

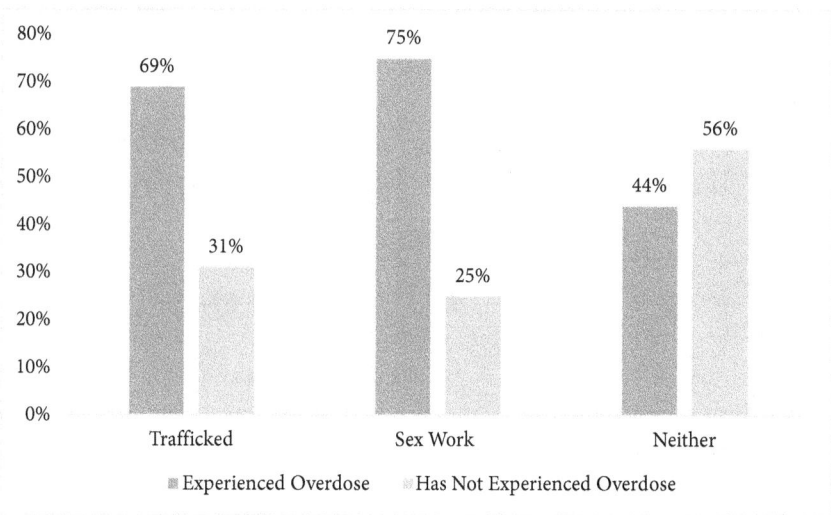

Figure 5 Drug overdose by status

One survivor said,

When I got arrested, I was finally free of my trafficker, but I still had all my other problems. I was still addicted, I didn't have any place to go to call home, I didn't know how to live. I had never had a bank account, never paid bills, never shopped or cleaned the house. I didn't know how to make money in any legitimate way. I realized that my worst fear wasn't being beaten by my trafficker. My worst fear was where would I go and what would I do if I got free of him?

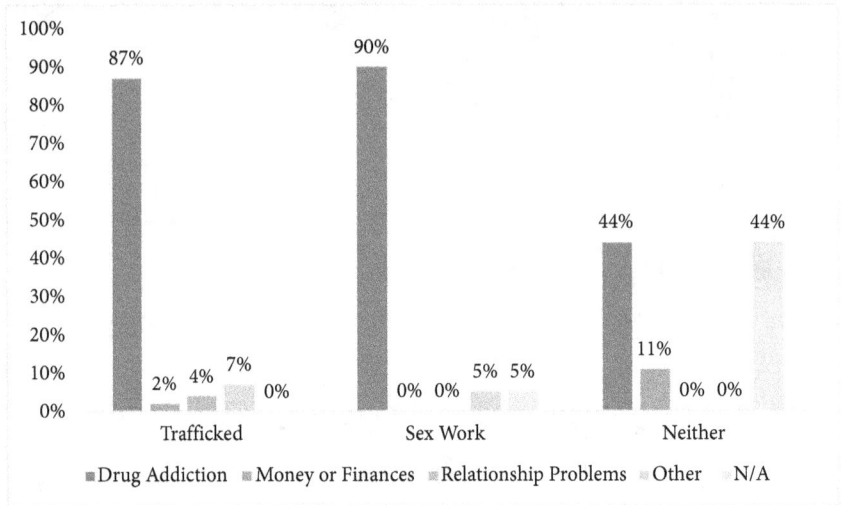

Figure 6 Respondents' main barriers to pursuing a different path by status

The respondents were asked about barriers to achieving those goals (Figure 6). None of the participants responded with "no barriers." Among all three groups, drug addiction emerged as the most prominent and significant barrier (Figure 5). Additional barriers such as financial constraints and relationship problems were also identified.

The women also were asked to list their top three current needs, revealing essential requirements for their well-being. They emphasized fundamental necessities such as food, clothing, shelter, and access to showers. They also said that medical care was high on the list of needs. Many expressed a need for drug detox and rehabilitation support. Additionally, some identified the need for legal assistance and assistance obtaining basic identity documents, such as IDs, social security cards, or copies of birth certificates. Last, they expressed a need for a caring community and a sense of belonging. These responses confirm the importance of developing comprehensive support systems that encompass a range of services tailored to the specific needs of individuals who have been trafficked or involved in commercial sex.

Another critical issue identified was the high percentage of women who have children. In all three categories, a majority of respondents reported being mothers.

In this survey, 80 percent of women who were trafficked and 75 percent of women who identified as engaged in sex work reported that they had children (Figure 7). These reports raise significant concerns regarding the resources

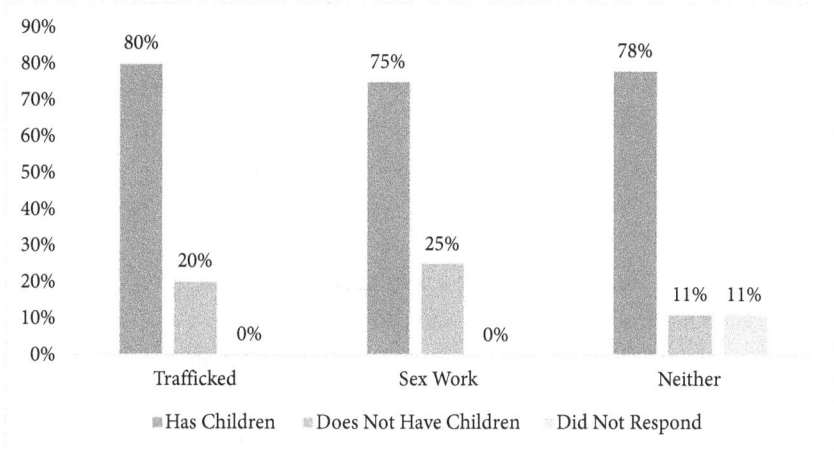

Figure 7 Respondents with children by status

available to these women during their pregnancies or during the early years of the children's lives, such as access to affordable childcare.

In a series of focus groups conducted about pregnancy in trafficking, women noted that service providers and other helper organizations are frequently not set up to assist women with children (Lederer et al. 2023). For example, one survivor of sex trafficking said that she would not go to the local shelters for trafficking victims because they did not accept children. She said that she slept with her two-year-old in an abandoned car over a winter in the Midwest to keep her two-year-old with her (Lederer et al. 2023). This is not the fault of the shelters; it is a systemic problem. It is difficult to obtain licenses for residential shelters for trafficking victims to keep mothers and children together. In order to get help, a mother must give up her child, or be separated from her child to obtain services.

Some agencies are pioneering new forms of care in which, as long as there is not child abuse, mother and child are never separated, and go to new kinds of foster care together (see e.g., Safe Families for Children n.d.). These agencies see homelessness, unemployment, domestic violence, incarceration, substance abuse, and human trafficking as sources of crisis that, in many government and nonprofit systems of care, separate families and particularly separate mothers from their children. Their approach is to provide a host family for the family in crisis. In this way both mother and child or children stay together and receive wrap around services tailored to their needs (see e.g., Safe Families for Children n.d.).

In this survey, a surprisingly large number of respondents (38–44 percent) could not access health care or other services because they did not have something as simple as identification papers or transportation to and from a service provider (Lederer et al. forthcoming). Social workers, legal aid, and other service providers should have interns or entry-level staff available to help remove these barriers, including obtaining basic identification documents such as duplicate birth certificates, social security cards and numbers, driver's licenses, or walker's IDs.

Specialized education and awareness programs tailored to the professionals who come into direct contact with clients and patients are another way to help service providers understand how they may encounter trafficking in their daily work and how to respond appropriately. In a 2023 survey on pregnancy and human trafficking, pregnant victims of trafficking were asked if they had sought help from many different kinds of health providers during the time they were trafficked (Lederer et al. 2023). Ninety percent of victims said that they sought health care; 80 percent sought health care in emergency rooms (ERs) in hospitals; 58 percent sought care in neighborhood or urgent care clinics; 35 percent sought care from private physicians.

Unfortunately, even though most reported interacting with medical professionals, when they were asked to characterize their general interactions with health-care providers, only 9.7 percent reported agreeing with the statement that medical professionals understood what was happening to them. Only 12.9 percent believed the care they received was "excellent." Only 9.7 percent reported that medical professionals were "trauma informed." Only 9.7 percent reported that the medical professional followed up with them or provided aftercare, and only 6.5 percent reported receiving helpful referrals (Lederer et al. 2023).

In research published in 2020 by the US Department of Health and Human Services National Institute of Health, three types of barriers trafficking victims face in obtaining health care were identified: extrinsic, intrinsic, and systemic barriers (Garg 2020). Extrinsic barriers included trafficker control, physical confinement, and influence of peers. Intrinsic barriers included discrimination, confidentiality, trust in health-care providers, knowledge of the health-care system, and emotional reluctance. Systemic issues inherent to the health-care system included health-care provider knowledge, complex registration processes, language barriers, appointment times, and service coordination.

In this survey, a combination of extrinsic, intrinsic, and systemic barriers are inextricably tied. Women who are trafficked or engaged in sex work also struggle with drug and alcohol addictions, experience homelessness or housing instability, and suffer from serious health problems. Recognizing the needs and realities of these patients and meeting them where they are—out on the street, in mobile and other health clinics, in rehab programs, and in temporary shelters—to assess their needs is key. Using individualized case management, and other holistic, whole-of-person assessment instruments is also critical. Unfortunately, many of the services that are available are siloed, making it difficult for women to receive sets of services tailored to their needs. Until the time when we can design housing and shelter services so that physical and mental health services, addiction and rehab services, life skills, and other related needs are all in a one-stop-and-shop center, we must explore other ways to ensure that multiple needs can be met. One possibility is more mobile clinics and services that meet women where they are—on the streets, in inexpensive motels, and other temporary residencies. Another possibility is a more sophisticated system of "warm hand-offs, in which Multi-disciplinary Teams (MDTs) of service providers from various fields come together on the front end to provide sets of needed services." In health care, a "warm handoff" is a handoff that is conducted in person, or live on-line, between two members of the health-care team, while the patient is present. This same technique can be extended to handing a person over to another service provider to find housing, rehabilitation center or residency treatment, or other sets of services.

Further Reading

Federal Bureau of Investigation (FBI). 2018. "Sober Home and Drug Treatment Center Owner Sentenced: Facilities Preyed on Vulnerable Adults Struggling with Addiction," February 21. https://www.fbi.gov/news/stories/florida-sober-home-owner-sentenced. Accessed June 25, 2023.

Garg, Anjali, Preeti Panda, Mandy Neudecker, and Sara Lee. 2020. "Barriers to the Access and Utilization of Healthcare for Trafficked Youth: A Systematic Review." *Child Abuse & Neglect: The International Journal* 100. https://doi.org/10.1016/j.chiabu.2019.104137.

Greene, Jody, "Prevalence and Correlates of Survival Sex Among Runaway and Homeless Youth." accessed at National Institute of Health, November 13, 2023, https://www.ncbi.nlm.nih.gov/pmc/articles/PMC1508758/pdf/amjph00009-0102.pdf.

Harris, Amy, and Shoshana Walter. 2017. "Rehab Scam: Defendants in Court-Ordered Rehab Work for Free." *Reveal*, October 4. https://revealnews.org/article/they-thought-they-were-going-to-rehab-they-ended-up-in-chicken-plants/. Accessed June 25, 2023.

Johnston, Caitlin. 2014. "Man Convicted of Human Trafficking Gets 34 Years in Prison." *Tampa Bay Times*, January 14. https://www.tampabay.com/news/courts/criminal/man-convicted-of-human-trafficking-gets-34-years-in-prison/2163311/. Accessed June 25, 2023.

Kelly, Annie. 2018. "Exclusive: UK Traffickers Using Drugs to Force People into Slavery, Report Finds." *The Guardian*, October 17. https://www.theguardian.com/global-deve lopment/2018/oct/17/exclusive-uk-traffickers-using-drugs-to-force-people-into-slav ery-report-finds. Accessed June 25, 2023.

Lederer, Laura J., and Christopher G. Wetzel. 2014. "The Health Consequences of Sex Trafficking and Their Implications for Identifying Victims in Healthcare Facilities." *Annals of Health Law* 23, no. 1). https://www.icmec.org/wp-content/uplo ads/2015/10/Health-Consequences-of-Sex-Trafficking-and-Implications-for-Iden tifying-Victims-Lederer.pdf. Accessed June 25, 2023.

Lederer, Laura J., Stanley Stinson, and McKamie J. Chandler, "Barriers to Escape: How Homelessness and Drug Addiction Prevent Women from Escaping Sex Trafficking and Commercial Sex." Journal Name Vol # (forthcoming).

Lederer, Laura J., Theresa Flores, and McKamie J. Chandler. 2023. "The Pregnancy Continuum in Domestic Sex Trafficking: Examining the Unspoken Gynecological, Reproductive, and Procreative Issues of Victims and Survivors." *Issues in Law and Medicine* 38, no. 1. https://www.globalcenturion.org/wp-content/uploads/2023/05/ The-Pregnancy-Continuum-in-Domestic-Sex-Trafficking-by-Laura-J-Lederer-Ther esa-Flores-McKamie-Chandler.pdf. Accessed June 25, 2023.

Murphy, Laura T. 2016. *Labor and Sex Trafficking among Homeless Youth.* New Orleans, LA: Loyola University Modern Slavery Research Project. https:// static1.squarespace.com/static/5887a2a61b631bfbbc1ad83a/t/5a7490fdc8302 508d6b76f1c/1517588734590/Labor+and+Sex+Trafficking+Among+Homel ess+Youth.pdf. Accessed June 25, 2023.

National Institute of Health. 2021. "Survival Sex Trading in Los Angeles, California," September 1. https://www.ncbi.nlm.nih.gov/pmc/articles/PMC 7334079/. Accessed June 25, 2023.

Office to Monitor and Combat Trafficking in Persons. 2020. "The Intersection of Human Trafficking and Addiction." Office to Combat and Monitor Trafficking in Persons. US Department of State. June. https://2017-2021.state.gov/wp-content/uplo ads/2020/10/TIP_Factsheet-The-Intersection-of-Human-Trafficking-and-Addict ion-1-508.pdf. Accessed June 25, 2023.

Office of Public Affairs. 2019. "Defendant Who Exploited Opioid Addictions of Young Women Convicted of Crimes Related to Drug Trafficking and Prostitution." Office of Public Affairs. March 25. www.justice.gov. U.S. Department of Justice.. https://www. justice.gov/opa/pr/defendant-who-exploited-opioid-addictions-young-women- convicted-crimes-related-drug. Accessed June 25, 2023.

Parkes, Neil. 2018. "A Few Doors Down the Links between Substance Misuse and Modern Slavery." *The Salvation Army*. https://www.salvationarmy.org.uk/ sites/default/files/resources/2019-09/A%20few%20doors%20down%20-%20 The%20links%20between%20substance%20misuse%20and%20modern%20slav ery.pdf. Accessed June 25, 2023.

Polaris Project. n.d. "Human Trafficking and the Opioid Crisis." Polaris Project. https://polarisproject.org/wp-content/uploads/2019/10/Human-Trafficking-and-the-Opioid-Crisis.pdf. Accessed July 18, 2023.

Safe Families for Children. n.d. "About Us." https://safe-families.org/about/.

Trail, Desiree. n.d. "Desiree Trail." Combating Trafficking in Persons. U.S. Department of Defense. https://ctip.defense.gov/Portals/12/Survivor%20Voices/Desiree%20Trail_Final.pdf?ver=kZTaFVwD1U5ixYf6UrVsoA%3d%3d&timestamp=1680890892201. Accessed June 25, 2023.

Whitbeck, Les, Melissa Welch Lazoritz, Devan Crawford, and Dane Hautala. 2014. *Street Outreach Program: Data Collection Project Executive Summary.* Lincoln: University of Nebraska. https://www.rhyttac.net/assets/docs/Research/research%20-%20sop%20data%20collection%20project.pdf. Accessed June 25, 2023.

Q21. What Negative Health Impacts Are Associated with Human Trafficking?

Answer: Numerous studies have shown that trafficking is both a public and private health issue. Victims and survivors of human trafficking have both physical and mental health problems. The health issues that arise from sex trafficking overlap with but also are distinct from the health issues that arise in labor trafficking.

The health issues most commonly reported by survivors can roughly be divided into three categories: illnesses, injuries, and impairments. Illnesses includes physical and mental illness, physical illnesses can be acute and/or chronic. Injuries include broken bones, bruises, and other injuries occurring as a result of violence in trafficking. Impairments include alcohol and drug use, misuse, and abuse, drug addiction, drug overdose, and related issues. The wide variety of health issues victims and survivors of human trafficking seek treatment for, and the frequency with which they seek treatment, demonstrates the importance for health-care providers who have direct contact with patients to understand how they present in health-care settings, to know the signs and indicators, and to respond appropriately.

The Facts: The earliest studies on health issues of trafficking victims were focused mainly on the spread of HIV/AIDS to and through trafficking victims. In his remarks at the release of the 2004 Trafficking in Persons Report, Secretary of State Colin Powell stated: "Aside from the intolerable human rights violations that trafficking involves, trafficking is linked to other very grave problems that we must not allow to persist, let alone to grow. Trafficking is a global public health threat that spreads HIV/AIDS and other infectious diseases" (Powell 2004).

Following the first national survey, published in 2014, which looked at self-reported health conditions of domestic sex trafficking victims, a number of studies have followed, looking at physical and mental health issues of sex trafficking and labor trafficking victims and survivors. For the most part, health complications in these studies were divided by the eleven major organ systems in the human body, or some combination thereof, including general health and health complications related to skeletal, muscular, nervous, endocrine, cardiovascular, lymphatic, respiratory, digestive, urinary, and reproductive systems. The major mental health disorders are classified as anxiety disorders, depression, bipolar disorders, PTSD, schizophrenia, eating disorders, disruptive behavior and dissocial disorders, and neurodevelopmental disorders (World Health Organization 2022). Since the first study, most studies have focused on a specific geographic area; a specific population (Greenbaum et al. 2015); or a specific type of condition, such as physical, mental, or behavioral health; specific type of health issues; health provider screening tools; health provider responses; and other related issues.

The findings of the first studies are now being replicated across the country and around the world. In the first survey in the United States, researchers found that survivors experienced serious physical health problems during trafficking. The most frequently reported physical problems were neurological. More than 90 percent of respondents reported at least one neurological symptom and 82.1 percent specifically reporting memory problems, insomnia, or poor concentration. Headaches or migraines (53.8 percent) and dizziness (34.0 percent) were also common symptoms. Trafficking negatively affected the general health of victims as well, with 85.7 percent reporting at least one symptom in the general health category. Severe weight loss (42.9 percent), malnutrition (35.2 percent), loss of appetite (46.7 percent), and eating disorders (36.2 percent) were especially common; 71.4 percent of respondents reporting at least one of these diet-related symptoms.

The toll of constant commercial sexual exploitation and physical abuse on the victims led to a range of additional conditions. Physical injuries were rampant, with nearly 70 percent of victims reported physical injuries, most commonly to the head or face. Symptoms not conventionally associated with sexual abuse were only slightly less common: 67.9 percent of respondents experienced some type of cardiovascular or respiratory difficulty and 61.3 percent suffered from gastrointestinal symptoms while being trafficked. More than half of the survivors (54.3 percent) reported dental problems, tooth loss being the most common problem (42.9 percent). In respondents, 71 percent reported at least one pregnancy, whereas 22 percent reported five pregnancies or more while being trafficked (Lederer and Wetzel 2014).

In the first study in the UK, women and adolescent girls were asked about twenty-six physical symptoms they experienced in the past two weeks and to rate how much this symptom bothered them. Headaches (82 percent), feeling easily tired (81 percent), dizzy spells (70 percent), back pain (69 percent), memory difficulty (62 percent), stomach pain (61 percent), pelvic pain (59 percent), and gynecological infections (58 percent) were among the most common and severely felt symptoms (Zimmerman 2008).

Another early study looked mainly at health-care interactions of survivors, including whether they were screened for human trafficking. This study found that the majority of interactions of survivors were at emergency rooms, urgent care, and slightly fewer at primary care health facilities. It found that the most common health problems experienced by participants while being trafficked included suffering physical abuse (66 percent, $n = 113$), self-diagnosed depression (65 percent, $n = 112$), headache (45 percent, $n = 78$), and back pain (42 percent, $n = 72$). Other common problems reported were weight loss, menstruation problems, and nausea/vomiting (Chisolm-Straker et al. 2016).

In the first national study, survivors were overwhelmingly traumatized not only physically but also mentally. Being trafficked created psychological conditions in many of these victims and exploited existing mental instability in others. All but two of those who responded to the survey (98.1 percent) reported at least one psychological issue during the time they were trafficked, and survivors noted an average of more than a dozen. The most frequently reported problems included depression (88.7 percent), anxiety (76.4 percent), nightmares (73.6 percent), flashbacks (68.0 percent), low self-esteem (81.1 percent), and feelings of shame or guilt (82.1 percent).

A substantial number of survivors suffered from other psychological disorders, including acute stress (38.7 percent), bipolar (30.2 percent), depersonalization (19.8 percent), multiple personality (13.2 percent), and borderline personality (13.2 percent) disorders. Two additional and particularly chilling reporting rates confirm the extent of mental trauma that survivors suffered: 41.5 percent had attempted suicide (one victim reported nine such attempts) and 54.7 percent suffered from PTSD.

The psychological consequences that the trafficking victims in these focus groups reported were wide-ranging, severe, and in some cases nearly universal. As with physical symptoms, the findings on the psychological consequences of trafficking are consistent with other studies. Even the escape from their trafficking circumstances was far from a remedy for the psychological suffering of survivors. When reporting on their health experiences after trafficking, 96.4 percent of survivors reported at least one psychological symptom and an average of 10.5 mental health issues. This indicates that there were only minor improvements in the number of psychological problems experienced following escape or exit from their trafficking situations. Sex trafficking took a lasting mental and emotional as well as physical toll on nearly every survivor in the study (Lederer and Wetzel 2014).

The first studies in Europe also noted mental health issues. Compared with a general US population of adult women, the study participants' symptoms were in the 95th percentile and in the 51st percentile compared with female psychiatric patients. Symptoms associated with depression were most often reported, with 39 percent of the participants acknowledging having had suicidal thoughts within the past seven days. The same study found that 57 percent of the women and adolescent girls were victims of PTSD according to criteria of the Harvard Trauma Questionnaire (Zimmerman 2008).

One international report reviewing a number of countries showed that depression, anxiety, PTSD, and self-harm and attempted suicide are common among survivors in contact with refuge services (Ottisova 2016). In another study in England, researchers found that symptoms of depression, anxiety and PTSD were reported by 78 percent of women and 40 percent of men survivors (Oram et al. 2015). In a study of trafficked people in Greater Mekong sub-region, 61 percent of men and 67 percent of women, as well as 57 percent of children, reported probable depression (i.e., symptoms indicative of depression as measured by a standardized screening tool) and probable PTSD was reported by 46 percent of men, 44 percent of women, and 27 percent of children (Kiss 2015).

The 2014 study was also the first to ask survivors about gynecological, reproductive, and procreative health issues. In the survey, survivors also reported significant numbers of reproductive health problems while they were being trafficked. Most notably, more than two-thirds of survivors (67.3 percent) contracted some form of sexually transmitted infection (STI). Survivors reported significantly higher rates of chlamydia (39.4 percent) and gonorrhea (26.9 percent) than the next most common disease (Hepatitis C, 15.4 percent). Well over half of the survivors (63.8 percent) reported at least one gynecological symptom other than STDs/STIs, with pain during sex (46.2 percent), urinary tract infections (43.8 percent), and vaginal discharge (33.3 percent) among the most common such symptoms. The extent of reproductive health issues that survivors reported is hardly surprising due to the extreme levels of sexual abuse these women endured. On average, the respondents reported being used for sex by approximately thirteen buyers per day (Lederer and Wetzel 2014).

Since that time, the same author conducted a pilot study of thirty-one survivors in four US cities looking at their gynecological, reproductive, and procreative health issues (Lederer, Flores, and Chandler 2023). It found that gynecological health issues were widespread and severe among the survivor participants. Out of thirty-one survivor participants, twenty-nine reported experiencing at least one gynecological infection, illness, or symptom while being trafficked. Some participants reported ten or more problems. Seventy-four percent of the survivors surveyed reported contracting at least one sexually transmitted infection (STI) while being trafficked. Shockingly, among the thirty-one survivor respondents, there were at least 119 pregnancies, with abortion and miscarriage as common pregnancy outcomes. Thirty-five percent of all pregnancies ended in abortion. Eighty-two percent of the survivor participants reported feeling regret over their past abortion, but only a small minority reported being aware of abortion alternatives: 22.6 percent knew about Pregnancy Resource Centers, 19.4 percent were aware of adoption alternatives, and only 3.2 percent were aware of Safe Havens and Safe Haven laws (Lederer, Flores, and Chandler 2023).

This pilot study also explored childbirth and childrearing in the context of trafficking. Among the survivors, forty-four children were born while they were being trafficked. Nineteen survivors reported keeping their child or children and raising them. Ten survivors reported that their children were raised by relatives, taken by authorities, or even taken by the trafficker. Thirty-seven percent of survivor participants reported receiving full prenatal care, while 13.4 percent received partial prenatal care while pregnant and being trafficked (Lederer, Flores, and Chandler 2023).

As to general health care, in the pilot study, 90 percent of victims said that they sought healthcare; 80 percent sought health care in Emergency Rooms in hospitals; 58 percent sought care in neighborhood or urgent care clinics; 35 percent sought care from private physicians. When they were asked to characterize their general interactions with health-care providers, only 9.7 percent reported agreeing with the statement that health-care providers understood what was happening to them. Only 12.9 percent believed the care they received was "excellent." Only 9.7 percent reported that medical professionals were "trauma informed" and only 9.7 percent reported that the medical professional followed up with them or provided aftercare, and only 6.5 percent reported receiving helpful referrals (Lederer, Flores, and Chandler 2023).

In the US study, researchers also looked at injuries from violence by the trafficker or the buyer. The survey asked survivors if they had experienced violence, listing twelve possible forms. These included being threatened with a weapon, shot, strangled, burned, kicked, punched, beaten, stabbed, raped, or penetrated with a foreign object. Nearly all the survivors (92.2 percent) reported being the victim of at least one form of physical violence. Many survivors had suffered more than half of these experiences. Respondents reported an average of 6.25 of the twelve forms of violence. Likewise, most of these abuses were the rule rather than the exception; eight of the twelve were reported by half or more of the respondents, including behaviors as extreme as strangulation (Lederer and Wetzel 2014).

In 2021, researchers analyzed data from the IOM Victim of Trafficking Database, the largest database on human trafficking worldwide, on 10,369 cases of trafficking victims who had reported violence. They found 54 percent reported physical and/or sexual violence; 50 percent physical violence; and 15 percent sexual violence, with 25 percent of women reporting sexual violence. Experiences of physical and sexual violence among trafficked victims were significantly higher among women and girls, individuals in sexual exploitation, and those experiencing other forms of abuse and deprivation, such as threats and forced use of alcohol and drugs. In labor trafficking, violence was frequently associated with trafficking into manufacturing, agriculture, and begging (greater than 55 percent) (Stöckl et al. 2021).

While few other studies specifically on violence in human trafficking have been conducted, a 2023 paper asserted that just as cases of intimate partner violence are being missed in screening when patients present with injuries, so too, human trafficking cases are not being identified when patients present with injuries. The authors give two examples, one a sex trafficking case and the second a labor trafficking case:

> Case 1: While awaiting imaging after a high-speed motor vehicle collision, the patient is asking how much longer she needs to be in hospital because she is concerned her partner will be upset that he has not heard from her. You explain that there is ongoing concern for possible serious injuries based on her abdominal pain. She becomes increasingly anxious and is requesting her telephone, repeating that her partner is going to be upset if she cannot reach him. You reassure the patient that you will provide her with a telephone to call her partner after she is taken to computed tomography (CT Scan).

> Case 2: The trauma team receives an alert that a man is being transported for a limb-threatening injury; his arm was caught in machinery at work. On arrival, paramedics relay additional information that the patient is concerned

about seeking medical attention because his temporary foreign worker permit expired, and he is no longer formally employed. As the team prepares to address the limb-threatening injury, the trauma physician identifies that after critical limb care is provided, efforts to reach his family were unsuccessful. (Sampsel, Deutscher, and Duchesne 2023)

Finally, substance use disorder, drug addiction, and drug overdose, are common health issues in human trafficking. In the US study, many survivors were dependent on drugs or alcohol while they were trafficked either because the substances were forced on them as a control mechanism by their traffickers or because substance use was a means of coping with the immense abuse they suffered. More than 84 percent used alcohol, drugs, or both during their captivity and more than a quarter (27.9 percent) said that forced substance use was a part of their trafficking experience. More than a quarter of victims reported injected drugs and overdoses (27.2 percent and 26.0 percent, respectively). Alcohol, marijuana, and cocaine were the most common substances, but others were prevalent as well.

Since the time of that study, with the prevalence of opioids, fentanyl, and other prescription drugs, new studies found that while 70 percent of participants engaged in daily heroin use, 11.6 percent reported daily opioid pill use (Footer et al. 2019). The opioid crisis is a public health epidemic for which structural factors need to be assessed. A human trafficker can exploit an individual's opioid addiction to coerce the individual into human trafficking. An anti-trafficking service provider in Maine reported that 66 percent of clients' substance abuse led to their being trafficked, whereas only 4.5 percent reported that their addiction was a result of being trafficked (Smith, Stoklosa, and Corrigan 2016).

Further Reading

Chisolm-Straker, Makini, Susie Baldwin, Bertille Gaïgbé-Togbé, Nneka Ndukwe, Pauline N. Johnson, and Lynne D. Richardson. 2016. "Health Care and Human Trafficking: We are Seeing the Unseen." *Journal of Health Care for the Poor and Underserved* 27, no. 3: 1220–33. doi: 10.1353/hpu.2016.0131.

Footer, Katherine H. A., Ju Nyeong Park, Sean T. Allen, Michele R. Decker, Bradley E. Silberzahn, Steve Huettner, Noya Galai, and Susan G. Sherman. 2019. "Police-Related Correlates of Client-Perpetrated Violence Among Female Sex Workers in Baltimore City, Maryland." *American Journal of Public Health* 109, no. 2: 289–95. https://doi.org/10.2105/AJPH.2018.304809.

Greenbaum, Jordan, James E. Crawford-Jakubiak, Committee On Child Abuse And Neglect, Cindy W. Christian, James E. Crawford-Jakubiak, Emalee G. Flaherty, John M. Leventhal, James L. Lukefahr, Robert D. Sege. 2015. "Child Sex Trafficking and Commercial Sexual Exploitation: Health Care Needs of Victims." *Pediatrics* 135, no. 3: 566–74. 10.1542/peds.2014–4138.

Kiss, Ligia, Nicola S Pocock, Varaporn Naisanguansri, Soksreymom Suos, Brett Dickson, Doan Thuy, Jobst Koehler, Kittiphan Sirisup, Nisakorn Pongrungsee, and Van Anh Nguyen. 2015. "Health of Men, Women, and Children in Post-Trafficking Services in Cambodia, Thailand, and Vietnam: An Observational Cross-sectional Study." *Lancet Global Health* 3, no. 3: 154–61. https://doi.org/10.1016/S2214-109X(15)70016-1.

Lederer, Laura J., and Christopher A. Wetzel. 2014. "The Health Consequences of Sex Trafficking and Their Implications for Identifying Victims in Healthcare Facilities." *Annals of Health Law* 23, no. 1: 61–91. https://www.icmec.org/wp-content/uplo ads/2015/10/Health-Consequences-of-Sex-Trafficking-and-Implications-for-Iden tifying-Victims-Lederer.pdf. Accessed June 25, 2023.

Lederer, Laura, Theresa Flores, and McKamie Chandler. 2023. "The Pregnancy Continuum in Domestic Sex Trafficking in the United States." *Issues in Law and Medicine* 38, no. 1. https://www.globalcenturion.org/the-pregnancy-continuum-in-domestic-sex-trafficking/. Accessed June 25, 2023.

Oram, Siân, Mizanur Khondoker, Melanie Abas, Matthew Broadbent, and Louise M Howard. 2015. "Characteristics of Trafficked Adults and Children with Severe Mental Illness: A Historical Cohort Study." *Lancet Psychiatry* 2, no. 12: 1084–91. https://doi.org/10.1016/S2215-0366(15)00290-4.

Ottisova, L., S. Hemmings, L. M. Howard, C. Zimmerman, and S. Oram. 2016. "Prevalence and Risk of Violence and the Mental, Physical and Sexual Health Problems Associated with Human Trafficking: an Updated Systematic Review." *Epidemiology and Psychiatric Sciences* 25, no. 4: 317–41. doi: 10.1017/S2045796016000135.

Powell, Colin L. 2002. *Remarks at the Rollout of the 2004 Trafficking in Persons Annual Report*. Presented in Washington, DC. June 14. https://2001-2009.state.gov/secret ary/former/powell/remarks/33525.htm. Accessed June 25, 2023.

Sampsel, Kari, Julianna Deutscher, and Emma Duchesne. 2023. "Intimate Partner Violence and Human Trafficking: Trauma We May Not Identify." *Emergency Medicine Clinics of North America* 41, no. 1: 101–16. https://doi.org/10.1016/j. emc.2022.09.013.

Smith A., H. Stoklosa, C. Corrigan, and L. Foley. 2016. "The Intersection of Substance Abuse and Human Trafficking." Paper presented at Office for Victims of Crime Human Trafficking Regional Training Forum. Providence, RI, August 24.

Stöckl, Heidi, Camilla Fabbri, Harry Cook, Claire Galez-Davis, Naomi Grant, Yuki Lo, Ligia Kiss, and Cathy Zimmerman. 2021. "Human Trafficking and Violence: Findings from the Largest Global Dataset of Trafficking Survivors." *Journal of Migration and Health* 4. https://doi.org/10.1016/j.jmh.2021.100073.

World Health Organization. 2022. "Mental Disorders." World Health Organization, June 8. https://www.who.int/news-room/fact-sheets/detail/mental-disorders. Accessed June 25, 2023.

Zimmerman, Cathy, Mazeda Hossain, Katherine Yun, Vasil Gajdadziev, Natalia Guzun, Maria Tchomarova, Rosa Angela Ciarrocchi, Anna Johansson, Anna Kefurtova, and Stefania Scodanibbio. 2008. "The Health of Trafficked Women: A Survey of Women Entering Posttrafficking Services in Europe." *American Journal of Public Health* 98, no. 1: 55–9. https://doi.org/10.2105/AJPH.2006.108357.

Q22. Do Other Forms of Human Trafficking Exist?

Answer: Yes, several other forms of trafficking are recognized in the Protocol to Prevent, Suppress, and Punish Trafficking in Persons, an international Protocol attached to the United Nations Convention against Transnational Organized Crime. These types of trafficking crimes—organ trafficking, organ harvesting, trafficking for purposes of begging and/or peddling—were not addressed in the Trafficking Victims Protection Act of 2000.

The legislation was the first legally binding instrument with an internationally recognized definition of human trafficking. This definition, according to the United Nations, "provides a vital tool for the identification of victims, whether men, women or children, and for the detection of all forms of exploitation which constitute human trafficking. Countries that ratify this treaty must criminalize human trafficking and develop anti-trafficking laws in line with the Protocol's legal provisions."

The US Trafficking Victims Protection Act prohibits the recruitment, harboring, transportation, provision, or obtaining persons (by force, fraud, or coercion) for two purposes: *forced labor and commercial sex*, whereas the definition of the Protocol says that the recruiting, transporting, harboring, or receipt of a person, for the purpose of "exploitation shall include, at a minimum, the exploitation of the prostitution of others or other forms of sexual exploitation, forced labour or services, slavery or practices similar to slavery, servitude or the removal of organs."

An older 1984 Organ and Transplant Act prohibits organ trafficking, but it may be insufficient to cover today's forms of trafficking. In recent years, legislators in the United States have introduced several bills to address organ trafficking and organ harvesting, but to date Congress has not passed any new law on the subject. Other forms of trafficking that are recognized under the international definition of trafficking, but not specifically addressed in the US definition are begging, peddling, forced drug trafficking (mules), and other forced illegal activities, especially when children are involved.

The Facts: Organ trafficking is a crime that is difficult to track for a number of reasons. First, though it shouldn't be, it has been unfairly associated with the legitimate lifesaving procedure of organ donation. In the United States, the trafficking of organs is prohibited in the larger National Organ and Transplant Act of 1984. The entire act is devoted to creating an infrastructure for the legal donation of and transplantation of human organs, defined as "the human (including fetal) kidney, liver, heart, lung, pancreas, bone marrow, cornea, eye, bone, and skin or any subpart thereof and any other human organ (or any subpart thereof, including that derived from a fetus)." The traffic in human organs is prohibited in Title III of the National Organ and Transplant Act of 1984 titled: Prohibition of Organ Purchases. It states that "It shall be unlawful for any person to knowingly acquire, receive, or otherwise transfer any *human organ for valuable consideration.*" And follows with the penalty: "Any person who violates (a) shall be *fined $50,000 or imprisoned 5 years* or both."

Some history will help shed light on the nature and scope of this growing problem. For many centuries, while various forms of slavery and trafficking in persons flourished, medical science had no ability to take a live organ from one person and transplant it into another person to keep the recipient alive. Only in the twentieth century did doctors make medical progress in this field. A short view of the first successful organ transplantations shows the development of the field over a century, and indeed, the rapid development of the field in the latter half of the twentieth century.

1905: First successful cornea transplant by Eduard Zirm (Czech Republic)

1954: First successful kidney transplant by J. Harrison and Joseph Murray (Boston, United States)

1966: First successful pancreas transplant by Richard Lillehei and William Kelly (Minnesota, United States)

1967: First successful liver transplant by Thomas Starzl (Denver, United States)

1967: First successful heart transplant by Christian Barnard (Cape Town, South Africa)

1981: First successful heart/lung transplant by Bruce Reitz (Stanford, United States)

1983: First successful lung lobe transplant by Joel Cooper (Toronto, Canada)

1984: First successful double organ transplant by Starzl and Bahnson (Pittsburgh, United States)

1986: First successful double-lung transplant (Ann Harrison) by Joel Cooper (Toronto, Canada)

1995: First successful laparoscopic live-donor nephrectomy by Ratner and Kavoussi (Balt, Maryland)

1997: First successful transplantation of a human knee joint by Gunther O. Hofmann

1998: First successful live-donor partial pancreas transplant by David Sutherland (Minnesota, United States)

1998: First successful hand transplant (France)

1999: First successful Tissue Engineered Bladder transplanted by Anthony Atala (Boston, United States)

2005: First successful partial face transplant (France)

2006: First jaw transplant combining donor jaw by Eric M. Genden Mount Sinai Hospital, New York)

2008: First successful complete full double arm transplant by Biemer et al. (Germany)

2008: First baby born from transplanted ovary by James Randerson

2008: First transplant of a trachea human windpipe by Paolo Macchiarini (Barcelona, Spain)

2008: First successful transplantation of 80 percent of face, by Maria Siemionow (Cleveland, United States)

2010: First full facial transplant, by Dr. Joan Pere Barret and team (Barcelona, Spain)

2011: First double leg transplant by Dr. Cavadas and team (Valencia's Hospital La Fe, Spain)

Today, the US Department of Health and Human Services keeps a running record of the number of people in the United States waiting for an organ transplant, the number of people who die each day waiting for a transplant, and the number of transplants performed each year (Figure 8). In 2022, 104,230 were on the official transplant waiting list. Over 42,000 transplants were performed in 2022. The gap in supply versus the demand for organs is what creates the market for illegal organ harvesting and organ trafficking. According to experts it is a thriving market.

A similar gap exists internationally. Statistics across nations worldwide are harder to come by, but the UN confirmed a total of 144,302 organ transplants worldwide in 2021, an increase of 5.9 percent from the year before. There is no known accurate figure for how many people need organ transplants worldwide,

Patients on the Waiting List by Organ
As of July 2023

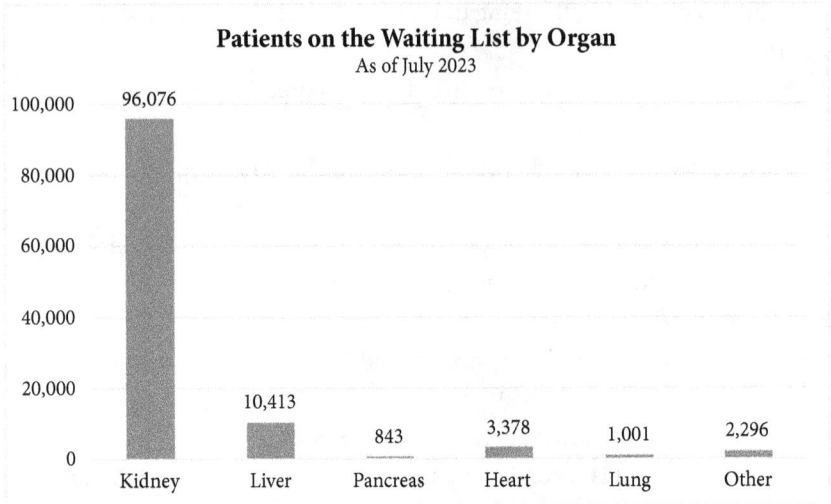

Figure 8 Patients on waiting list by organ, July 2023.

Transplants Performed by Organ
In 2022

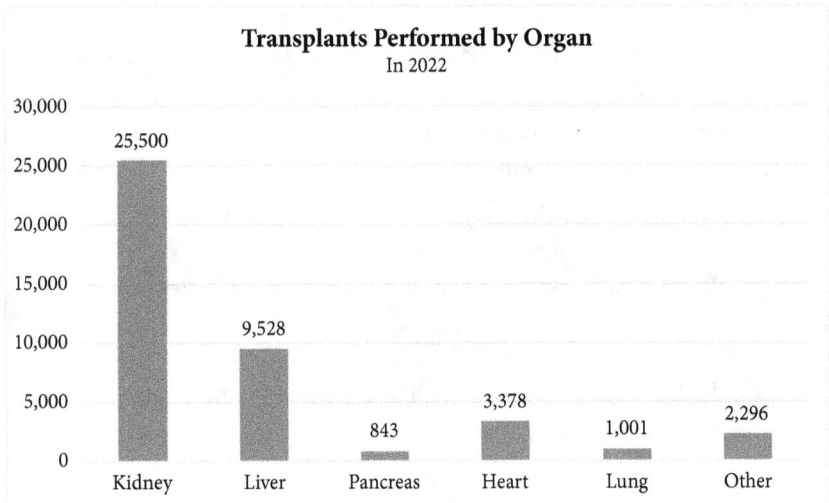

Figure 9 Transplants performed by organ, 2022.

but the demand is great. The most wanted organs are kidneys, livers, lungs, skin, eyes, and ovaries. Donor bases vary in developing nations. Organ transplantation is frequently the best or only treatment for end-stage organ failure. The need for organs, especially from potential recipients in resource-rich countries, has led to a black market (sometimes known as the "red market" in organ harvesting and trafficking) (Carney 2011).

Reports of trafficking for organs began surfacing in the early twenty-first century, especially in resource-poor countries. In India, in 2008, police arrested an organ trafficking and harvesting ring in New Delhi that allegedly used force, fraud, or coercion to obtain kidneys from laborers. By the time the ring was busted it had taken more than 500 kidneys from mostly male workers and sold them on the black market. Investigators say the ring operated for years and included a doctor who scouted potential locations where multiple men could be operated on at a time. The men complained that they went into the hospital for checkups and came out without a kidney.

India subsequently passed a law strictly prohibiting organ harvesting and organ trafficking, but as recently as 2016, there was another case, also in New Delhi, in which a prestigious Indian hospital was duped by traffickers into removing the kidneys of victims who were falsely presented as relatives of needy patients. Police arrested five people, including two assistants of a senior doctor of the hospital. The traffickers allegedly lured poor people into selling their kidneys for 300,000 rupees ($4,480) and then sold the organs on the black market at huge profit (Bhalla 2016).

In the Philippines, the National Bureau of Investigation (NBI) sent out an alert about the smuggling of kidneys. The NBI said organ traffickers even kidnapped children and took them abroad, where valuable organs were surgically removed and sold to foreign nationals.

In the United States a kidney trafficking ring allegedly operating for over ten years was raided by the FBI. Organ traffickers obtained "donors" from Israel paying them $10,000 per kidney. They sold the kidneys to recipients in the United States for $160,000, making approximately $150,000 per kidney. The trafficker admitted that from January 2006 through February 2009, he conspired with others to provide a service, in exchange for large payments, to individuals seeking kidney transplants by obtaining kidneys from paid donors. The defendant admitted that he was paid approximately $120,000, $150,000, and $140,000, respectively, on behalf of these three recipients. He pled guilty in the first ever US federal conviction on charges of brokering illegal kidney transplants for profit (US Attorney's Office 2011). Other black market rings trafficking in kidneys have been found in South Africa, China, Pakistan, Turkey, Brazil, and Columbia.

In 2006 alone, 11,000 transplants were performed in China using organs taken from executed prisoners. There were 8,000 kidney transplants, 3,000 liver transplants, and approximately 200 hundred heart transplants (Budiani-Saberi and Delmonico 2008).

Many of those executed were political prisoners (including members of the Falun Gong religious movement) (Treasure 2007). One doctor who performs heart transplants explored the plausibility of this claim in a peer-reviewed journal article and said that factors that make the allegations plausible are the partitioning of the logistic elements and technical steps just as described for transplantation anywhere, and the necessity for haste. What makes it credible in his view is the numerical gap between the reported number of transplants compared with what is possible in other countries, the short waiting times and the confidence with which operations are offered in the global health market, and the routine blood testing of the Falun Gong (Treasure 2007).

Some researchers believe that as many as 41,500 organs of political prisoners were harvested in China. Upon execution their organs were harvested and taken to hospitals, some of them built across the street from the prisons, where "transplant tourists" awaited them. The term "transplant tourism" was coined to describe a patient in need of a transplant who flies to another country to purchase an organ and have it transplanted. In 2007 China adopted the Human Transplantation Act that bans commercialism around organ transplants. Since then, China reportedly has reduced the number of transplants to foreign patients by 50 percent. However, experts note that the reduction in Chinese activity has presumably been supplanted by transplant tourism and organ trafficking in other countries where laws against organ trafficking do not exist or are poorly enforced (Matas and Kilgour 2007).

In 2015 China implemented a new set of rules they claim stopped the removal of organs for transplantation from executed prisoners and replaced it with a voluntary system (Congressional Research Service [CRS] 2021). In 2021, China adopted a provision in its first Civil Code that prohibited the sale of human organs and any donations obtained by force or coercion (CRS 2021).

Corneal transplantation is a surgical procedure where a damaged or diseased cornea is replaced by donated corneal tissue. It is one of the earliest successful transplant techniques developed. The surgical procedure is performed by an ophthalmologist, but can be done on an outpatient basis (the patient goes home following surgery). The donor can be of any age.

Dozens of cases of human trafficking involving the cornea have been reported, mainly in countries where other forms of organ trafficking are flourishing. In 2010 authorities in Yemen arrested a broker involved in trafficking human organs of Yemeni citizens. Over 200 Yemeni victims of human organ trade sold their kidneys or corneas of their eyes for amounts ranging between $5,000 and $7,000. In China in 2019, an egregious case was reported of a young boy having his eyes gouged out for organ trafficking (Mail Foreign Service 2013). Over 300,000 are awaiting corneal transplants in China alone (Mail Foreign Service 2013).

In Cyprus, in 2010, police closed a fertility clinic under charges of trafficking in human eggs. The Petra Clinic, as it was known locally, imported women from Ukraine and Russia for egg harvesting and sold the genetic material to foreign fertility tourists. This "reproductive trafficking" is another form of human trafficking that is apparently flourishing. Allegations in this case, and several other in Spain, the United States, Mexico, and Israel include operating a fertility clinic without a license, paying donors coercive sums, and performing non-medically necessary sex selection. In the Petra Clinic, egg donors were being routinely hyper-stimulated to produce sixty or more eggs, and batches were split up between multiple recipients. Most doctors consider more than fourteen eggs dangerous. In another case in Romania, doctors were removing victims' eggs and selling them to foreign couples eager to pay large sums for in vitro and other reproductive technologies.

Between 2003 and 2004, five employees at a tissue bank in the Czech Republic sold over 7 million crowns (Czech currency = $450,000) of skin grafts to Dutch companies. In the United States, a terrible case of trafficking of skin from across the border in Tijuana, Mexico, to US burn graft clinics was uncovered in 2010. A former police officer-turned-private detective and a doctor were charged in the case.

Since the first terrible case was reported in the early 2000s, many countries have taken action. Internationally, the Transplantation Society held an International Summit on Transplant Tourism and Organ Trafficking in Istanbul in 2008. The summit sought to address, "the urgent and growing problems of organ sales, transplant tourism and trafficking in organ donors." Out of the Summit came "The Declaration of Istanbul on Organ Trafficking and Transplant Tourism." The Istanbul Declaration included principles and proposals relating to strengthening legal and ethical organ transplants and preventing organ trafficking, transplant commercialism, and transplant tourism. The declaration includes provisions calling for countries to maximize the number of organs available for transplantation and prohibiting advertising for organ trafficking, organ tourism, and related activities.

In the United States, meanwhile, Congress has introduced several pieces of legislation related to organ trafficking. The Stop Predatory Organ Trafficking Act (H.R. 1434) and the Stop Forced Organ Trafficking Act (H.R. 1592 and S. 602) would authorize various visa and passport restrictions on individuals identified as being involved in organ trafficking and require reporting by the State Department on organ trafficking, in addition to other provisions. A discussion draft before the House Committee on Financial Services, the Organ Trafficking and Suspicious Activity Reports (SARs) Form Act, would direct Treasury's Financial Crimes Enforcement Network to inform financial institutions that organ trafficking is considered a type of human trafficking for the purpose of filing a Suspicious Activity Report (SAR). Legislation introduced in previous Congresses has also sought to address organ trafficking, such as the STOP Organ Trafficking Act (H.R. 2121), which included passport restrictions and would have amended the TVPA to include "trafficking in persons for purposes of the removal of organs" to the definition of severe forms of trafficking in persons, as well as other provisions."

None of these bills have passed, but they do create a background and infrastructure in which further action can be taken. For example, the STOP Organ Trafficking Act stipulated the following:

- kidnapping or coercion of individuals to extract their organs for profit contradicts the standards for ethical behavior upon which the United States has based its laws;
- harvesting of organs from living children, regardless of the level of brain activity, is a violation of the human rights of the child and is a breach of internationally accepted medical ethical standards;
- illegal harvesting and trafficking of human organs violates the Universal Declaration of Human Rights; and
- efficient national organ donation systems with effective enforcement mechanisms that ensure voluntary organ donations are the most effective way to combat trafficking in human organs.

It also defined trafficking in human organs, which has been a continuing problem in international criminal justice and law enforcement communities. Experts have debated the difference between organ trafficking, organ harvesting, and organ tourism, with no agreed-upon definitions to date.

The STOP Act defined "trafficking in human organs" as:

- the recruitment, transportation, transfer, harboring, or receipt of a person, either living or dead, for the purpose of removing one or more of the person's organs by coercion, abduction, deception, abuse of power, or transfer of payments or benefits; or
- the illicit transportation and transplantation of those organs in one or more other persons for profit or any other purpose.

"Organ" is defined as the human (including fetal) kidney, liver, heart, lung, pancreas, bone marrow, cornea, eye, bone, and skin or any subpart thereof, and any other human organ or subpart (including that derived from a fetus) specified by the president.

Two other provisions in the act provided for "trafficking in human organs" to be included in the definition of "severe forms of trafficking in persons," and for "the Interagency Task Force To Monitor and Combat Trafficking to be is tasked with collecting and organizing data from human rights officers at U.S. embassies on host country's laws against trafficking in human organs and any instances of violations of such laws."

Other recommendations for combating organ trafficking included harmonizing all the various phrases and definitions currently in use around organ trafficking, filling in information gaps pertaining to the nature and scope of organ trafficking globally, reducing US demand for trafficked organs, and restricting US-funded medical training and sale of medical equipment that could be used for organ trafficking and organ transplantation. It also called upon professional medical organizations and human rights NGOs to play a bigger role in countering organ trafficking (Congressional Research Service 2021).

Further Reading

Bhalla, Nita. 2016. "Top Indian Hospital Says Duped into Removing Kidneys for Organ Traffickers." *Reuters*, June 6. https://www.reuters.com/article/us-india-trafficking-org ans/top-indian-hospital-says-duped-into-removing-kidneys-for-organ-traffickers-idUSKCN0YS1Z9. Accessed June 25, 2023.

Budiani-Saberi, D. A., and F. L. Delmonico. 2008. "Organ Trafficking and Transplant Tourism: A Commentary on the Global Realities." *American Journal of Transplantation* 8, no. 5: 925–9. https://doi.org/10.1111/j.1600-6143.2008.02200.x.

Carney, Scott. 2011. "Blood, Bones and Organs: An Interview with Author Scott Carney (The Red Market)." By NPR. npr.org. June 10. https://www.npr.org/2011/06/10/136931615/blood-bones-and-organs-the-gruesome-red-market.

Congressional Research Service. 2021. *International Organ Trafficking: In Brief.* R46996: 1–13. https://sgp.fas.org/crs/row/R46996.pdf.

Mail Foreign Service. 2013. "Parents' Horror as Chinese boy, 6, Has His Eyes Gouged Out After Being 'Kidnapped by Organ Trafficker Who Stole Both His Corneas.'" *Daily Mail*, August 27. https://www.dailymail.co.uk/news/article-2402741/Parents-horror-Chinese-boy-6-eyes-GOUGED-OUT-kidnapped-organ-trafficker-stole-corn eas.html. Accessed June 25, 2023.

Matas, David, and David Kilgour. 2007. *An Independent Investigation into Allegations of Organ Harvesting of Falun Gong Practitioners in China.* January 31. https://organh arvestinvestigation.net/. Accessed June 25, 2023.

Treasure, Tom. 2007. "The Falun Gong, Organ Transplantation, the Holocaust and Ourselves." *Journal of the Royal Society of Medicine* 100, no. 3:119–21. doi:10.1177/014107680710000308.

US Attorney's Office. 2011. "Brooklyn Man Pleads Guilty in First Ever Federal Conviction for Brokering Illegal Kidney Transplants for Profit." Federal Bureau of Investigation. https://archives.fbi.gov/archives/newark/press-releases/2011/brook lyn-man-pleads-guilty-in-first-ever-federal-conviction-for-brokering-illegal-kidney-transplants-for-profit. Accessed June 25, 2023.

6

The Long Arc of Slavery

Man is the only Slave. And he is the only animal who enslaves. He has always been a slave in one form or another and has always held other slaves in bondage under him in one way or another.

—Mark Twain

The Reverend Martin Luther King said that "the arc of the moral universe is long, but it bends toward justice." The first article in this closing chapter explores the history of slavery. It is a subject that has been studied by a multitude of scholars—perhaps most famously Orlando Patterson, a historical and cultural sociologist at Harvard University. In his book *Slavery and Social Death* (1982), Patterson provided what was and is still considered the definitive historical analysis of the institution of slavery.

Patterson built on the work of earlier scholars—such as George Murdock, who provided a comparative study of 185 world cultures, in which he identified 65 cultures he considered slave-holding cultures, and Ephraim Isaac, also at Harvard, who taught a course titled, The History and Concept of Slavery—to demonstrate that "slavery was firmly established in all the great early centers of human civilization," and that "far from declining [it] actually increased in significance with the growth of all the epochs and cultures that modern Western peoples consider watersheds in their historical development."

The closing article examines the history and evolution of the anti-slavery movement in the United States. It looks at four approaches to ending African Chattel slavery in the United States: (1) the first faith-based efforts to eradicate slavery in church communities, (2) the secular abolitionists who emerged from the faith-based movements, (3) feminist activists who had roots in the secular abolitionist movements, and (4) an emerging human rights movement that defined trafficking and modern-day slavery as an abuse of human rights. These early anti-slavery advocates each had their own thought leaders, their own primary source materials that motivated them, and their own programs of action that propelled them. Through their lives and works they demonstrated the timeless words of the late Congressman John Lewis: "Freedom is the continuous action we all must take, and each generation must do its part to create an even more fair, more just society."

Q23. How Long Has Slavery Been in Existence?

Answer: Historians say slavery existed in even the earliest and simplest societies, and that it was widespread in almost every ancient civilization, from Babylonian, Sumerian, Egyptian, and other ancient Middle Eastern societies to the city states of classical Greece, the Roman Empire, China and Japan, Africa, South Asia, and the Americas (Hunt 2002). As far back as 6800 BCE there were signs of slavery in Mesopotamia, where conquered peoples were forced into slavery (Bales 2005). In 2575 BCE Egyptian temple art celebrated the capture of Nubian slaves in battle (History Press 2023). Egyptians capture slaves by sending special expeditions up the Nile River (Bales 2005). The Bible mentions the Jewish people were enslaved by the Egyptians, escaping probably around 1186 BCE (Exod. 13:1 and 14:29) With a few exceptions, in almost every early culture, slavery existed, and in many civilizations, it was an accepted way of life. Even before there were written languages, there were depictions of slavery in the arts and crafts of societies, as well as objects used to enslave. Finally, with written records came documentation of the enslavement itself.

The Facts: It is generally believed that slavery existed over 6,000 years BCE in the Sumerian and Mesopotamian civilizations in what is now known as Iraq. The oldest known *written* reference to slavery is found in Law #15 in the Hammurabi Code of 1754 BCE: "If anyone takes a male or female slave of the court, or a male or female slave of a freed man, outside the city gates, he shall be put to death" (Yale University n.d.). In Greece, there is evidence that over 20,000 slaves were used to mine silver in ancient times (Bressan 2018), including a painting depicting enslaved people working in the mines in Laurium, Greece (Lowe 2019). In addition, in his description of the silver mines, Aristotle reported that one of the mine owners, Nikias, owned 6,000 slaves who worked in his mines. He also talked about other mine owners who owned 1,000 or 2,000 slaves (Aristotle). Other documentation is found in the mines themselves and on stone documentation (Hunt 2002; British Museum n.d.). A clay cuneiform tablet from 1480 BCE, now located in Room 54 of the British Museum in London, is a fugitive slave treaty between Idrimi of Alakakh and Pillia of Kizzuwatna (ancient Anatolia, what is now Turkey) (British Museum).

Scholars estimate that in Athens "as many as 80,000 to 100,000 people were enslaved between 450 and 210 BCE, amounting to one in four inhabitants, with an average household possessing three to four slaves (Emory University 2021). Slaves in ancient Athens were the property of their masters under Athenian law. By the late first century BCE in Rome and other parts of Italy, 1–1.5 million people were enslaved, representing 15–25 percent of the population. Both societies practiced "chattel slavery," a form of absolute servitude in which enslaved persons were owned as property and could be subjected to physical violence, sexual exploitation, torture, and death with impunity (Emory University 2021; Lowe 2019).

The Old Kingdom in Egypt is the period spanning *ca.* 2700–2200 BCE. The written record is sparse, but there is documentary evidence that rulers exempted certain classes of people (priests, royal family) from forced labor and that slaves were subjected to beatings (Loprieno 2012). One text, the *Instruction of Dua-Khety*, also known as The Satire of the Trades, was composed in the Middle Kingdom, which lasted from 2040 to 1782 BCE. This is a collection of sayings and instructions mostly ascribed to famous sages, and they discuss general matters of life and moral principles. According to one European scholar, "the human condition of the slave ... is alluded to in the Satire of Trades (also known as the Instruction of Khety, after the name of the narrator), a classical literary text of the early New Kingdom composed in order to describe the advantages of the scribal profession over all others" (Loprieno 2012). Here, different forms of forced labor are thematized: peasants are "drawn to work" or "obliged to work in the fields," the carpenter's children do not benefit from their father's hard work, a weaver is punished with fifty lashes for a day of absence from work, and a gardener is subject to a yoke (Loprieno 2012). In spite of the lack of explicit references to slavery, the text provides ample evidence for large-scale coercive labor (Loprieno 2012).

By the time of the New Kingdom, which ran from 712 to 332 BCE, thousands of references to slaves can be found in documents. A papyrus from the nineteenth Dynasty of Egypt references Syrian slaves, slave girls, foreign slaves captured as spoils of war, male and female slaves forced to labor in the temples, workhouses full of male and female slaves, slaves being bought and sold in slave markets, the branding of slaves to ascertain ownership, a captain's sale of foreign slaves, and many other references to a civilization that accepted slavery, especially slavery of foreign nationals (Archeological Museum of Bologna n.d.). Many such documents are found in the Egyptian Middle Kingdom era and particularly the New Kingdom era (Loprieno 2012). At the same time, paintings, sculpture, carvings in bas relief, and other artistic depictions include images of slave markets, slave beatings, captive slaves in chains, slave girls from brothels, and many other images that corroborate slave life in Egypt (Loprieno 2012).

A depiction in marble relief of Roman collared slaves in chains in 200 CE (Common Era), which was found in then Smyrna, of Hellenistic Greece (now Izmir, Turkey) is in the Ashmolean Museum of Art and Archaeology in Oxford, England (Ashmolean Museum of Art and Archaeology n.d.). In the National Museum of Rome-Baths of Diocletian, a slave collar from the fourth century CE is on display. Made of metal, the message on the metal tag reads, "UGI. TENE ME. CUM REVOCAVERIS ME D. M. ZONINO, ACCIPIS SOLIDUM," which means, "I have run away. Catch me. If you return me to my master Zoninus, you will receive a solidus." Slaves in Roman culture were tattooed with their master's name (Loprieno 2012). The Bible also tells of slavery of the Jewish people, and their exodus from Egypt in or around 1186 BCE.

At the same time in Asia and South Asia, ancient civilizations of the East also built slavery into their societies. For example, the first recognized dynasty in China, the Qin dynasty, ran from 221 to 205 BCE. While slavery was reported in China before that, in the Qin dynasty large numbers of slaves were used to build roads and canals, work the land, and construct buildings and walls. During the Qin dynasty, the Great Wall of China was built and fortified using as many as 300,000 slaves. Slave labor was quite extensive during this period. It is estimated that as much as 5 percent of the Chinese population was enslaved. According to scholars, this slave population was built up through capture during war, slave raiding, and enslavement of insolvent debtors. Many documents confirm that slavery was commonplace in China. The National Museum for Chinese Writing in Anyang, China, holds a slave contract written in Old Uyghur script. As another example, the Silk Museum collection in Hangzhou, China, includes a contract for the purchase of a slave during the Tang dynasty (661 CE) in Turpan, Xinjiang. The contract records the purchase of a fifteen-year-old slave for six bolts of plain silk and five Chinese coins.

There were a number of types of slaves in ancient India: (1) those born to enslaved mothers, (2) those purchased, (3) those captured in war or raids, and (4) those who voluntarily became slaves, such as to escape starvation during times of famine. Buddha, who lived between the sixth and fourth centuries BCE, mentions slavery in his discourses discussing slaves being beaten, put in chains, branded, or fed scraps as punishment for making mistakes.

Scholars note that although Buddhism was one of the earliest religions to condemn slavery, the practice was widespread in all Buddhist countries for centuries. Slavery is also referenced in the Sanskrit *Laws of Manu* of the first century BCE. The Edicts of Ashoka—a set of fourteen edicts handed down *ca.* third century BCE by Emperor Ashoka, a follower of Buddha—refer to the obligations of slaves to their masters. By the nineteenth century, when the British began to document the extent of slavery in its colonies, there were an estimated 8–9 million slaves in India.

Slavery was widely practiced in other areas of Asia including Thailand, Burma, the Philippines, Nepal, Indonesia, and Japan as well as by Central Asian advanced civilizations such as the Mongols, Kazakhs, and others. Whether Buddhist, Hindu, Islamic, or other religion, slavery seems to have been a part of all these civilizations (Hunt 2002).

In Europe, slavery was also a part of life. In 1086, King William carried out one of the first country-wide surveys of his kingdom. Records show that about 10 percent of the population entered in the survey were slaves, with the proportion reaching as much as 20 percent in some places. The Vikings (800–1050 CE) took slaves when they raided other countries. They used them in their homes, in fields, in construction, and traded them in international slave markets (Price 2020b). There are records of slavery in Scandinavia before the Viking era too. Mainland Europe (France, Germany, Poland, Spain, and other countries) also had slavery. Again, the Swedish Museum and other Scandinavian museums have shackles from the Viking towns of Birka, Sweden; Neu Nieköhr, Germany; and Trelleborg, Slagelse, Denmark (Raffield 2019). Experts note that Russia was essentially founded during the slave raiding by the Vikings, who moved from Scandinavia down through Southeastern Europe, and slavery remained a major institution there until the early 1720s, when the state converted the household slaves into house serfs in order to tax them.

The slave trade also thrived in ancient Africa. Slavery in Northern Africa is documented as far back as 1550–1080 BCE, when the Egyptians were bringing large numbers of slaves to work in agriculture and construction. Egyptians brought prisoners of war from Asia as far back as 2030 BCE to be traded as slaves. Long before the Atlantic slave trade began (sixteenth century), there was a flourishing slave trade in many parts of Africa. By the sixth century and up through medieval times, numerous slave trade routes were established. The trade is generally divided into indigenous trading (slaves traded in Africa to other Africans, usually by tribe or through kinship networks) and export trading (slaves traded from Africa to other countries and other parts of the world).

A map of the main slave trade routes in Arica in medieval times shows dozens of internal and external slave trade routes in the north, south, east, and west regions of Africa. In Central Africa there is a record of one king capturing and enslaving an entire village of people in what became the early "Kingdom of Kongo" (Thornton 2001). Precolonial Congo, also called the lower Congo, or the Kongo Kingdom together with the Gold Coast was the main source for the transatlantic slave trade for about 300 years. Native tribes of Africa assisted slave traders from other parts of the world to ship about 5 million slaves to Spanish, Portuguese, Dutch, Danish, French, British, and American territories of the New World. In addition, by the sixth century and up through medieval times, Arab slave traders established numerous slave trade routes. The east and north of the Congo were ravaged by the Arab slave trade for about 2,500 years.

Internally, a Central African slave trade, which consisted mainly of the enslavement of prisoners of war between African tribes, lasted over 10,000 years. Many museums in Africa and Europe have evidence of the slave trade, including neck chains, arm and hand chains, ankle and foot chains and rings, iron locks, and other examples of the mechanisms used to chain and transport chattel slaves. For example, the Netherlands Tropen Museum displays an iron ankle/foot ring used to imprison people in villages in the Upper Volta.

Before the Atlantic slave trade in the sixteenth century, scholars estimates that 18 million Africans were traded in Arab and African slave trade routes. Then, as the Atlantic slave trade began, another 7–10 million Africans were shipped as slaves to the Americas (Thornton 2001).

In the Americas some of the best-documented slave-owning societies were the Klamath, Pawnee, and the fishing societies, such as the Yurok, that lived along the Pacific coast. Some early records show that slaves were given away, traded, or even killed in potlatches—gift-giving ceremonies held by the Pacific Northwest indigenous peoples. Slavery is documented in dozens of other indigenous Indian societies in the Americas. During the four centuries between the arrival of Columbus and the beginning of the twentieth century, the Europeans enslaved 2.5–5 million Native peoples before the trans-Atlantic slave trade began as they were colonizing the Americas.

The sad fact is that slavery has been an institution in many ancient civilizations, societies, and communities, across race, religion, tribes, kinship networks, ethnicities, nationalities, countries, and regions around the world, and up through the twenty-first century. Although slavery is prohibited in every country in the world now, it still continues in practice.

Further Reading

Archeological Museum of Bologna. n.d. "Ancient Egypt Collection: Hieratic Papyrus with a Letter by Bakenamon to Ramose." http://www.museibologna.it/archeologic oen/percorsi/66288/id/74985/oggetto/74988/. Accessed June 25, 2023.

Ashmolean Museum of Art and Archaeology. n.d. *A Depiction in Marble Relief of Roman Collared Claves in Chains in 200 C.E.* Oxford, England. https://collecti ons.ashmolean.org/collection/search/new; https://commons.wikimedia.org/wiki/ File:Roman_collared_slaves_-_Ashmolean_Museum.jpg. Accessed June 25, 2023.

Bales, Kevin. 2005. *New Slavery: A Reference Handbook (Contemporary World Issues).* Stuttgart, Germany: Holtzbrinck.

Bressan, David. 2018. "How the Mines of Laurion Saved Ancient Greece and Made Western Civilization Possible." *Forbes*, December 17. https://www.forbes.com/sites/ davidbressan/2018/12/17/how-the-mines-of-laurion-saved-greece-and-by-extens ion-made-western-civilization-possible/?sh=3ca3f4595dae. Accessed September 19, 2023.

British Museum. n.d.a. *Slave 'Tag' or Collar. Fourth Century.* Rome. https://www.britis hmuseum.org/collection/object/G_1975-0902-6. Accessed September 19, 2023.

British Museum. n.d.b. Clay Tablet. 1480 BC. Hittites. https://www.britishmuseum.org/ collection/object/W_1953-0711-2. Accessed September 19, 2023.

Chinese Museum of Chinese Writing. "A Slave Contract Written in Old Uyghur Scripts." https://en.wikipedia.org/wiki/Old_Uyghur_alphabet#/media/File:%E5%9 B%9E%E9%B9%98%E6%96%87_%E5%AE%9A%E6%85%A7%E5%A4%A7%E5%B 8%88%E5%8D%96%E5%A5%B4%E5%A5%91.JPG. Accessed September 19, 2023.

Emory University, Michael C. Carlos Museum. 2021. "Confronting Slavery in the Classical World." https://carlos.emory.edu/exhibition/confronting-slavery-classi cal-world#:~:text=Estimates%20suggest%20that%20in%20Athens,25%20perc ent%20of%20the%20population. Accessed September 19, 2023.

Hunt, Peter. 2002. *Slaves, Warfare, and Ideology in the Greek Historians.* Boulder, CO: Cambridge University Press.

Loprieno, Antonio. 2012. "Slavery and Servitude," in *UCLA Encyclopedia of Egyptology.* Los Angeles: University of California. http://digital2.library.ucla.edu/viewItem. do?ark=21198/zz002djg3j.

Lowe, Dan. 2019. "Aristotle's Defense of Slavery." *1000-Word Philosophy.* https://1000wor dphilosophy.com/2019/09/10/aristotles-defense-of-slavery/. Accessed June 25, 2023.

Price, Neil. 2020a. *Children of Ash and Elm: A History of the Vikings.* New York: Basic Books.

Price, Neil. 2020b. "The Little-Known Role of Slavery in Viking Society." *Smithsonian Magazine,* August 25. https://www.smithsonianmag.com/history/little-known-role-slavery-viking-society-180975597/. Accessed June 25, 2023.

Raffield, Ben. 2019. "The Slave Markets of the Viking world: Comparative Perspectives on an 'Invisible Archaeology'" *Slavery & Abolition: A Journal of Slave and Post-Slave Studies* 40, 4: 682–705.

"Slavery in History," The History Press, online article, https://www.thehistorypress. co.uk/articles/slavery-in-history/

Thornton, John. 2001. "The Origins and Early History of the Kingdom of Kongo, c. 1350-1550." *International Journal of African Historical Studies* 34, no. 1: 89–120. https://doi.org/10.2307/3097288.

Yale University. n.d. The Lillian Goldman Law Library, The Avalon Project. "The Hammurabi Code." https://avalon.law.yale.edu/ancient/hamframe.asp. Accessed June 25, 2023.

Q24. How Did the Modern Anti-Slavery Movement Develop?

In the fight against modern-day slavery, four distinct anti-slavery approaches have emerged—*faith-based, secular abolitionist, feminist, and human rights.* Each of these unique traditions plays an important role in combating human trafficking. They played off one another; strengthened one another; borrowed language, concepts, advocacy, and activism from one another, often building on each other's prior work. Most importantly, they delivered speeches, wrote articles and books, organized protests, and devised other ways to capture the public's attention and make the issue of modern-day slavery visible.

Primary source materials demonstrate how each of the advocates from these different traditions relied on foundational documents to make their arguments against slavery. Christians had the Bible; secular abolitionists referred to the Declaration of Independence and other founding documents from the formation of the United States of America; feminists cited the Declaration of Sentiments, a statement of women's equality patterned on the Declaration of Independence that was forged at the 1848 Seneca Falls Convention, the birthplace of women's suffrage; and human rights advocates championed the Universal Declaration of Human Rights and many other documents drafted in the League of Nations and subsequently in the United Nations.

"Liberty is the right of every human creature, as soon as he breathes the vital air; and no human law can deprive him of that right which he derives from the law of nature," wrote John Wesley, an eighteenth-century Methodist preacher. He believed that God was on the side of the abolitionists. He described slavery as a sin and referred to it as "the execrable sum of all villainies" (Wesley 1775). The last letter he wrote before he died was in 1791 to William Wilberforce, a fellow Christian, abolitionist, and parliamentary member in England, in which he said, "Go on, is in the name of God and in the power of his might, till even American slavery (the vilest that ever saw the sun) shall vanish away before it" (Wesley 1791).

One hundred years before that, Benjamin Lay, a Quaker in the United States, used an eerily modern method—a boycott—to demonstrate against African American chattel slavery. One of the earliest abolitionists in the United States, he proclaimed that he wore nothing, ate nothing, used nothing made even partially from slave labor (Rediker 2018). He published over two hundred anti-slavery pamphlets in his lifetime, which he handed out to fellow Quakers to persuade them to stand against slavery (Rediker 2018). With a keen understanding of how to get attention, he stood in winter outside a Quaker meeting with no coat and one foot bare in the snow. When people expressed concern for his health, Lay gave an impromptu speech about how slaves were forced to work outdoors in winter with little or no protection from the elements and advocated for Quakers speaking out about their lack of freedom (Rediker 2017).One Sunday, he concluded a diatribe against slavery by plunging a sword into a Bible containing a sack of red pokeberry juice, splattering those nearby with the metaphorical blood of slaves (Rediker 2018).

On another occasion, Lay briefly kidnapped the child of slaveholders to show them how slaves felt when they were separated from their families and sold. Today, his portrait hangs on the first floor in the National Portrait Gallery in Washington, DC, where he is identified as a Quaker abolitionist and humanitarian, "known for his strident anti-slavery actions and protests." He was successful in his efforts: Quakers became the first denomination in the United States to publish a statement condemning slavery. In 1688 the first American public document condemning slavery was passed in Germantown, Pennsylvania.

The document, the 1688 Germantown Quaker Petition against Slavery, is available at the Haverford College Quaker and Special Collection (Quaker and Special Collections 2023). Benjamin Lay kept up his advocacy and activism, and also published his own booklet in 1737, entitled, *All Slave-Keepers That Keep Innocents in Bondage, Apostates"* (Lay et al. 1737). In it, he made a passionate argument against slavery anywhere, but especially for Quakers and other Christians. It took almost a century of activism, but by 1774 Quakers had to choose: they could no longer own slaves and remain members of the Quaker faith (Quakers in the World n.d.). While there were many other individual Christians in the United States and Europe who had written and spoken out against slavery, the 1688 Petition was the first official written statement by a Christian denomination in what was to become the United States condemning slavery.

One hundred years later, some anti-slavery activists began using non-theological arguments for freeing the slaves. They may still have been Christian, but by the late 1700s, these secular abolitionists had the founding documents of the United States of America to support their position, including the Declaration of Independence, the Articles of Confederation, the Constitution of the United States, and the Bill of Rights. All of these documents contained moral and legal arguments for condemning slavery.

Coming together in 1833, they formed the American Anti-Slavery Society, which was one of the first secular organizations to advance the notion of freedom for slaves in the United States. It grew from a few founding members the first year to a membership of over 150,000 by 1840. Its founder, William Lloyd Garrison, a passionate abolitionist, was also a journalist, and the Society regularly published journals, printed leaflets and pamphlets, and published articles in newspapers to advance its cause. From 1840 to 1870 it published its own newspaper, *The National Anti-Slavery Standard*.

In its Declaration of Sentiments, published on July 19, 1848, it clearly relies on the Declaration of Independence:

> More than 57 years have elapsed since a band of patriots convened in this place to devise measures for a deliverance of this country from a foreign yoke. The cornerstone upon which they devised this Temple of Freedom was broadly this – that all men are created equal, and they are endowed by their Creator with certain inalienable rights, that among these are life, LIBERTY and the pursuit of happiness. (American Anti-Slavery Society 1833)

The declaration goes on,

> At the sound of their trumpet call three millions [*sic*] people rose up as from the sleep of death; and rushed to the strife of blood; deeming it more glorious to die instantly as freeman, than desirable to live one hour as slaves....their measures were physical resistance –the marshalling in arms—the hostile array—the mortal encounter. Ours shall be ... the overthrow of prejudice by the power of love—and the abolition of slavery by the spirit of repentance. (American Anti-Slavery Society 1833)

One of the most famous members of the American Anti-slavery Society was Frederick Douglass, a former slave. In a moving speech on July 4, 1852, entitled, "What to the Slave Is the Fourth of July?" he delivered an impassioned call for freedom by juxtaposing the way a slave experienced the Fourth of July with how it is experienced by US citizens. He condemns the passage of the Fugitive Slave Act, saying it "obliterated the Mason Dixon line," effectively nationalizing slavery.

Douglass framed the Constitution of the United States as a document of liberty. He says that the arguments made by fellow abolitionists

> clearly vindicated the Constitution from any design to support slavery for an hour.... In that instrument I hold there is neither warrant, license, nor sanction of the hateful things; but interpreted, as it ought to be interpreted, the Constitution is a glorious liberty document. Read its preamble, consider its purposes. Is slavery among them? ... if the Constitution were intended to be, by its framers and adopters, a slaveholding instrument, why neither slavery, slaveholding, nor slave can anywhere be found in it. (Douglas 1852)

Abolitionists also used drawings and etchings to illustrate the inhumanity of slavery, such as the now famous woodcut of a man in chains that accompanied John Greenleaf Whittier's anti-slavery poem, "Our Countrymen in Chains" (American Anti-slavery Society 1837). These secular arguments against slavery, combined with the faith-based professions and resolutions built to a climax in the Civil War. In its aftermath, the Emancipation Proclamation and shortly after, the 13th Amendment to the Constitution, proclaimed all slaves free and prohibited slavery and involuntary servitude in the United States. Curiously, the motto of the American Anti-slavery society foreshadowed by over one hundred years the global human rights approach to slavery with its motto, "Our country is the world—our countrymen are mankind."

The feminist perspective on slavery, particularly sex slavery (and today sex trafficking), came from women who considered themselves both Christians and abolitionists. Yet despite the anti-slavery focus on both those traditions, something was missing that made possible a terrible exploitation of women and children.

Josephine Butler, born and raised in England, was active with her husband in the British abolitionist movement. She was also a Christian. She remembered walking through a part of London where poor women and children were being bought and sold for sex. Soon she volunteered in those neighborhoods and found herself hearing women's stories. She made the connection between females who were compelled to sell sex and the African chattel slavery that she and her husband had worked to eradicate. In fact, Butler was a pioneer in presenting cogent arguments against sex trafficking and commercial sexual exploitation of women and children.

By the mid-nineteenth century formal petitions had been submitted (England) and the first convention held (in the United States), demanding women's right to vote. As with the secular abolitionists, the women gathering at Seneca Falls in 1848 drafted and passed a "Declaration of Sentiments." Modeled on the Declaration of Independence, the document put forth an agenda for the women's rights movement. A set of twelve resolutions was adopted calling for equal treatment of women and men under the law and voting rights for women. Sixty-eight women and thirty-two men signed it.

In Britain, the earliest formal petition for women's rights was introduced in the Parliament by MP Hunt. According to the record,

> It came from a lady of rank and fortune—Mary Smith, of Stanmore, in the county of York. The petitioner stated that she paid taxes, and therefore did not see why she should not have a share in the election of a Representative; she also stated that women were liable to all the punishments of the law, not accepting death, and ought to have a voice in the making of them; but so far from this, even upon their trials, both judges and jurors were all of the opposite sex. She could see no good reason for the exclusion of women from social rights. (Minutes of the Meeting 1832)

Josephine Butler and others who joined together to stop the commercial sexual exploitation of women and children were aware of the suffrage movement taking place on both sides of the Atlantic Ocean and borrowed freely from the language of suffragists and suffragettes to make their case against what they saw as a new form of slavery.

She fought her first big battle in the Contagious Disease Acts of 1866–9. These acts were purported to be passed to prevent men who frequented women in prostitution from getting sexually transmitted infections and bringing them home to their wives and children. However, the focus of the acts was on the females. The government envisioned a "great register" of all women who, in Ms. Butler's words, "come under the denomination of common prostitutes." Anyone on the register was subject to government mandated vaginal exams. They gave government officials the right to pull any woman off the street at any time and "examine" them—in a police station, a doctor's office, or even in an alley.

She founded a new organization, the Ladies National Association for the Abolition of Government Regulation of Prostitution," known for short as the LNA, and held regular meetings where she gave the podium to young women and girls who had been brutalized physically by the state-mandated compulsory exams. The details were gruesome and shocking. Like some of her predecessors protesting African Chattel slavery, she used props, including displaying of chains and locks and crude gynecological tools used on the women and children in what Butler described as "surgical rape." With these props and pictures, she was able to demonstrate the loss of liberty baked into the Contagious Disease Acts.

Butler's goal was to repeal the Contagious Disease Acts by exposing the two-tiered standard in the Contagious Disease Acts—one for women and the other for men, who were subject to no exam, no register, no "diabolical record," as she termed it. She and the LNA campaigned for almost twenty years. The Contagious Diseases Acts were repealed in 1886. Before that time, however, Butler and others had noticed an international trade in females. In one of her speeches, she described what she saw in France:

> You know that wherever there is a slavery there must be a slave trade, because you need slaves to fill up the market; and so in this case, women are sent from one country to another as slaves, bought and sold .... At Liege, two trucks were found at the railway station crowded with young girls—quite young, many of them not more than thirteen, crowded like cattle. They were under the charge of one of the policemen of the system. He was conveying them from a certain brothel in Liege to hand them over wholesale to another brothel in Paris. These poor girls did not wish to be taken to Paris. ... some of them began to cry, and they all became hysterical and said they would not go. The policeman thereupon put manacles upon their hands and fastened them behind their back and they were thus taken as slaves in chains. (Butler 1876)

Butler spent her final decades taking this "New Abolitionists" battle internationally. Her last organizing effort was the founding of the International Abolitionist Federation in 1875. It began its work in England as the British and continental Federal for the Abolition of Prostitution arguing that state-regulated prostitution was responsible for enslaving women in prostitution. They documented the many types of state regulations of prostitution that bordered on slavery or were themselves enslaving women. Among these were forced vaginal exams conducted by government authorities; registration of women involved or thought to be involved in prostitution, including minors; imprisonment of women who refused vaginal exams; and forced hospitalization of women found to have disease. They also documented cases of debt bondage where women were sold to brothels and could not escape from the debt owed.

The organization also trained its fire on what is commonly called the "White Slave Trade." Although mainstream scholarship in the latter half of the twentieth century deemed the men and women opposed to this early sex industry as puritanical, moralistic, prudish, arising as it did out of Victorian society, new research and writing of scholars in the twenty-first century is showing a much richer tapestry of advocates, including suffragettes, faith-based and secular abolitionists, socialists, and others who understood trafficking of women and girls to be another form of slavery (Attwood 2021).

Butler herself documented the international nature of the slave trade and began organizing women in a dozen countries in Europe as well as those who were a part of the British Empire. By the turn of the century, regular meetings of international associations tracked the traffic of women and girls in countries all around the world. For example, at the International Congress on the White Slave Trade held in June 1899, over a dozen countries participated and gave reports on the legal, diplomatic, moral, and social aspects of the problem. One speaker noted:

> There is a regular trade in young girls who are bought and sold, imported and exported, to and from the ports and cities of Europe. It will naturally occur to remark that such a traffic involves slavery.... The business is an international trade, kept up very much by the movement of girls from one country to another and in a very large number of cases ... the movement of persons under stress of fear or fraud, [and] minors incapable of consent. (International Congress on the White Slave Trade 1899)

Representatives from various nations began meeting together on various causes such as peace following the Napoleonic Wars and the First World War, and the prototype was set for a more formal gathering of international organizations addressing world problems. The International Abolitionist Federation, formed in 1875, was one of the first and it has survived into the twenty-first century. It was instrumental in helping to draft and pass the UN Protocol to Prevent, Suppress, and Punish Trafficking in Persons in 2000. But scholars consider the League of Nations, formed on January 10, 1920, to be the first formal Intergovernmental Organization. The League of Nations was the precursor to the formation of the United Nations, founded in 1945 to prevent war and advance human rights and dignity. One of its key documents is the Universal Declaration of Human Rights, considered a landmark document setting out the basic human rights of all people on earth (United Nations [UN] 1948).

Today there are 192 member states of the United Nations, all of whom have signed the Universal Declaration of Human Rights. Since that time, more than 70 conventions have been introduced, including many addressing slavery and slavery-like practices such as forced labor, worst forms of child labor, international trafficking in persons.

Anti-slavery and anti-trafficking human rights organizations refer to the Universal Declaration of Human Rights and other related conventions, treaties and protocols in the work they do to stop slavery. The document lays out in the preamble its raison d'etre:

- Whereas recognition of the inherent dignity and of the equal and inalienable rights of all members of the human family is the foundation of freedom, justice, and peace in the world,
- Whereas disregard and contempt for human rights have resulted in barbarous acts which have outraged the conscience of mankind, and the advent of a world in which human beings shall enjoy freedom of speech and belief and freedom from fear and want has been proclaimed as the highest aspiration of the common people,
- Whereas it is essential, if man is not to be compelled to have recourse ... to rebellion against tyranny and oppression, that human rights should be protected by the rule of law,
- Whereas it is essential to promote the development of friendly relations between nations,
- Whereas the peoples of the United Nations have in the Charter reaffirmed their faith in fundamental human rights, in the dignity and worth of the human person and in the equal rights of men and women and have determined to promote social progress and better standards of life in larger freedom. (UN 1948)

It then lays out in a series of thirty articles, the basic universal rights of human beings, starting with the first four articles:

Article 1—All human beings are born free and equal in dignity and rights. They are endowed with reason and conscience and should act towards one another in a spirit of brotherhood.

Article 2—Everyone is entitled to all the rights and freedoms set forth in this Declaration, without distinction of any kind, such as race, color, sex, language, religion, political or other opinion, national or social origin, property, birth or other status.

Article 3 – Everyone has the right to life, liberty, and security of person.

Article 4 – No one shall be held in slavery or servitude; slavery and the slave trade shall be prohibited in all their forms. (UN 1948)

The emphasis on life and liberty, the insistence on rights, and the prohibition of any kind of slavery or servitude are the foundational articles in the Universal Declaration of Human Rights. This language is drawn from a long anti-slavery tradition and reshaped for use in an international arena by all member states of the United States. Human rights organizations and activists use this document, and others based on this document, to make their case against slavery and human trafficking. One key focus of human rights advocates was on taking the rights outlined in the Universal Declaration and applying them to victims of trafficking. In one key document, "Human Rights Standards for the Treatment of Trafficked Persons," an early anti-trafficking advocate drew from international human rights instruments to draft a document "to protect and promote respect for the human rights of individuals who have been victims of trafficking" (Global Alliance Against Traffic in Women 1999).

Examining the early antecedents of today's anti-slavery movement and understanding our historical traditions give us an analytic context and help us make sense of some of today's debates on policy, program, priorities, and perspectives to abolish modern-day slavery. Fascinatingly, the language developed sometimes centuries ago by religious, abolitionist, feminist, and human rights anti-slavery advocates created frameworks for twenty-first-century anti-trafficking and anti-slavery advocates. The foundation of today's anti-slavery work was laid in the early efforts from these four traditions, each of which had developed anti-slavery arguments based on the tradition in which they were rooted. They protested, wrote, spoke, and persevered until their cries were heard (Lederer 2018).

Further Reading

1688 Germantown Quaker Petition Against Slavery, Haverford College Quaker and Special Collection. https://guides.tricolib.brynmawr.edu/abolitionHC. Accessed September 19, 2023.

American Anti-Slavery Society. 1833. *Declaration of Sentiments of the American Anti-Slavery Society*. Adopted in Philadelphia, December 4, 1833. New York: Gilder Lehrman Institute of American History. https://www.gilderlehrman.org/collection/glc06200?gclid=CjwKCAjwvNaYBhA3EiwACgndggE3lDxruzbLXTQa4_k3F6U5NoFNaz6vu4M7y25zXTHWVT7Xk-dZSRoCjyMQAvD_BwE. Accessed September 19, 2023.

American Anti-Slavery Society, and Anti-Slavery Office. 1837. *Am I Not a Man and a Brother?* Photograph. https://www.loc.gov/item/2008661312/.

Attwood, Rachael. 2021. "A Very Un-English Predicament: 'The White Slave Traffic' and the Construction of National Identity in the Suffragist and Socialist Movements' Coverage of the 1912 Criminal Law Amendment Bill." *National Identities* 24 (3): 217–46. doi: 10.1080/14608944.2021.1895096.

Butler, Josephine. 1876. "Grave Words to Electors and Non-Electors, and Moral Reformers, on Immoral and Unjust Legislation," Speech, Annual Meeting of the Ladies National Association for the Repeal of the Contagious Diseases Acts, October 19. Hull, England. https://speakingwhilefemale.co/virtue-butler1/. Accessed September 19, 2023.

Douglass, Frederick. 1852. "What to the Slave is the Fourth of July?" Speech, Ladies Anti-Slavery Society, July 5. Rochester, New York.

Emancipation Proclamation, January 1, 1863. National Archives, Washington, DC. https://www.archives.gov/exhibits/featured-documents/emancipation-proclamation#:~:text=President%20Abraham%20Lincoln%20issued%20the,and%20henceforward%20shall%20be%20free.%22. Accessed June 25, 2023.

Global Alliance Against Traffic in Women (GAATW), Foundation Against Trafficking and International Human Rights Law Group. 1999. "Human Rights Standards for the Treatment of Trafficked Persons." https://gaatw.org/resources/publications/902-human-rights-standards-for-the-treatment-of-trafficked-persons. Accessed September 19, 2023.

International Congress on the White Slave Trade, National Vigilance Association. 1899. "White Slave Trade: Transactions of International Congress on the White Slave Trade, held in London on 21st, 22nd and 23 of June, 1899. London. https://babel.hathitrust.org/cgi/pt?id=hvd.32044103257614&view=1up&seq=5. Accessed September 19, 2023.

Lay, Benjamin, Benjamin Franklin, Nathan Harper, and Benjamin Franklin Collection. 1738. *All Slave-Keepers That Keep the Innocent in Bondage: Apostates…* Philadelphia: Printed for the author. Pdf. https://www.loc.gov/item/66038906/.

Lederer, Laura. 2018. *Modern Slavery: A Documentary and Reference Guide.* Westport, CT: Greenwood. http://publisher.abc-clio.com/9781440844997.

Minutes of the Meeting, UK Parliament, August 3, 1832. http://hansard.millbanksystems.com/commons/1832/aug/03/rights-of-women. Accessed September 19, 2023.

National Vigilance Association. 1899. "Transactions of the International Congress on the White Slave Trade," held in London on 21–3 of June. London: National Vigilance Association, 17.

Quaker and Special Collections. n.d. Haverford College. Protests Against Slavery (HC. MC 975.11.55). Haverford, PA. https://archives.tricolib.brynmawr.edu//repositories/5/resources/8784. Accessed September 19, 2023.

Quakers in the World. n.d. "Eliminating Slavery amongst Quakers." *Quakers in the World.* https://www.quakersintheworld.org/quakers-in-action/58/Eliminating-Slavery-amongst-Quakers. Accessed September 19, 2023.

Rediker, Marcus. 2017. "The Quaker Comet Was the Greatest Abolitionist You Never Heard Of." *Smithsonian Magazine,* September. https://www.smithsonianmag.com/history/quaker-comet-greatest-abolitionist-never-heard-180964401/. Accessed September 19, 2023.

Rediker, Marcus. 2018. *The Fearless Benjamin Lay: The Quaker Dwarf Who Became the First Revolutionary Abolitionist*. Boston, MA: Beacon Press.

United Kingdom Parliament, Minutes of the Meeting, August 3, 1832. http://hansard. millbanksystems.com/commons/1832/aug/03/rights-of-women. Accessed September 19, 2023.

United Nations. 1948. "Universal Declaration of Human Rights." *United Nations*. https://www.un.org/en/about-us/universal-declaration-of-human-rights. Accessed September 19, 2023.

Wesley, John. 1791. Letter to William Wilberforce. February 22. https://www. wesleysheritage.org.uk/object/letter-written-by-john-wesley-1791/. Accessed September 19, 2023.

Wesley, John. 1775. *Thoughts Upon Slavery*. https://www.google.com/books/edition/ Thoughts_Upon_Slavery/iTdcAAAAQAAJ?hl=en&gbpv=1&pg=PA4&printsec=fro ntcover. Accessed September 19, 2023.

Yale Law School, Lillian Goldman Law Library. 1924. "The Covenant of the League of Nations. Including Amendments Adopted to December, 1924." *Avalon*. https://ava lon.law.yale.edu/20th_century/leagcov.asp. Accessed September 19, 2023.

Index

About the Author

Laura J. Lederer, J.D., is a subject matter expert on Human Trafficking and president of Global Centurion, an anti-trafficking NGO. She serves as subject matter expert on Trafficking in Persons for US government agencies including the US Department of Defense, Department of Health and Human Services, and Department of Justice. Recent projects have included the development of a data collection instrument for tracking labor and sex trafficking cases in the Department of Defense; the development of the HHS SOAR to Health and Wellness training on human trafficking for health-care professionals; training and technical assistance efforts on human trafficking for HHS' Family Youth Services Bureau (FSYB); and specialized training and supplemental materials on human trafficking for the Office of Population Affairs (OPA) Title X Family Planning Clinics.

Prior to her work at Global Centurion, she served for eight years in the US Department of State as senior advisor on Trafficking in Persons to Under Secretary of State for Democracy and Global Affairs where she helped to stand up the Office to Monitor and Combat Trafficking in Persons. From 2002 to 2009, she was also the Executive Directorship of the Senior Policy Operating Group on Trafficking in Persons, a policy group that staffed the president's cabinet-level Interagency Task Force on Trafficking in Persons.

Over the past fifteen years she worked extensively with survivors of human trafficking to document their experiences with first responders, particularly in health care. She is the primary investigator and author of a landmark study entitled, "The Health Consequences of Sex Trafficking," published in the Health Policy and Law Review of Loyola University Chicago School of Law, *Annals of Health Law and Life Sciences*, in which she interviewed domestic survivors of sex trafficking about their physical and mental health problems. In 2014 she testified in the House of Representatives at a hearing for a bill on training, referral, reporting, and rescue issues for health providers. This testimony helped support passage of Title VII of the Justice for Victims of Trafficking Act of 2015.

Lederer founded and directed The Protection Project at Harvard University's John F. Kennedy School of Government in 1997 and moved it to Johns Hopkins University School of Advanced International Studies (SAIS) in 2000.

At Georgetown Law Center, she developed and co-taught the first law school course on international human trafficking. She taught the course at Georgetown Law Center from 2001 to 2014.

She was an expert consultant for *The Day My God Died*, a feature-length documentary film that casts a spotlight on the devastating impact child sex trafficking has upon the lives of children trafficked from Nepal to India. She was an advisor for the *New York Times* article that served as the basis for *Trade*, a feature-length drama based on real cases of international sex trafficking starring Kevin Kline.

She is the author of numerous articles on trafficking and commercial sexual exploitation including "Sold for Sex; the Link Between Street Gangs and Human Trafficking," "Addressing Demand: Why and How Policymakers Should Utilize Law and Law Enforcement to Target Customers of Commercial Sexual Exploitation," and "The Pregnancy Continuum in Human Trafficking." During the course of her work, she has spoken at over 500 governmental, intergovernmental, and nongovernmental events.

Lederer's most recent book is *Modern Slavery: A Documentary and Reference Guide to the Development of the 21st Anti-Trafficking Movement*, published in 2018 by Greenwood Publishing. It tells the story of the modern-day anti-slavery movement through primary-source materials including documents, speeches, pamphlets, treaties, laws, and articles spanning more than 300 years. The collection tracks rising consciousness about the many forms of modern-day slavery and the efforts of people who are working to combat trafficking in all its forms.